DATE

S

A

Literature in context

ENGLISH ROMANTIC HELLENISM
1700–1824

Literature in context series

General Editor
DOUGLAS BROOKS-DAVIES

Jonathan Swift:
the contemporary background
CLIVE T. PROBYN

Renaissance Latin poetry
IAN MACFARLANE

Petrarch and Petrarchism: the
English and French traditions
STEPHEN MINTA

Forthcoming:

The Courtly Love Tradition
BERNARD O'DONOGHUE

ENGLISH ROMANTIC HELLENISM
1700–1824

Timothy Webb

Literature
in context

Manchester University Press

Barnes & Noble Books · New York

First published 1982
by Manchester University Press
Oxford Road, Manchester M13 9PL

British Library cataloguing in publication data

English romantic Hellenism, 1700–1824. –
   (Literature in context series).
   1. English literature – 18th century
   I. Webb, Timothy   II. Series
   820.8'005   PR445

   ISBN 0–7190–0772–0

Published in the United States of America
by Barnes & Noble Books
a division of Littlefield, Adams & Co. Inc.
81 Adams Drive, Totowa, New Jersey, 07512

ISBN 0–389–20029–8

Computerised Phototypesetting
by G C Typeset Ltd., Bolton, Greater Manchester

Printed in Great Britain by
Redwood Burn Limited, Trowbridge
and bound by Pegasus Bookbinding, Melksham

Contents

General Editor's Preface—*page vii*

Prefatory Note— *ix*

Chronology— *xi*

Introduction— *1*

v

General editor's preface

One of the basic problems in reading literature is that of establishing a context for it. In the end the context of any work is infinite and unknowable. But if we approach the problem more simple-mindedly (and ignore questions posed by biography) we can say that a work's context is to a large extent definable by the ideas – theological, philosophical, political, and so on – current in the period in which it was written, and by the literary forms and genres that a period fosters and prefers. It is the ultimate aim of this series to try to help the student of English literature place works of all periods in their various contexts by providing volumes containing annotated selections of important background texts on the assumption that it is through contact with original texts only that true understanding may develop. Some of the volumes will be wide-ranging within a given period, containing a variety of texts (some in full, some extracts) illustrating dominant ideas and themes or forms; others will be more specialised, offering background material to the ideas and forms embodied in individual works of a particular author or concentrating on one or two thematic obsessions of a period. Although the emphasis is on English literature, much of the background material adduced will be of European origin. This will be presented in translation and, in appropriate cases (usually verse), the original will be printed with a translation on the facing page. The series should thus be of use to students pursuing comparative literature courses as well as interdisciplinary courses involving literature. In each volume there will be a substantial introduction, explanatory headnotes to the texts, and a bibliography of suggested further reading.

Douglas Brooks-Davies

Good taste was first formed under Grecian skies.
J. J. Winckelmann, *Gedancken* (1755)

We prepared to read the Iliad and the Odyssey in the countries, where Achilles fought, where Ulysses travelled, and where Homer sung.
Robert Wood, *Essay on the Original Genius of Homer* (1767)

. . . the purpose for which alone I live . . . is . . . to renew the lost Art of the Greeks.
William Blake, Letter of 16 August 1799

We are all Greeks—our laws, our literature, our religion, our arts have their roots in Greece.
P. B. Shelley, Preface to *Hellas* (1821)

Prefatory note

The title of this book requires some explanation. English Romantic Hellenism is used here in the broadest sense to indicate a phase of interest in Greece and its culture and history which is to be distinguished from that of the Renaissance at one boundary and the Victorian period at the other. Traditionally, the classification has been used either to describe a phenomenon which has been confined to the second half of the eighteenth century and the earlier part of the nineteenth or to isolate a certain idealized and often sentimental attitude which was common in that period. My purpose here is to suggest that what is normally identified as Romantic Hellenism should be seen as part of a continuum which can be traced back to the end of the seventeenth century. I also want to suggest some of the diversity and complexity of response to the Greek example: among the topics involved are history, politics, landscape, travel, the influence of the environment, primitivism, ruins, architecture, sculpture, drama, philosophy, mythology and the role of the poet. Much interest was also focused on Homer and the problems and philosophy of translation.

Although my main concern is with English reactions, I have found it impossible to ignore the influence of European thinking, particularly that of the French and the Germans. The passages from Fénelon, Winckelmann, Barthélemy and Schlegel have been included because of their unavoidable significance; where possible, I have presented them in contemporary English translations, though many English readers might have read the French in the original and Winckelmann perhaps in a French translation. The Chronology pays particular attention to the details of translation both from French and German into English and from English into European languages; this is intended to show the close connections between English and European conceptions of Greece. The Chronology also provides what is, in effect, a contemporary bibliography of primary sources while the Select Bibliography provides a list of modern editions and of secondary works.

I have tried to reproduce the original texts, though with some slight modifications in the interests of convenience and intelligibility. Original conventions have been followed wherever possible, except in the case of large capitals, which have been translated into italics. I have also removed long and detailed footnotes in a small number of cases (notably those of Blackwell and Spence) but retained those notes which seem to be of particular interest and made use of the references in my own endnotes. In a few cases I have also found it necessary to remove some Greek quotations from the text while retaining the translations provided in the original. Unless otherwise indicated in the notes, books have been published in London; capitals indicate that the full details may be found in the Select Bibliography.

I should like to record a particular debt to the invaluable work of a number of predecessors, notably M. L. Clarke, J. Mordaunt Crook, Donald M. Foerster and T. J. B. Spencer. My thanks are also due to Barbara Parry for her exemplary typing and to Philip Healy and Ruth Webb for generous assistance in reading proofs.

Quotations are made from *The Letters of Percy Bysshe Shelley*, ed. Frederick L. Jones (1964), *The Complete Letters of Lady Mary Wortley Montagu*, ed. Robert Halsband (1965), and *The Collected Letters of Samuel Taylor Coleridge*, ed. Earl Leslie Griggs (1956–71) by permission of Oxford University Press; from Alexander Pope, *Homer's Iliad and Odyssey* (Twickenham Edition), ed. Maynard Mack (1967) by permission of Methuen and Co. Ltd.; from Dora Wiebenson, *Sources of Greek Revival Architecture* (1969) by permission of A. Zwemmer Ltd.

Chronology

Télémaque (tr. Isaac Littlebury 1699; also tr. by Ozell, Des Maiseaux, J. Kelly, J. Hawkesworth, W. H. Melmoth, P. Proctor and T. Smollett, all by 1776; verse translations by G. Bagnall 1790, M. A. Meilan 1792–4, J. Youde ?1793; tr. into German 1700, Italian 1704, Spanish 1713, Dutch 1720, Greek 1742, Russian 1747, Hungarian 1755, and Polish; tr. into Latin verse 1743, 1764, 1808, Italian ottava rima 1747, and into French verse in part or in whole four times since 1817)

1700 Matthieu Souverain, *Le Platonisme dévoilé* (tr. as *Platonism Unveil'd*, 1700)

1701 Edmund Chishull, *Iter Asiae Poeticum* (printed in *Antiquitates Asiaticae*, 1728)

1709 Aaron Hill, *A Full Account of the Present State of the Ottoman Empire*
Temple Stanyan, *The Grecian History* (2nd ed. 1739, new ed. 1781)

1710 William King, *History of the Heathen Gods and Heroes* (5 eds. by 1731)

1711 Joshua Barnes (ed.), *The Iliad* and *The Odyssey*
Anne Lefèvre Dacier, *L'Iliade d'Homère* (tr. into English 1712)

1713 Proposals issued for Pope's translation of the *Iliad* (which appears in 6 vols. between 1715 and 1720)

1715 Thomas Parnell, *An Essay on the Life, Writings and Learning of Homer* (prefixed to Pope's translation)

1716 Anne Lefèvre Dacier, *L'Odyssée d'Homère*

1718 Anthony Blackwall, *An Introduction to the Classics* (6 eds. by 1746)
*Lady Mary Wortley Montagu at Troy (letters published 1763)

1719 Bernard de Montfaucon, *L'antiquité expliquée et représentée en figures* (10 vols. to 1724, including supplements; tr. D. Humphreys from Latin and French as *Antiquity explained, and represented in sculptures*, 10 vols. to 1725)

1720 *Alexander Pope, *The Iliad of Homer* (completed)
Lady Mary Wortley Montagu, 'Verses Written in the Chiask at Pera' (1718) (published)

1724 Fontenelle, *Discours sur l'origine des fables* (addendum to *Entretiens sur la pluralité des mondes*; originally written in the 1690s)

Joseph François Lafitau, *Moeurs des sauvages amériquains comparées aux moeurs des premiers temps* (tr. into Dutch 1751, German 1752)

1725 Giambattista Vico, *Principi di una Scienza Nuova*
      Alexander Pope, Broome and Fenton, *The Odyssey of Homer,* vols. 1–3 (vols. 4 and 5 in 1726)

1727 Andrew Ramsay, *Les Voyages de Cyrus* (including long essays on the theology and mythology of the ancients) (tr. N. Hooke as *A New Cyropaedia,* or *The Travels of Cyrus, 1727,* 10 eds. by 1778; over 30 eds. in English and French before 1800; tr. into German 1728, Spanish 1738, Italian 1753, Greek 1783)

1728 Joseph Spence, *Essay on Pope's* Odyssey

1729 Samuel Clarke (ed.), *The Iliad (The Odyssey,* 1740)

1730 Charles Rollin, *Histoire Ancienne* (13 vols. to 1738; tr. into English ?1737–9, 15 eds. by 1823)

1732 Foundation of the Society of Dilettanti

1733 Thomas Lisle, *Letter from Smyrna to his sisters at Crux Easton* (Dodsley's *Collection,* 1782, vi. 182–8)

1735 *Thomas Blackwell, *An Enquiry into the Life and Writings of Homer* (tr. J. H. Voss into German 1776; tr. into French 1798)

      James Thomson, *Greece* (second part of *Liberty, A Poem*)

1737 Richard Glover, *Leonidas* (5th enlarged ed. in 1770; further eds. in 1798, 1804; tr. into French prose 1738, German prose 1749)

1738 Excavations begin at Herculaneum
      John Breval, *Remarks on Several Parts of Europe* (includes Agrigentum and Paestum; earlier version, 1726)
      Antoine Banier, *La Mythologie et les fables expliquées par l'histoire* (3 vols. to 1740; tr. as *The Mythology and Fables of the Ancients,* 4 vols., 1739–40; shorter versions in 1711, 1715)

1740 *John Dyer, *The Ruins of Rome*

1743 Charles Perry, *A View of the Levant* (tr. into German 1754, 1765)
      Richard Pococke, *Description of the East,* vol. 1 (vol. 2, 1745) (tr. into French 1772–3, German 1754–5)

1744 *The Travels of the late Charles Thompson* (probably fictional; 4 eds. by 1798)

1747 *Joseph Spence, *Polymetis* (3 eds. by 1774; abridged

version 1764, reaching 6 eds. by 1802; tr. into French 1773–6)
Edmund Chishull, *Travels in Turkey and back to England*

1748 *James Stuart and Nicholas Revett issue their proposals for an expedition to Greece

Thomas Blackwell, *Letters Concerning Mythology* (tr. into French 1771)

Excavations begin at Pompeii

1749 Samuel Johnson's *Irene* produced at Drury Lane

1751 Stuart and Revett arrive in Athens

1752 Richard Dalton, *Museum Graecum et Aegyptiacum*
Foundation of Accademia Ercolanese
Comte de Caylus, *Recueil d'Antiquités Égyptiennes Étrusques, Grecques, Romaines* (7 vols. to 1767)

1753 Samuel Boyse, *A New Pantheon*
*Robert Wood, *The Ruins of Palmyra, otherwise Tedmor, in the Desart* (tr. into French 1753)

1754 Alexander Drummond, *Travels through Different Cities of Germany, Italy, Greece . . .*

1755 *Johann Joachim Winckelmann, *Gedancken über die Nachahmung der griechischen Wercke in der Mahlerey und Bildhauer-Kunst* (tr. Henry Fuseli in *Reflections on the Painting and Sculpture of the Greeks*, 1765, 1767; tr. anonymously 1766)

1757 Robert Wood, *The Ruins of Balbec* (tr. into French 1757, German 1769)

Comte de Caylus, *Tableaux tirés de l'Iliade, de l'Odyssée d'Homère et de l'Énéide de Virgile*

First of 8 vols. of *Le Antichità di Ercolano esposte* (to 1792)

1758 Mark Akenside, *Hymn to the Naiads* (written 1746)
Julien Davide Le Roy, *Les Ruines des plus beaux monuments de la Grèce* (2nd. ed. 1770; tr. into English 1759)

Elizabeth Carter, *All the Works of Epictetus* (4th. ed. 1807)

1759 *J. J. Winckelmann, 'Beschreibung des Torso im Belvedere zu Rom' (tr. Fuseli 1765); 'Beschreibung des Apollo im Belvedere' (tr. Fuseli 1768)

Richard Sayer, *Ruins of Athens* (an English version of Le Roy; in 1764 this in turn appeared in an abbreviated German version published by G. C. Kilian)

Floyer Sydenham (tr.), Plato's *Io* (eight other dialogues tr. by 1780)

1760   James Macpherson, *Fragments of Ancient Poetry* (*Fingal* 1762; *Temora* 1763; *Works of Ossian* 1765)

1761   Giovanni Battista Piranesi, *Della Magnificenza ed' Architettura de' Romani*

1762   George III purchases collection of drawings and prints from Cardinal Albani

*James Stuart and Nicholas Revett, *The Antiquities of Athens*, vol. 1 (later volumes in 1789, 1794, 1814, 1830; French tr. by Feuillet 1808–22, German tr. 1829–31)

J. J. Winckelmann, *Anmerkungen über die Baukunst der Alten* (tr. into French 1783)

J. J. Winckelmann, *Sendschreiben von den Herculanischen Entdeckungen* (tr. into French 1764, English 1771)

William Falconer, *The Shipwreck*

1763   Richard Chandler, *Marmora Oxoniensia*

1764   'Ionian Mission' of the Society of Dilettanti (Chandler, Revett and Pars are abroad till 1766)

J. J. Winckelmann, *Geschichte der Kunst des Alterthums* (tr. G. H. Lodge as *The History of Ancient Art among the Greeks*, partially 1849, completely 1880; tr. into French 1766, 1781, 1790–1803; tr. into Italian 1779)

Robert Adam, *Ruins of the Palace of the Emperor Diocletian, at Spalatro, in Dalmatia*

1766   G. E. Lessing, *Laokoon* (not tr. into English till 1836; tr. into French 1802)

P. F. Hugues (D' Hancarville), *Collection of Etruscan, Greek, and Roman Antiquities, from the Cabinet of the Hon. W. Hamilton* (French and English, 4 vols. to 1767; reprinted 1785–8, 1801–8)

Christoph Martin Wieland, *Geschichte des Agathon* (to 1767; tr. as *The History of Agathon*, 1773; tr. into French 1768, 1802; Greek 1814)

1767   *Robert Wood, *A Comparative View of the Antient and Present State of the Troade. To which is prefixed an Essay on the Original Genius of Homer* (limited edition; revised and enlarged versions with the emphasis on Homer in 1769 and posthumously in 1775 with the assistance of Jacob Bryant; 1769 version tr. into German by C. F. Michaelis 1773 (including review 1770 by C. G. Heyne), this version reviewed by Goethe;

German version of expanded 1775 text, 1778; tr. into French 1777, also into Spanish and Italian)

J. J. Winckelmann, *Monumenti Antichi Inediti* (2 vols. tr. into French 1808–9)

1768 Thomas Major, *The Ruins of Paestum* (English and French)

Stephen Riou, *The Grecian Orders of Architecture*

1769 *Ionian Antiquities: or Ruins of Magnificent and Famous Buildings in Ionia*, vol. 1

Josiah Wedgwood opens pottery factory at Etruria

1770 Rising in the Morea, supported by Catherine the Great

1771 P.-A. Guys, *Voyage littéraire de la Grèce* (tr. as *A Sentimental Journey through Greece*, 1772)

1772 J. H. Riedesel, *Reise durch Sicilien und Grossgriechenland* (tr. J. R. Forster as *Travels through Sicily and ... Magna Graecia*, 1773; tr. into French 1773, 1802)

British Museum purchases collection of Greek vases, bronzes and other antiquities from Sir William Hamilton for £8,400

1773 Patrick Brydone, *A Tour through Sicily and Malta*

James Macpherson (tr.), *The Iliad* (prose)

1774 Richard Chandler, *Inscriptiones Antiquae*

Jacob Bryant, *A New System, or, an Analysis of Ancient Mythology* (3 vols. to 1776; 3rd. ed. 1807, 6 vols.)

Oliver Goldsmith, *The Grecian History* (10 eds. by 1809)

1775 *Richard Chandler, *Travels in Asia Minor*

1776 *Richard Chandler, *Travels in Greece* (reprinted with *Travels in Asia Minor* 1776, 1817, 1825; both vols. tr. into French 1806, and German)

Edward Gibbon, *The Decline and Fall of the Roman Empire* (8 vols. to 1788)

1777 William Hamilton, *Account of the Discoveries at Pompeii*

William Young, *The Spirit of Athens*

Robert Potter (tr.), *Tragedies of Aeschylus* (4 more eds. by 1812)

1778 G. B. Piranesi, *Différentes Vues de ... Pesto*

1780 Uvedale Price, *An Account of the Statues ... in Greece* (tr. from Pausanias)

Eyles Irwin, *A Series of Adventures* (3rd ed. 1787; tr. into French 1792)

1781 Russia and Austria conclude a treaty with a view to driving the Turks out of Europe and restoring a Greek empire

Robert Potter (tr.), *Tragedies of Euripides,* vol. 1 (vols. 2 and 3 to 1783)

Johann Heinrich Voss, German translation of the *Odyssey*

1782 M. G. A. F. Choiseul-Gouffier, *Voyage pittoresque de la Grèce,* vol. 1 (vol. 2, 1809; vol. 3, 1822)

1784 William Mitford, *History of Greece,* vol. 1 (2, 1790; 3, 1797; 4, 1808; 5, 1810; tr. into German 1818)

1785 P. F. Hugues (D'Hancarville), *Recherches sur l'origine, l'espirit, et les progrès des arts de la Grèce* (3 vols.)

William Jones, 'On the Gods of Greece, Italy, and India' (printed in *Asiatick Researches,* 1799)

1786 *John Gillies, *History of Ancient Greece* (2 vols.; 3rd ed. 1792–3; tr. into French 1787–8)

Richard Payne Knight, *An Account of the Remains of the Worship of Priapus*

L.-F.-S. Fauvel takes up residence in Athens where he collects antiquities till 1801

1787 *Thomas Taylor (tr.), *Concerning the Beautiful* and *The Mystical Initiations; or, Hymns of Orpheus*

1788 Richard Potter (tr.), *Tragedies of Sophocles* (Thomas Francklin's version of Sophocles ran into five editions between 1759 and 1809)

John Lemprière, *Bibliotheca Classica; or, a Classical Dictionary* (10 eds. by 1818)

*Jean-Jacques Barthélemy, *Les Voyages du jeune Anacharsis en Grèce* (tr. W. Beaumont ?1791; 6 eds. by 1799; 5 eds. of tr. by 1817; 7 eds. of new tr. by 1818; tr. into Greek 1819)

Thomas Taylor, *The Commentaries of Proclus* (2 vols. to 1789)

1789 *The Antiquities of Athens,* vol. 2 (ed. William Newton)

1790 Thomas Taylor (tr.), *A Dissertation on the Eleusinian and Bacchic Mysteries* (2nd. ed. 1813)

John Bell, *Bell's New Pantheon* (2 vols.)

1791 J. B. Lechevalier, *Description of the Plain of Troy* (tr. Andrew Dalzel)

William Cowper (tr.), *The Iliad* and *The Odyssey*

Sir William Hamilton (text) and J. H. W. Tischbein (plates), *Collection of Engravings from Ancient Vases of Greek*

Workmanship (English and French, 4 vols. to 1795; reprinted 1800–3 (Italian and French), 1803–9)

Christoph Martin Wieland, *Geheime Geschichte des Philosophen Peregrinus Proteus* (tr. as *Private History of Peregrinus Proteus the Philosopher,* 1796)

1792   Thomas Watkins, *Travels* (2 vols., 2nd. ed. 1794)

1793   Johann Heinrich Voss, German translation of the *Iliad*
John Flaxman, *The Odyssey of Homer* (engraved by T. Piroli)
Richard Porson appointed Regius Professor of Greek at Cambridge

1794   Richard Worsley, *Museum Worsleyanum* (2 vols. to 1803)
The Antiquities of Athens, vol. 3 (ed. Willey Reveley)
*J. B. S. Morritt travelling in Greece (till 1796; journal partially published 1817, letters 1914)

1795   Friedrich August Wolf, *Prolegomena ad Homerum*
John Flaxman, *The Iliad of Homer* (engraved by T. Piroli)
John Flaxman, *Compositions from the Tragedies of Aeschylus* (engraved by T. Piroli)

1796   Jacob Bryant, *A Dissertation concerning the War of Troy* (*Observations*, 1795; Bryant continued the argument in a variety of publications)

1797   James Dallaway, *Constantinople Ancient and Modern, with Excursions*
Ionian Antiquities, vol. 2

1798   Execution of Pheraios Rhigas (b. 1760), Greek patriotic poet and revolutionary whose 'War Song' was translated by Byron

1799   J. Montagu (Earl of Sandwich), *A Voyage ... round the Mediterranean ... in 1738 and 1739*
Second collection of Greek vases from Sir William Hamilton wrecked off Scilly Isles (eight cases lost; sixteen purchased by Thomas Hope)

1800   William Hayley, *Essay on Sculpture*
William Franklin, *Remarks and Observations on the Plain of Troy*
Lord Elgin sends his team to make plaster-casts of the Parthenon

1804   Thomas Kirk, *Outlines from ... Greek, Roman and Etruscan Vases* (based on Hamilton collection; 2nd. ed. 1814)

Thomas Taylor and Floyer Sydenham (trs.), *The Works of Plato*
William Gell, *The Topography of Troy*
1805   Sculptures and bronzes collected by Charles Townley sold to the British Museum (further purchases in 1814)
Joseph Dacre Carlyle, *Poems, suggested chiefly by scenes in Asia-Minor, Syria and Greece* (Carlyle was scholarly adviser to Lord Elgin's mission, 1799–1801)
1806   Edward Baldwin [William Godwin], *The Pantheon*
Richard Polwhele, *Grecian Prospects*
John Sibthorp, *Florae Graecae Prodromus* (10 vols. to 1840)
1807   William Wilkins, *The Antiquities of Magna Graecia*
William Gell, *The Geography and Antiquities of Ithaca*
Thomas Hope, *Household Furniture and Interior Decoration*
Elgin Marbles on display at Elgin's house in Park Lane
1808   Aubin Louis Millin, *Peintures de vases antiques,* vol. 1 (vol. 2, 1810)
1809   *A. W. Schlegel, *Vorlesungen über dramatische Kunst und Literatur* (to 1811; tr. J. Black as *Lectures on Dramatic Art and Literature*, 2 vols., 1815; tr. into French 1814)
Richard Payne Knight, *Select Specimens of Antient Sculpture* (for the Society of Dilettanti)
Thomas Hope, *Costume of the Ancients* (2 vols.; 2nd. ed. 1812)
W. R. Wright, *Horae Ionicae*
Sydney Owenson (later Lady Morgan), *Woman: or, Ida of Athens*
1810   W. R. Hamilton, *Memorandum on the Earl of Elgin's Pursuits in Greece*
William Gell, *The Itinerary of Greece* (reviewed by Byron in *Monthly Review*, August 1811)
E. D. Clarke, *Travels in Various Countries* (6 vols. to 1823)
C. R. Cockerell, *Travels in Southern Europe and the Levant 1810–1817* (ed. S. P. Cockerell, 1903)
1811   John Galt, *Voyages and Travels in the years 1809, 1810, and 1811*
J. W. Goethe, *Tagebuch einer Reise nach Sizilien von Henry Knight* (tr. from the journal of Richard Payne Knight, 1777, in *Philipp Hackert*)
1812   Second 'Ionian Mission' of the Society of Dilettanti
Second collection of Elgin Marbles arrives in England and is

displayed at Burlington House

Aegina Marbles purchased by Ludwig of Bavaria

Lord Byron, *Childe Harold's Pilgrimage,* Cantos 1 and 2

Charles Kelsall, *A Letter from Athens* (verse)

1813   John Cam Hobhouse, *A Journey through Albania* ...
(made with Byron in 1809–10)

Lord Byron, *The Giaour*; *The Bride of Abydos*

F. S. N. Douglas, *An Essay on certain points of resemblance
between the ancient and modern Greeks* (2nd ed.)

1814   Phigaleian Marbles (5th century B. C.) acquired by British
Museum

James Rennell, *Observations on the Topography of the Plain of
Troy*

Lord Byron, *The Corsair*; *Lara*

W. M. Leake, *Researches in Greece*

Henry Moses, *A Collection of Antique Vases* ...

William Haygarth, *Greece, a Poem*

1815   Lord Byron, *The Curse of Minerva* (written 1811)

Walter Savage Landor, *Idyllia Nova Quinque Heroum atque
Heroidum*

William Wordsworth, 'Laodamia' (written 1814)

R. Twedell (ed.), *The Remains of the late John Twedell*

1816   Lord Byron, 'Prometheus'

Benjamin R. Haydon, *The Judgement of Connoisseurs upon
Works of Art compared with that of Professional Men*

The Antiquities of Athens, vol. 4 (ed. Joseph Woods)

John Hamilton Reynolds, *The Naiad and Other Poems*

After Select Committee hearing, Parliament purchases the Elgin
Marbles for £35,000 (*Report* published)

William Wilkins, *Atheniensia*

1817   Henry Moses, *Select Greek and Roman Antiquities*

J. P. Gandy and Bedford, *The unedited Antiquities of Attica* (tr.
into French 1832)

J. P. Gandy and W. Gell, *Pompeiana* (to 1819)

Felicia Hemans, *Modern Greece*

John Flaxman, *Compositions from the Works [and] Days, and
Theogony of Hesiod* (engraved by William Blake)

Illustrated books on the Elgin Marbles by E. I. Burrow, J. L.
Combe and William Sharp

1818 John Keats, *Endymion*
Leigh Hunt, *Foliage* (including *The Nymphs*)
Thomas Love Peacock, *Rhododaphne*
P. B. Shelley translates Plato's *Symposium* (published in severely edited version, 1840)
Richard Lawrence, *Elgin Marbles*
Richard Payne Knight, *An Inquiry into the Symbolical Language of Ancient Art and Mythology*

1819 John Keats, *The Fall of Hyperion. A Dream* (published in 1856)
Leigh Hunt, *Hero and Leander*; *Bacchus and Ariadne*
Edward Dodwell, *A Classical and Topographical Tour through Greece*
Thomas Hope, *Anastasius; or, Memoirs of a Greek* (2nd ed. 1820)

1820 P. B. Shelley, *Prometheus Unbound*; *The Witch of Atlas* (published 1824)
Henry Moses, *Vases from the Collection of Sir Henry Englefield Bt.* (English and French)
John Keats, *Lamia, Isabella, The Eve of St. Agnes, and other Poems* (including *Hyperion*, 'Ode on a Grecian Urn')
William Wordsworth, 'Dion' (written 1816); 'Ode to Lycoris' (written 1817)
Walter Savage Landor, *Idyllia Heroica*
Elizabeth Barrett, *The Battle of Marathon*
T. S. Hughes, *Travels in Sicily, Greece, and Albania*
H. W. Williams, *Travels in Italy, Greece, and the Ionian Islands*
B. W. Procter ('Barry Cornwall'), *A Sicilian Story*

1821 Proclamation of revolt by Alexandros Ypsilantis on 24 February; beginning of Greek War of Independence
Edward Dodwell, *Views in Greece*
P. B. Shelley, *Adonais*; *Hellas*
W. M. Leake, *The Topography of Athens*

1822 Formal proclamation of Greek Independence
Turks massacre Christian inhabitants of Chios; Turkish invasion of Greece begins
C. Maclaren, *Dissertation on ... the Plain of Troy*

1823 British Government recognizes Greeks as belligerents in War of Independence

B. W. Proctor, *The Flood of Thessaly*
1824 Death of Byron at Missolonghi
P.B. Shelley, *Posthumous Poems*

Introduction

I

In 1675 a French writer described his feelings on first seeing the city of Athens:

At the first sight of this Famous Town . . . I started immediately, and was taken with an universal shivering all over my Body. Nor was I Singular in my Commotion, we all of us stared, but could see nothing, our imaginations were too full of the Great Men which that City had produced. [1]

The sentimental traveller called himself de la Guilletière but his real name was Georges Guillet de Saint-George and, in spite of the vivid catalogue of physical symptoms, he had never been to Athens. His travels were fictional but his picture of the city was based on a variety of sources including eye-witness accounts provided by the French Capuchins who had settled in Athens. This curious gallimaufry of fact and fiction was reprinted several times and was regarded as authoritative by more than one unsuspecting scholar who had no opportunity of testing its veracity. *Athènes ancienne et nouvelle* marks the end of one phase of writing about Greece and heralds the beginning of another; the factual basis of de la Guilletière's account was soon to be tested in person by travellers of a more empirical temperament, while his emotional prostration at the sight of Athens was to be echoed in a variety of postures by a long succession of Romantic Hellenists.

Of course, as Dr Charles Perry was to point out nearly seventy years later, first-hand experience did not always guarantee accuracy of observation. The emotional impact of an encounter with the classical past sometimes distorted the vision. [2] Travellers to Greece could rarely avoid the sigh of regret for the departed glories of the past or the strong tug of identification with the Greeks of the present day, miserably subservient to the tyranny of the Ottoman Empire. A century and a half of these responses was later to receive its most complete and most powerful expression in Byron's *Childe*

Harold:

> Fair Greece! sad relic of departed worth!
> Immortal, though no more; though fallen, great!
> Who now shall lead thy scatter'd children forth,
> And long accustom'd bondage uncreate? [3]

Yet the attractions of the landscape, the suggestiveness of ruins and the touching political plight of the Greeks were also to be held in balance by an increasing desire to discover the truth, a scientific curiosity to collect and assess the evidence of Greece both as it had been in the days of its glory and as it now was in the time of its sad decline.

In the year in which *Athènes ancienne et nouvelle* appeared, another Frenchman, Jacob Spon, and an Englishman, George Wheler, were touring Greece and the Levant and recording their impressions in some detail; in particular, they were able to present a first-hand account of Athens and to report on the Parthenon, part of which was to be destroyed in an explosion in 1687. Spon's book appeared between 1678 and 1680, Wheler's in 1682; together they provided the first extensive, authoritative description of modern Greece. Spon's account, in particular, became an important work of reference for later travellers and archaeologists. They were not without prejudices; Wheler offered an emotional dedication to Charles II, which looked over its shoulder at the Civil War and which helped to procure a knighthood for its author. Yet although they were not always objective, Spon was a doctor and antiquarian and Wheler a zoologist and botanist and they approached their subject with a curiosity not unallied to the spirit of scientific enquiry. The keynote was stuck by Wheler when he complained that previous travellers 'have perhaps seen it [Athens] only from Sea, through the wrong end of their Perspective-Glass'. [4] Whatever the motes in their respective eyes, Spon and Wheler did make their own observations and their enquiries were not conditioned by the goals of a simple-minded search for the picturesque.

In their emphasis on the pragmatic, Spon and Wheler might be regarded as the originators of a new and influential approach to the understanding of Greece. Undoubtedly, the history of neo-classicism and of its close relation Romantic Hellenism was partly shaped by subjectivity, emotionalism and a predilection for *lontani* and the wrong end of the perspective-glass; but the eighteenth and early nineteenth-century view of Greece was also firmly grounded on the endeavours of travellers, archaeologists, cultural historians and scholars. Although Athens retained its potency as an ideal city of the mind 'Based on the crystàlline sea / Of thought and its eternity'[5] and although neo-classical theory consistently propounded the virtues of ideal beauty, there was an increasing interest in discovering the reality of Greece both past and present.

This interest can be traced very clearly in the epoch-making *Antiquities of Athens* by James Stuart and Nicholas Revett (first vol. 1762, second vol. 1789, three other vols. to 1830): these beautifully-produced volumes which were sponsored by the aristocratic art-lóvers of the Society of Dilettanti (see Appendix) provided the first adequately detailed and accurate visual record of Greek architectural remains at Athens and in Asia Minor (see No. 9). Stuart and Revett were impelled not only by the desire to elevate Greece at the expense of Rome but also by their concern to establish the architectural and archaeological facts:

We have carefully examined as low as to the Foundation of every Building that we have copied, tho' to perform this, it was generally necessary to get a great quantity of earth and rubbish removed; an operation which was sometimes attended with very considerable expence.

When they found that they could not get an unobstructed view of the Tower of the Winds, they arranged to have an interfering building demolished and rebuilt after they had finished their investigation. Even the six engaging plates in the first volume which are based on the drawings of Stuart were conditioned by the pursuit of accuracy:

The Views were also finished on the spot; and in these, preferring Truth to every other consideration, I have taken none of the Liberties with which Painters are apt to indulge themselves, from a desire of rendering their representation of Places more agreeable to the Eye and better Pictures. Not an object is here embellished by strokes of Fancy.

This scrupulous exactitude exerted its influence on the Ionian Mission which was officially sponsored by the Society of Dilettanti and whose members were Revett, Richard Chandler and the artist William Pars. The Mission eventually resulted in the *Ionian Antiquities* (first vol. 1769, second vol. 1797) which, like the *Antiquities of Athens*, was elegant and influential (see No. 28). Like its predecessor, it helped to create a new taste for Grecian architecture and decoration which appealed to the aesthetic sensibility but which was founded on a scientific attention to fact. Together with the *Antiquities of Athens* it provided a detailed reservoir not only of architectural ideas but of the precise details and measurements of the elevations. The joint impact of these publications made its mark both on interior decoration and more gradually on architecture; some of the resulting buildings at first appeared exotically inappropriate to the English scene but by the early years of the nineteenth century the Greek style had been established as one of the dominant standards of architectural excellence.

Ionian Antiquities included a number of engravings from the sensitive watercolours of William Pars (the younger brother of Blake's drawing master) which removed the architectural remains from the scientific vacuum in which they were presented for architectural purposes and portrayed them as buildings in a landscape. While the linear purity of the designs and elevations was certainly inspiring to architects and neo-classical seekers after the pleasures of contour or outline, the engravings provided a balance by introducing the narrative, the human and the exotic. Without these softening influences, the *Antiquities* would be a work of almost abstract severity, an act of homage to intellectual beauty as well as to archaeographical and architectural exactitude. The contribution of Pars is to remind the reader or the student of architecture that the antiquities of Ionia were originally designed to interpenetrate with the landscapes and to draw attention to the present state of the buildings, many of which were ruined. Pars was obviously influenced by James Stuart who, for all his dedication to Nature and Truth as opposed to Fancy, introduced into his pictures some splashes of local colour and a number of figures, including members of his own party variously equipped with tape-measures and sketching materials.

If *Ionian Antiquities* maintains a balance between the imaginative and the scientific response, so does the individual work of its leading contributor, Richard Chandler (see No. 19). Chandler is not primarily concerned with the aesthetic delights of the picturesque or the exotic, or with the pleasurable sadness pursued by the sentimental traveller; instead, he exhibits an almost puritanical dedication to the correction of poetic misapprehensions. Athens, for example, has encouraged extravagant flights of the imagination from those who have never seen it (see pp. 165–6); in deliberate contrast, Chandler asserts the supremacy of empirically tested reality and of local truth.

Similar corrections are made by other writers such as J. B. S. Morritt (see No. 27), though sometimes in a different spirit and with different intentions. Many of the pioneering travellers had taken in Greece as part of their travels in the Levant (indeed a number of them had worked for the Levant Company or had been attached to the embassies at the Sublime Porte). As a result, the earlier narratives usually devoted more attention to wet Greece than to dry (or mainland) Greece. After the great artistic/archaeographic expeditions and towards the end of the eighteenth century, there was an increase in the number of travellers to the mainland; this was to culminate in the activities of the topographers in the early nineteenth century. One consequence was that the poets' evocations of the Golden Age could be set more clearly against the criteria of those who had actually travelled in Greece. On one occasion we even find a painter approaching Athens and matching the colours of the landscape and the buildings against the palettes of Poussin, Lodovico Caracci and Titian. [6]

The most celebrated of these later travellers was, of course, Lord Byron, whose first-hand experience of Greece and Asia Minor entitled him to the pleasures of correcting 'poetic geography'; the correction was given added piquancy because it provided an opportunity to find Wordsworth at fault both in his idealization of the 'still seclusion' of Turkish cemeteries and in his sense of place:

He says of Greece in the body of his book—that it is a land of
  rivers—fertile plains—& *sounding* shores
  Under a cope of *variegated* sky
The rivers are dry half the year—the plains are barren—and shores *still* & *tideless* as the Mediterranean can make them—the Sky is anything but variegated—being for months & months—but "darkly—deeply —beautifully blue."

Here Byron is exhibiting his own predilection for fact while he gleefully accuses Wordsworth of substituting a soft and charming English pastoral for the vivid but harsher realities of the Greek landscape. Yet, although Byron generally employs his experiences of Greece to satisfy a highly personal need to deflate the falsely 'poetic' and the complacent, he also uses his knowledge to defend Pope's Homer against ignorant detractors. Having 'read it on the spot', he records authoritatively that 'there is a burst—and a lightness—and a glow—about the night in the Troad'.[7] In such consultations of the realities, Byron is part of a tradition which goes back to the eighteenth-century travellers, to *Antiquities of Athens* and to its successors.

These travellers included poets as well as prose writers and students of history and manners. As a poet, Byron was in a position to draw, directly or indirectly, on the Greek experiences of predecessors such as William Falconer, W. R. Wright, Richard Polwhele and J. D. Carlyle. He had a particular regard for Falconer, a sailor who produced the first extensive treatment of modern Greece in English poetry. Byron admired Falconer because of 'the strength and reality of his poem'[8] but, although the topographical passages of *The Shipwreck* (1762) are tinged with a precise evocativeness derived from genuine experience, they remain somewhat idealized. In contrast the success of the Greek passages in *Childe Harold* is based on Byron's ability to present a powerful and convincing picture of the present-day country set against glimpses and nostalgic intimations of its past. Byron's sentiment is kept in check by the sharpness and the authenticity of his observations, while the topographical descriptions of the traveller and the political reflections of the Philhellene are animated by the drive of the verse and the immediacy of the feeling. It was a balance achieved by few of his predecessors or his contemporaries in the tradition of Greek travel.

II

The search for truth also played an important part in the revaluation of Homer. Much of the early interpretation tended to isolate the poems both from social and cultural circumstances and from their geographical settings. Few scholars were personally familiar with the geography of the *Iliad* or of those sections of the *Odyssey* which are set in Greece. Gradually, a shift in thinking began to take place as it was recognized that Homer was the product of a specific environment and that a careful study of the Greek landscape and of those factors which had helped to produce him could throw much light both on the details and perhaps on the very nature of his poetry.

One of the first writers to make first-hand use of local evidence was Lady Mary Wortley Montagu (see Nos. 3 and 4). Writing to Alexander Pope from Adrianople in 1717 she noted that she was living 'in a place where Truth for once furnishes all the Ideas of Pastorall'. She had been reading the latest volume of Pope's translation and had been struck by the exact correspondences between certain descriptions in Homer and contemporary Turkish life. In a second letter Lady Mary reports on her visit to Troy in a manner which is commonsensical and robustly humorous but which remains susceptible to the spirit of place and the promptings of the historical imagination. Her respect for Homer is enhanced by her observations: 'While I view'd these celebrated Fields and Rivers, I admir'd the exact Geography of Homer, whom I had in my hand'. This letter was not published till 1763 but the tribute to Homer is significant; it marks the prelude to a fresh series of attempts to match the poem to the available facts, an investigation which perhaps reached its climax with Schliemann's excavations of Troy and Mycenae but which is still continuing today.

One of the most important contributions to the rediscovery of Homer in this period was made by Robert Wood (see Nos. 11 and 16). Wood's travels in Greece and Asia Minor had convinced him that 'the Iliad has new beauties on the banks of the Scamander; and the Odyssey is most pleasing in the countries where Ulysses travelled and Homer sung'. Experience of the classical sites was a pleasure in itself but Wood recognized that its implications reached beyond the sentimental indulgences of the tourist and could sometimes 'help us to understand them [the poet or historian] better'. Little allowance is made for originality or poetic imagination: Wood's *Essay on the Original Genius of Homer* (1767) is based on the premise that Homer's poems are an accurate representation of reality. Unlike Le Bossu and many of the French critics, Wood sees the *Iliad* as a work without moral design; instead, it is 'an exact transcript' both geographically and in matters of history. Wood finds fault with Pope's translation because it ignores these facts and treats Homer's geographical precisions as if they were arbitrary adjectival decorations. His lengthy account of the geographical details of the Catalogue of Ships (see pp. 141–3) is intended to show how Pope's poetical liberties have distorted and sometimes confused the particularities of Homeric geography; Wood acknowledges that some of these deviations can be attributed to the imperatives of the rhyme scheme but he insists that, for all its spirit, Pope's translation perverts the verisimilitude of the original.

Not everyone agreed: as late as 1808, Anna Seward observed that Pope's version of the Catalogue of Ships 'shows what genius and judgement can do with the most *barren* materials'. The Swan of Lichfield maintained that it was better to sin against truth than against beauty and she had no doubt that 'Pope's Homer was, as *poetry*, very superior to its Original . . .'.[9] Yet, in spite of such firmly asserted preferences, there was a growing tendency to apply the criteria of verifiable reality. Homer was no longer regarded primarily as an allegorist or a master of mythological generalities but as a clear-eyed observer of the world around him. Writing in 1771 P.-A. Guys insisted on the value of reading Homer and the Greek poets on Greek soil where one can recover even the smallest details by using one's eyes—'C'est en Grèce qu'il faut relire l'Iliade & l'Odyssée . . .'; after a visit to Troy in the company of the *Iliad*, he responded enthusiastically: 'Quelle vérité! quelle énergie! quel choix dans toutes ses images!'[10] Travelling in Greece in 1776 the Comte de Choiseul-Gouffier also attempted to relate the landscape to the Homeric poems; the result was a beautifully-produced folio, the first volume of which appeared in 1782. A similar enlightenment came to Goethe, who never visited Greece but who discovered that the landscape of Magna Graecia brought Homer vividly to life. He told Herder:

A word about Homer. The scales have fallen from my eyes. His descriptions, his similes, etc., which to us seem merely poetic, are in fact utterly natural though drawn, of course, with an inner comprehension which takes one's breath away. Even when the events he narrates are fabulous and fictitious, they have a naturalness about them which I have never felt so strongly as in the presence of the settings he describes. Let me say briefly what I think about the ancient writers and us moderns. *They* represented things and persons as they are in themselves, *we* usually represent only their subjective effect . . . [11]

Perhaps the most popular site for the student of Homer was the plain of Troy. Robert Wood had experienced some difficulty in identifying the site of the city and later visitors and classical scholars were not slow to put forward rival theories. Le Chevalier, Jacob Bryant, Gilbert Wakefield, James Dallaway, J. B. S. Morritt, William Francklin and Henry Hope among others all expressed their views before 1800; the early nineteenth century saw the productions of Edward Clarke, Edward Dodwell, J. Rennell and C. Maclaren, and of eminent topographers such as William Gell and William Leake. Some found fault with Homer, and Bryant even concluded that the Trojan War had not taken place and that the city of Troy had never existed. Bryant had never been to Troy and was firmly refuted by others who had. Among the believers was Lord Byron. For him, as for Robert Wood, Mary Wortley Montagu and others, one of the prime virtues of Homer was his veracity: '... we *do* care about "the authenticity of the tale of Troy". I have stood upon that plain *daily*, for more than a month, in 1810; and, if any thing diminished my pleasure, it was that the blackguard Bryant had impugned its veracity ... I still venerated the grand original as the truth of *history* (in the material *facts*) and of *place*. Otherwise, it would have given me no delight.' [12]

This gradual discovery of Homer's veracity makes an interesting counterpoint to the views of the eighteenth-century novelists. The novel was establishing itself at this time by creating its own identity and teleology; this involved an emphasis on realism as opposed to romance, and on contemporary relevance and immediacy rather than adherence to classical models. One result was an attempt to discredit the classics in general and Homer in particular. For instance, Daniel Defoe diagnosed a damaging lack of morality in classical literature: the siege of Troy was all for 'the Rescue of a Whore' and there was 'not a Moralist among the *Greeks* but *Plutarch*'. Homer was a superstitious wandering bard who had transformed the story of 'the Wars of the Greeks ... from a Reality, into a meer Fiction ...'. [13]

Henry Fielding's views were more complex. He admired classical literature and recognized that it still had its uses: as he explains in *Tom Jones* (xii.1), the ancients are 'to be esteemed among us writers as so many wealthy squires, from whom we, the poor of Parnassus, claim an immemorial custom of taking whatever we can come at'.

Homer was a particular favourite: Parson Adams's discourse on his virtues (*Joseph Andrews*, iii.2) is not uninfluenced by Fielding's own preferences. Fielding employs Homer as a model in *Joseph Andrews*, for structural and thematic purposes, while in *Tom Jones* he uses the epic both as a subject for burlesque and as a standard by which the action of the novel may be measured. Fielding began by equating *Joseph Andrews* with the *Odyssey* and Fénelon's *Télémaque* as opposed to the French romance (Preface to *Joseph Andrews*, 1742). By the time he came to write *The Journal of a Voyage to Lisbon* (1755) he had completely reversed his position:

But in reality, the *Odyssey*, the *Telemachus*, and all of that kind, are to the voyage-writing I here intend, what romance is to true history, the former being the confounder and corrupter of the latter . . . (Preface).

However one may wish to qualify this statement by noting, for example, that it does not mention the *Iliad* and that the needs of a journal are different from those of a novel, it is clear that Fielding sides with Defoe in finding Homer wanting by the criteria of the historian and the realist.

Thirty years later, this point was developed by the novelist Clara Reeve in *The Progress of Romance* (1785) where she draws parallels between the *Odyssey* and the adventures of Sinbad the Sailor and declares that, in spite of her veneration for Homer, she finds little to choose between the two narratives. One of the speakers in the dialogue makes a claim which is disputed but never successfully controverted: 'Homer was the parent of Romance; where ever his works have been known, they have been imitated by the Poets and Romance writers.' [14]

Clearly, there were two ways of seeing Homer. For the novelists, he was a writer of outmoded romances, the product of a barbarous age which had little interest or relevance for the recorders and analysts of contemporary British society; for many poets, travellers and men of letters, he was not only the most meticulous of observers but the historian of a world which, though undoubtedly alien, was irresistibly attractive.

III

The fluctuating reputation of Homer is a useful index of changing (and sometimes conflicting) attitudes towards Greece and the classical past. The French scholars, critics and writers who engaged in the Battle of the Ancients and the Moderns devoted much of their energy to discussing his faults and virtues. Many of them showed a tendency to idealize Homer and to concentrate on the simplicity of heroic manners. Fénelon believed that 'Rien n'est si aimable que cette vie des premiers hommes';[15] for him, as for Mme Anne Dacier, the simplicity of Homeric manners seemed to bring back the Golden Age. Fénelon's influential didactic romance *Télémaque* (1699; see No. 1) was designed to reproach his courtly contemporaries for their luxury and corruption by presenting an idealized narrative which distils a pastoral serenity from passages in the *Odyssey*, while Mme Dacier's view was based on an unfavourable contrast with her own times ('Pour moy, . . . je trouve ces temps anciens d'autant plus beaux, qu'ils ressemblent moins au nostre').[16] The calmer episodes of the *Odyssey* provided the main imaginative stimulus for those who preferred to idealize the Homeric world; both the *Iliad* and the more violent incidents of the *Odyssey* were usually ignored or tactfully kept in the background. Conversely, those who found fault with Homer tended to concentrate on the *Iliad* and on the barbarity and uncouthness of its heroes and their language. Both sides acknowledged that Homer's society bore only the slightest resemblance to their own. One of the most significant effects of the Battle was to bring out more clearly the importance of understanding the true nature of that ancient society: the Battle 'emphasized uniqueness, difference, change, and development, not permanence or universality'.[17]

In English criticism an early example of the developing historical sense can be found in Pope's Preface (see No. 2) and Notes, in marked contrast to the translations themselves which tend to transmogrify Homer in conformity to the principles of Augustan taste. In the translations, the harsher or cruder or 'lower' aspects of Homeric life, language and style are either omitted or elevated by the use of elegant poetic diction so that they lose their capacity to shock or to arrest us by their strangeness. Pope's prose accounts of Homer are sympathetic and alert us to the cultural differences between Homeric society and his own, though this sense of difference sometimes leads him to emphasize the virtues of a pastoral way of life. Like Fénelon and Mme Dacier, he responds to the intimations of a Golden Age with an enthusiasm which may seem uncritical: 'There is a Pleasure in taking a View of that Simplicity in Opposition to the Luxury of succeeding Ages . . .' The Notes are marked by a tendency to allegorize but they also display a willingness to explain what may seem disturbingly alien to the modern reader. Pope's admiration for Homer leads him to acknowledge qualities which lie beyond the precincts of Augustan decorum. He also refuses to idealize the Homeric world by ignoring those features which are more brutal and less comfortably 'uncivilized':

Who can be so prejudiced in their Favour as to magnify the Felicity of those Ages, when a Spirit of Revenge and Cruelty, join'd with the practice of Rapine and Robbery, reign'd thro' the World, when no Mercy was shown but for the sake of Lucre, when the greatest Princes were put to the Sword, and their Wives and Daughters made Slaves and Concubines?

Pope's commentary is often revealing but it remains subsidiary to the translation. The historical approach was given a more continuous and extensive formulation in Thomas Blackwell's *An Enquiry into the Life and Writings of Homer* (1735; see No. 6). According to Blackwell, the life of the wandering bard was 'the likest to the plentiful state of the Golden Age'. Blackwell's attractive representation of the bardic life was influential both among the Scottish primitivists, who detected parallels with Macpherson's Ossian (Macpherson himself translated the *Iliad*) and among the German critics. Blackwell's Homer was the product of the society he portrayed and for whom he performed—not the 'Inhabitants of a *great luxurious City*' but smaller groups not far removed from the nomadic, balanced between total barbarism and the more settled institutions associated with commercial prosperity. The Greeks *lived naturally,* and were governed by the *natural Poise* of the Passions, as it is settled in every human Breast'; their language was artless and unaffected, far removed from the verbal dexterities of more sophisticated societies. Blackwell insists on the naturalness of this society which he contrasts with the greenhouse artificialities of his own. Yet, although the whole trend of this argument would seem to align Blackwell with Fénelon and other seekers after the Golden Age, he is alert to the price exacted by the 'natural' and the primitive. If Homer had the advantage of living at a time when men's passions were close to the surface, he suffered the disadvantage of living in a violent and warlike society. If 'polishing diminishes a Language' and 'coops a Man up in a Corner', it also marks his separation from a society in which 'living by Plunder gave a Reputation for Spirit and Bravery'.

Blackwell's book derives much of its impetus from the contrast between the Greek way of life as portrayed by Homer and the life of contemporary Western Europe. His investigations were conducted from Aberdeen and based on the authority of his library but their implications were confirmed by more adventurous students. For example, Robert Wood (whose geographical findings we have already encountered) travelled both in Greece and the Near East and was able to record from personal experience the manners of the Arabs which so closely resembled those of the Homeric poems and which represented 'a perpetual and inexhaustible store of the aboriginal modes and customs of primeval life'. In listing the main features of these societies, he exposes not only their deficiencies and crudities according to the criteria of contemporary 'polite' society, but also their cruelty and violence and their cheap regard for women, for heterosexual love and for human life. If judged by the standards of Wood's own society, 'the courage of Achilles must appear brutal ferocity, and the wisdom of Ulysses low cunning'.

While Homer was being reinterpreted in the light of these new contexts, travel writers and missionaries were gradually working their way towards the science of comparative ethnology. The first stirrings can be traced back at least as far as the seventeenth century when a number of travellers (most of them missionaries) began to record their experiences in various parts of the world: among them were Richard Blome (America; 1687), Abraham Roger (India; 1670), Arnoldus Montanus (China and Japan; tr. 1670–1), Joannes Schefferus (Lapland; tr. 1674), Willem Bosman (Guinea; tr. 1705) and La Créquinière (India; tr. 1705). One of their main concerns was the savage customs and cult practices which they encountered and which as missionaries they were anxious to eradicate. Their accounts of these practices consistently invoke the ancient world by way of analogy: it was, says Frank E.

13

Manuel, 'virtually impossible to examine a strange savage religion without noting disparities and conformities with what one knew about ancient paganism'.[18]

Such comparisons can be found, for example, in the letters and reports of Jesuit missionaries, most notably perhaps in the highly important account by Joseph François Lafitau of his experiences among the Iroquois (*Moeurs des sauvages amériquains comparées aux moeurs des premiers temps* (1724)). Lafitau's book was designed to destroy the atheistical notion that there were many primitive nations who had no religion at all, and no knowledge of divinity. For such purposes, the Iroquois and the ancient Greeks threw a revealing light on one another. The sacrifices, initiations and rituals of the Indians brought to mind what he had read about similar practices among the Pelasgians. For instance, the myth of the satyr was given a plausible origin in the Indian custom of wearing the skins and horns of animals; the connection was illustrated by an engraving which placed two satyrs between an ancient German and an American Indian. Here and elsewhere the illustrations represent the Indians in the posture of classical sculpture. When confronted with naked flesh, Europeans often tended to invoke the Greco-Roman tradition; long before Lafitau, the explorer Verrazzano had seen in the Indians an 'aria dolcie e suave imitando molto l'antico' (a judgement which was ironically qualified when the Indians abandoned their classical poses to eat him).[19] The same artistic influences can be found in J. G. Forster's account of the inhabitants of Tahiti whom he observed on Cook's expedition to the South Seas (see p. 168). In Lafitau's case the engravings conferred on his subjects a dignity and nobility which seems rather oddly to transcend those brutal tendencies which he acknowledged both in the Indians and the Homeric warriors ('Quoi de plus inhumain que les Héros de l'Iliade?')[20]

An even more illuminating perspective on the Greeks was advanced in an essay which appeared in the same year as Lafitau's book, the *Discours sur l'origine des fables* by Fontenelle. Like Lafitau, Fontenelle compared the ancient Greeks to the American Indians; the idea had occurred to him as early as 1680 and the essay had originally been written in the 1690's. He made a number of comparisons between the myths of the Greeks and the American Indians and concluded that the Greeks had once been as savage and uncivilized as the Indians were now. What distinguished Fontenelle's approach from that of Lafitau and other predecessors and contemporaries was his premise of a progressive paganism. Fontenelle was especially concerned to trace the origins of myth by examining the operations of the primitive mind; his examination was based not only on Homer and the Greek writers and on the reports of travellers but also on observations of peasants and children. Fontenelle concluded that the Homeric gods were crude, brutal and warlike because they reflected the minds of their creators. He did not idealize: his Greeks were neither love-lorn shepherds nor gentlemen in pastoral disguises.[21]

The gradual recognition of the less civilized aspects of the Homeric poems was partly responsible for the declining popularity of Pope's translation and the rediscovery by the Romantics of the virtues of George Chapman. Even as late as the Romantic period, Pope still had his champions and defenders (Byron combatively declared that the Pope version had 'more of the spirit of Homer than all the other translations . . . put together')[22] but by the second half of the eighteenth century his translation seemed increasingly vulnerable to a variety of criticisms. Many critics found that their newly developed historical sense was offended by the way in which Pope had transformed the simplicity and natural vigour of the original into the fop-finery of a gentleman of the eighteenth century. Some, such as William Cowper, objected to Pope's tying the bells of rhyme round Homer's neck so that Pope's Homer resembled Homer just as Homer resembled himself when dead. 'I never', said Cowper, 'saw a copy so unlike the original.'[23] Others, such as Wordsworth and Coleridge, objected to Pope's poetic diction which, in their view, was intimately connected with his failure to observe even the most obvious natural phenomena.[24] Yet other readers objected specifically that Pope had deprived the original of its primitive brutality. Lord Kames complained that Pope considered it below the dignity of Achilles to 'act the butcher', forgetting that one of our greatest pleasures in reading Homer arises from his 'lively picture of ancient manners'.[25] Charles Lamb expressed a similar point of view in a letter to his friend Charles Lloyd, who had attempted to translate some Homer. Lamb suspected that Lloyd's principles and turn of mind would lead him 'to *civilize* his [Homer's] phrases, and sometimes to *half christen* them'. The deficiencies in his work in progress were obvious:

> What I seem to miss, and what certainly everybody misses in Pope, is a certain savage-like plainness of speaking in Achilles—a sort of indelicacy—the heroes in Homer are not half-civilised, they utter all the cruel, all the selfish, all the *mean thoughts* even of their nature, which it is the fashion of our great men to keep in.[26]

Taste had changed dramatically since Lord Chesterfield had told his son that 'Achilles, was both a brute and a scoundrel, and, consequently, an improper character for the hero of an epic poem' and had spoken disparagingly of 'the porter-like language of Homer's heroes . . .'.[27]

The dwindling popularity of Pope's Homer was balanced by a rise in the fortunes of George Chapman, whose translation was much less concerned with the 'milkiness of the best good manners' (see p. 178) and much more accommodating to the savage vitality of the original. Pope himself had acknowledged in Chapman a 'daring fiery Spirit that animates his Translation, which is something like what one might imagine *Homer* himself would have writ before he arriv'd to Years of Discretion' (Preface). That child-like forthrightness and animation must have recommended Chapman to the poets and critics of the Romantic age, who showed remarkable unanimity in their admiration for his poetic achievements. Coleridge: '. . . it has no look, no air, of a translation. It is as truly an original poem as the Fairy Queen'. Lamb: 'Chapman gallops off with you his own free pace . . . (what *Endless egression of phrases* the Dog commands)!' and later: 'I shall die in the belief that he has improved upon Homer, in the Odyssey in particular . . .' Keats borrowed a copy from Haydon, and was inspired to write his famous sonnet when he first read Chapman in 1816. Shelley ordered Chapman's *Homeric Hymns* in 1818 and adopted several turns of phrase in his own translation of the Hymns. Even Blake had his own copy of Chapman. The main feature which everyone remarked about this extraordinary translator was that he was 'thoroughly invested and penetrated with the sacredness of the poetic character'.[28] His poetic gifts compensated to all but the niggling few for the occasional harshness of his verse, for his interpolations, and for his frequent departures from the original Greek.

IV

At the beginning of the eighteenth century the status of mythology was precarious. Under pressure from the growing tendency to value the factual and the verifiable, defenders of mythology often resorted to allegorical interpretation and claimed that the stories concealed significant moral truths; but this did not satisfy hard-headed interpreters such as Pierre Bayle who claimed that the Greek myths were literally true and whose interpretations were deliberately calculated to deflate. An English equivalent can be found in Daniel Defoe, whose version of the Prometheus myth involves a well-meaning but absent-minded astronomer who contracts consumption by staying out at night on Mount Caucasus. [29] This bluntly reductive reading is not uncharacteristic of a number of English mythographers in the first half of the eighteenth century who approached the subject with heavy-handed rationality and deprived it of any imaginative appeal.

In spite of these pressures, classical mythology was still very much in evidence, especially in the earlier stages of the century. The main influences were still Roman: Virgil and Ovid were an important part of the mental furniture of the cultured man. The prestige of Ovid had declined since the Elizabethan period yet, as Douglas Bush records, 'every gentleman of letters translated parts of the *Metamorphoses* or the *Heroides* or the *Ars Amatoria*'. [30] The classical gods could still be encountered regularly in the immensely popular *Pantheon* which Andrew Tooke had translated from the French of Fr F. A. Pomey in 1698 and which was to appear in twenty-three editions by 1771. The divinities received further publicity from Pope's friend Joseph Spence, whose *Polymetis* first appeared in 1747 (see No. 8). This detailed and didactic work attempted to examine the connections between Roman poetry and 'the remains of the antient artists': its emphasis on the picturesque qualities of Roman poetry accorded well with the taste of many of Spence's contemporaries. Outside literature, classical mythology exerted its influence in a variety of locations. One observer noted in 1756: 'While infidelity has expunged the Christian theology from our creed, taste has introduced the heathen mythology into our gardens'; [31] the gods could still be detected in paintings, in the details of interior decoration and occasionally even in church.

In poetry and in prose, classical mythology was a rich source of vitality for the mock-heroic; otherwise its vigour was greatly diminished and the purposes it served were mostly decorative or superficial. Poetry, in particular, was debilitated by the system of poetic diction which Lord Chesterfield explained in an approving letter to his son.[32] This predilection for making 'translations of prose thoughts into poetic language', as Coleridge called it,[33] usually involved a thin coating of mythological varnish and produced results which were often grotesquely inappropriate. The habit must still have been infectious when Coleridge was at school since his teacher delivered a vigorous denunciation of mythological periphrasis.[34] It is easy to understand why William Blake could lament in 1783 the cessation of ancient melody in a poem which itself invokes the world of classical mythology as a beautiful but distant reality: 'The languid strings do scarcely move! / The sound is forc'd, the notes are few!'[35]

Not surprisingly, the novelists kept their distance. Daniel Defoe, who prided himself on his veracity and unassuming style, had no sympathy with the mythological method. Surveying the Thames from Hampton Court, he assures his readers: 'I shall sing you no Songs here of the River in the first Person of a Water Nymph, a Goddess, (and I know not what) according to the Humour of the ancient Poets.'[36] Here Defoe is in reaction not only against topographical writers such as Camden and Drayton but against mythology and the deceptive delights of the pastoral setting which so often accompanied it. Fielding's mythological burlesques in *Joseph Andrews* and *Tom Jones* are affectionate but their potency is generated by forcing a gap between the sublimity of the diction and the inescapably mundane nature of the subject matter. (Byron was later to follow this example in *Don Juan*.) Nearly forty years after Fielding and sixty years after Defoe, Henry Mackenzie, author of *The Man of Feeling*, objected to the continuing recourse to mythology in terms which seem to anticipate Wordsworth's attack on Pope's poetical diction in the Preface to *Lyrical Ballads*: 'Another bad consequence of this servile imitation of the ancients ... has been to prevent modern authors from studying nature as it is, from attempting to draw it as it really appears; and, instead of giving genuine descriptions, it leads them to give those only which are false and artificial.'[37]

In criticizing the prevalence of classical myth, the novelists were issuing a declaration of independence which helped to define the territory of the novel and to mark it off from the realm of poetry. Yet the shortcomings of classical mythology were equally evident to many poets. William Blake, for instance, provides a short and telling history of the subject in Plate 11 of *The Marriage of Heaven and Hell*. His analysis owes an obvious debt to the eighteenth-century debates on polytheism, on the origins of religion and on the dangerous potency of priestly imposture. Directly or indirectly, Blake's ideas can be traced to the concerns of Bayle, Fontenelle, Hume, and Holbach in *L'Enfer détruit* (1769). Yet there is a crucial divergence in emphasis. Fontenelle, for example, was interested in the way in which Greek myths had taken root in the imagination with such tenacity that even contemporary Christians resorted to them continually in art and literature: 'Nothing proves better that imagination and reason hardly have converse with each other and things of which reason is completely disabused lose none of their attractions for the imagination.'[38] It is at this point that Blake takes leave of the philosophers; where Fontenelle had regretted the failure of the reason to triumph over the imagination, the emphasis of Blake's compressed history is on the creative faculty of mind as opposed to the disabling constraints of system. Blake's own poetic career was to provide one of the most remarkable examples of one man's attempt to create a personal mythology of cosmic significance; his objection was not to the mythological method but to the unimaginative application of a prefabricated system of ciphers.

In a letter of 1802 Coleridge addresses himself to the same problem. Like Blake, he detects a dearth of imaginative involvement but, where Blake is partly concerned with the manipulation of power, Coleridge invokes those critical/psychological standards which were to be formulated so powerfully in *Biographia Literaria*:

It must occur to every Reader that the Greeks in their religious poems address always the Numina Loci, the Genii, the Dryads, the Naiads, &c &c—All natural objects were *dead*—mere hollow Statues—but there was a Godkin or Goddessling *included* in each—In the Hebrew Poetry you find nothing of this poor Stuff—as poor in genuine Imagination, as it is mean in Intellect—At best, it is but Fancy, or the aggregating Faculty of

19

the mind—not *Imagination*, or the *modifying*, and *co-adunating* Faculty. [39]

Here, as in his criticism of Gray, and as in Wordsworth's Preface, there is a close connection between the use of an inherited mythology and the employment of a traditional poetic diction: both imply a failure to observe accurately and a crippling deficiency of the imagination. The social implications of adhering to classical mythology were also evident to the Romantic poets: in particular, the connections between the delusions of mythology and the complacencies of pastoral were examined by poets who knew the countryside at first hand. The Arcadian idyll, the image of the country as a garden populated by nymphs, shepherds and classical divinities, was just as offensive to George Crabbe as it had been to Daniel Defoe. Crabbe refuses to hide the 'real ills' of the 'poor laborious natives' in the 'tinsel trappings of poetic pride'; his aim is to 'paint the Cot, / As Truth will paint it, and as Bards will not' (*The Village*). [40] Much of Wordsworth's poetry could be said to pursue the same goals; the insensitivity and selfishness of his own age may have caused him to think regretfully of pagan times when one might 'Have sight of Proteus rising from the sea; / Or hear old Triton blow his wreathèd horn' yet he too rejected the temptations of classical pastoral, and the rich mythology of his poetry is the product of his own imagination working on personal experience. Like Crabbe and Wordsworth, John Clare also rejected the conventions and chose instead 'A language that is ever green / That feelings unto all impart'. [41]

A number of writers were also exercized by an uneasy feeling that Greek mythology was the product of paganism and therefore unsuitable for the poetry of a Christian country. Several valiant scholars attempted to close the breach, working from the assumption that 'whenever there was any resemblance between classical and sacred literature the former had borrowed from the latter'. [42] The results were often preposterously unhistorical: for instance, in *Omeros Ebraios: sive historia Hebraeorum ab Homero conscripta* (1704) Gerhard Croese claimed that the *Iliad* was a pagan version of Joshua's attack on Jericho and that the story of Odysseus was derived from the wanderings of the patriarchs. The gardens of Alcinous he equated with Eden, while Mars and Venus suggested Samson and Delilah, and the fall of Troy represented the destruction of Sodom and Gomorrah. Fanciful theories such as this probably resulted from a desire to discover an underlying principle of unity, perhaps even a universal religion, behind the seeming heterogeneity of myth.

Many Christian writers were unimpressed. Joseph Spence advised in *Polymetis* that pagan mythology should be segregated from Christian truth in poetry to avoid the dangers of contamination. Coleridge and Wordsworth were much more sympathetic to the spirit of Greek poetry but, in the end, they too found that its religious implications were unacceptable, and its artistic achievements correspondingly limited. Clearly, they were both profoundly attracted by the beauty they found it necessary to reject. There are at least three passages in *The Excursion* (1804) and one in *The Prelude* where Wordsworth reveals his affection for Greek mythology and for its pastoral setting.[43] One of the passages irritated Byron by its idealization of the Greek landscape and its susceptibility to the Mediterranean dream (see p. 5); much more important is its account of the workings of the mythological imagination:

> And doubtless, sometimes, when the hair was shed
> Upon the flowing stream, a thought arose
> Of Life continuous, Being unimpaired;
> That hath been, is, and where it was and is
> There shall endure . . . [44]

Wordsworth here acknowledges the creative origins of Greek mythology yet, for his own purposes, the pastoral 'pleasure-ground' was less inviting than the moors, mountains, headlands and hollow vales of his own bleaker northern landscape which 'seize / The heart with firmer grasp'. Finally, Wordsworth was repelled by 'the anthropomorphitism of the Pagan religion'.[45]

The drift of Coleridge's sympathies was not dissimilar. The lines he freely translated from Schiller for *The Piccolomini* (1800) evoke the world of Greek mythology with an almost wistful sense of loss:

> The intelligible forms of ancient poets,
> The fair humanities of old religion,
> The Power, the Beauty, and the Majesty,
> That had their haunts in dale, or piny mountain,
> Or forest by slow stream, or pebbly spring,

> Or chasms and wat'ry depths; all those have vanished;
> They live no longer in the faith of reason!

Yet Coleridge maintained that Greek poetry was inferior both to Hebrew poetry and to English because it lacked imaginative force. This point he often repeated, discriminating between the limitations of the Greek mythology and the infinite suggestiveness of the Christian:

The Greeks changed the ideas into finites, and these finites into *anthropomorphi*, or forms of men. Hence their religion, their poetry, nay, their very pictures, became statuesque. With them the form was the end. The reverse of this was the natural effect of Christianity; in which finites, even the human form, must, in order to satisfy the mind, be brought into connexion with, and be in fact symbolical of, the infinite; and must be considered in some enduring, however shadowy and indistinct, point of view, as the vehicle or representative of moral truth.[46]

It would appear that the seam of classical mythology had been exhausted and that poetry could expect no further enrichment from that source. Yet when Joseph Cottle pronounced in the Preface to the second edition of *Alfred* (1804) 'whoever in these times, founds a machinery on the mythology of the Greeks, will do so at his peril', he was not delivering an epitaph; perilous though the enterprise might be, Greek mythology was about to enjoy a rich poetic revival. In retrospect, it appears that, although it was much weakened, it had never really died even in the eighteenth century. The first stirrings of a new life can be identified in the work of Mark Akenside (1721–70) and William Collins (1721–59). Neither achieved major poetic significance yet both produced poetry which was traditional and inventive. Akenside acknowledged a debt to the Greek lyric poets in his shorter works while he based the *Hymn to the Naiads* (1746) on the model of Callimachus, whose hymns he admired for 'the mysterious solemnity with which they affect the mind'. Characteristically, Akenside experiences no Keatsian delight at the appearance of Bacchus and his pards who are dismissed in favour of the cool and unimpassioned serenities represented by the Naiads; yet, for all its restraint, his *Hymn* demonstrates the rich potential of Greek mythology. Collins shared Akenside's preference for the neo-classical; he even composed an ode to simplicity in which that poetic ideal appeared as 'a decent maid / In Attic robe arrayed'. His odes are abstract in conception yet they

22

often exhibit a sensuousness, an imaginative power and an instinct for the suggestive and the undefined which transcends the limitations of their allegorical framework and which seems to look forward to the symbolic creations of the Romantics. Collins, like Akenside, finds his inspiration in Greece rather than in Rome — this gradual tilt of favour is an important feature of the second half of the eighteenth century.

It seems clear that the interest of Shelley and Keats in the possibilities of Greek mythology can be traced back in part at least to those eighteenth-century forebears. But there were other factors which helped directly or indirectly to create a favourable climate of thought for the production of *Endymion*, the two versions of *Hyperion*, 'Ode on a Grecian Urn', *Prometheus Unbound, The Witch of Atlas*, and many shorter poems and translations. One of these was the work of Thomas Taylor, who not only translated Plato and many of the Neoplatonists but who provided a key for the reading of symbolic narrative (see Nos. 23, 25 and 26). Plato's reputation had been depressed throughout the eighteenth century. In 1700 Matthieu Souverain had denounced him in *Le Platonisme dévoilé*, dismissing his doctrine because it was as 'absurd as the Theology of the Poets, and as unpolish'd as the Religion of the most superstitious vulgar' (English tr., 1700). Eighteenth-century rationalism found little to admire in what Monboddo described as 'the enthusiasm and mystic genius of Plato'.[47] Taylor's rediscovery of Plato and the Platonic tradition marked the slow re-emergence of a sense of the mysterious and the numinous which was to characterize the Romantic movement. It also heralded a shift from the frozen clarity of the eighteenth-century personification to the more suggestive connotations of the symbol. Although it was derided by many of his contemporaries, Taylor's work seems to be intuitively in touch with the direction which poetry was to take; in spite of his pedantry and his awkward style, he seems to have possessed some creative insight and his translations and essays were harbingers, if not necessarily promoters, of the symbolic narratives of the great Romantic poets.

The significance of Greek mythology was further underlined by the mythological handbooks of Lemprière (1788) and John Bell (1790), by William Godwin's book for children (published under the name of Edward Baldwin, 1806) and by interpretative works such as Richard Payne Knight's *An Inquiry* (1818). The two dictionaries are more objective and less opinionated than most of their predecessors in the art of interpretation; here, the nature of Greek mythology is accepted rather than attacked for its immorality or idolatry or explained away through various interpretative devices. Godwin's study displays a distinct sympathy with the Greek outlook, while Knight eludes the old-fashioned ethical emphases and devotes himself to unravelling cosmological and metaphysical symbols. The same period witnessed the growth of the rather speculative science of syncretic mythology which was based on the premise that 'beneath the seemingly disparate and heterogeneous elements of ancient universal mythico-religious and historical traditions there lay a harmonious tradition'.[48] George Eliot's Mr Casaubon was a late follower of this system; its best known exemplar was Jacob Bryant, who began to publish *A New System; or, An Analysis of Ancient Mythology* in 1774. Studies such as these were often absurdly fanciful or misguided yet they were part of a movement of thought which accorded significance and value to Greek mythology.

Greek influences also made themselves felt in the world of art: *The Antiquities of Athens* and *Ionian Antiquities* had helped to create a new interest in Greek design and architecture, while Winckelmann celebrated the achievements of Greek sculpture as the products of a happy climate and a favonian democracy (see Nos. 12–15). A variety of illustrated books on Pompeii, Herculaneum, Paestum and Magna Graecia as well as on Greece itself continued to shift the balance of attention from Rome to Greece in spite of the resistance of Piranesi, Robert Adam, William Chambers and others (see No. 17). The arrival in London of the Elgin Marbles confirmed the trend and provided tangible manifestations of the Greek spirit which had a profound effect on artists such as Haydon (see No. 31) and on his friend Keats. Greek pottery also emerged from obscurity through books and collections and through the artistic enterprise of Josiah Wedgwood and his protégé John Flaxman (for details, see Chronology).

Of course, Shelley and Keats came to discover Greek mythology by routes which were highly personal and which cannot be adequately accounted for in terms of this brief and general perspective. Yet their poetry was written in an age which abandoned the preconceptions of eighteenth-century poetry, preconceptions founded, as Leigh Hunt expressed it, on 'their gross mistake about what they called classical, which was Horace and the Latin breeding, instead of the elementary inspiration of Greece'.[49] What liberated their imaginations was the discovery that mythology need not be merely decorative or superficial but that it could be used to investigate the deepest human concerns. Byron, who had little sympathy either for the implications of Greek mythology or for his social 'inferiors', observed condescendingly of Keats that he had 'without Greek / Contrived to talk about the Gods of late'.[50] Francis Jeffrey was more understanding, and in an extremely perceptive essay in *The Edinburgh Review* for August 1820 acknowledged Keats's originality in his exploration of 'the loves and sorrows and perplexities' of mythological beings. As Jeffrey recognized, Greek mythology was no longer a fixed pantheon of marble postures but a point of entry to a world of moral and psychological significance. *Endymion, Lamia* and the two *Hyperions* go some way towards repairing that damaging dissociation of sensibility so precisely diagnosed by Coleridge: they combine the picturesque elements of Greek mythology with the 'inwardness or subjectivity, which principally and most fundamentally distinguishes all the classic from all the modern poetry'.[51] In the case of Keats, Greek mythology was also closely associated with his own feeling for natural beauty (as in 'I stood tip-toe') and with his delight in the combination of mythological story and natural setting in the works of Claude, Poussin and his other favourite artists. The conjunction between myth and the beauties of nature also made its impact on Keats's friends and contemporaries: Hazlitt, Wordsworth and Leigh Hunt all recorded the attractions of what Hunt described as 'the fair forms and leafy luxuries of ancient imagination'.[52]

Shelley, too, was susceptible to these attractions and his later poetry is often centred on a pastoral world which owes much to his constant recourse to Greek literature as 'the only sure remedy' for diseases of the mind. Shelley's search for a New Jerusalem involves a return to the image of the Golden Age: he did not share the nostalgic resignation of friends like Peacock, Hunt and Thomas Jefferson Hogg to the death of the mythological faculty but found that Greek mythology and Greek literature afforded satisfying images both of what man had achieved in the past and of a potential which might yet be realized again. If Keats's use of Greek mythology in *Hyperion* is focused on the problems of poetry and on the harsh but necessary processes of evolution, Shelley's characteristic focus is often related to his political concerns and to his deep and much challenged allegiance to Hope. Shelley was interested in the past largely because of its implications for the future: 'What the Greeks were, was a reality, not a promise. And what we are and hope to be, is derived, as it were, from the influence and inspiration of these glorious generations.'[53] Both *Hellas* and, particularly and outstandingly, *Prometheus Unbound*, take Aeschylus as their starting point and evolve into highly complex revisionary versions of their originals. Here Shelley is rescuing Greek literature from the confines of classicism and liberating the positive potential which is trapped within. Just as the Promethean trilogy had been used as a pretext for justifying the *status quo*, so Greek mythology had been wilfully misunderstood by Christian interpreters who had 'contrived to turn the wrecks of the Greek mythology, as well as the little they understood of their philosophy, to purposes of deformity and falsehood'.[54]

Shelley's affirmation of the power of mythology is both a refusal to accept the grim orthodoxies of Christianity with its degrading notion of eternal punishment in hell and an expression of the spirit of joy as manifested in the powers and forces of nature. This involves his translations from the Homeric Hymns, the crystalline neo-classical clarity of 'Arethusa', the sensuously realized dialectical balance of the Hymns of Pan and Apollo (intended for his wife's play *Midas*), the visionary invention of *The Witch of Atlas* and the Ionian island-paradise which marks the climax of *Epipsychidion*. Shelley also produced a number of poems in which the mythological imagination is allowed to work directly on the phenomena of the natural world without the intervening influence of a Greek original. Both 'Ode to the West Wind' and 'The Cloud' are freshly observed and both display a vivid use of mythological invention which has been informed by the example of Greek art and literature but which is never derivative or heavy-footed. Shelley's own desire to capture and to express 'the animation of delight' was reinforced and its achievement made possible by his sympathetic response to the joyous creativity of the Greeks. In contrast to a system centred on the image of a tyrannical and elderly father (see Winckelmann's version on p. 130), Shelley envisages a world informed by divinities who are young and beautiful and whose energy never deprives them of that serene poise and self-confidence which is aesthetically as well as morally pleasing. These poems give vital embodiment to 'the Religion of the Beautiful, the Religion of Joy' as Keats used to call it. Shelley would have been in sympathy with Keats's remarks to the painter Joseph Severn. 'Keats', said Severn, 'made me in love with the real living Spirit of the past.' ' " It's an immortal youth", he would say, "just as there is no *Now* or *Then* for the Holy Ghost".' [55]

V

If mythology could give rise to such varying interpretations, so too could the record of Greek literature and history. The Greek tradition was used not only as an encouraging pretext for reform but as an endorsement and justification of the *status quo*. This might seem surprising to the modern reader who is likely to remember the enthusiastic support which the Greeks received from the English Philhellenes during the War of Independence, Shelley's prophetic anticipation of a Greek victory in *Hellas*, and Byron's death in the Greek cause at Missolonghi. Yet in England it was always clear that a love of the classics was not necessarily associated with a love of liberty or a desire for social equality. Certainly, a knowledge of the classics and of Greek in particular was often associated with feelings of superiority—see Lord Chesterfield's advice to his son on the social value of Greek [56] and, eighty years later, the reactions of Lord Byron and the reviewers to Keats's attempt to revive Greek mythology without the advantages of a classical education.

The compliment could, of course, be reversed: although one of his contemporaries considered it a 'misfortune' for Samuel Richardson that 'he did not know the Antients', [57] the novelist prized his originality and cultivated a freedom from tradition whose consequences were ethical as well as aesthetic. Richardson vehemently disapproved of the morality of classical literature and of the epic in particular: the *Iliad* and the *Aeneid* were largely

27

responsible for 'the savage spirit that has actuated, from the earliest ages to this time, the fighting fellows, that, worse than lions or tigers, have ravaged the earth, and made it a field of blood'.[58] Similar views can be found not only among the novelists, who may have connected the classics with a world of privilege and power from which they were excluded, but among poets of a radical persuasion. Blake, for example, identified the classics with military imperialism: 'The Classics! it is the Classics, & not Goths nor Monks, that Desolate Europe with Wars.'[59]

Some admirers of Greece seem to have combined their admiration with a dislike for the changing society in which they lived, finding in Greek literature either a refuge from unpleasant social and political realities or a justification of things as they were. Shelley's friends Peacock and Hogg both had recourse to Greek as an antidote. Peacock's response was less reactionary and more intelligently flexible than that of Hogg, as his novels show, but he too was somewhat susceptible to the allure of the pastoral idyll. A much more extreme interpreter of the Greek tradition was Thomas Taylor, the Platonist. His attempt to restore the lost philosophy of Greece may have helped the progress of poetry and may even have appealed to radical poets such as Shelley and Blake but Taylor himself was profoundly anti-democratic and his researches into Greek literature and philosophy only confirmed his prejudice. The main trend of his thinking emerges very clearly in a passage in the preface to his translation of Pausanias, which was printed in 1794 (see No. 26). Here the formal excellence of Greek style is set in counterpoint to those licences which have helped to cause the French Revolution: for Taylor the best safeguard against the horrors of anarchy was the cultivation of the classics. Perhaps it is no accident that John Flaxman, who helped to popularize Greek mythology through the neo-classical finesse of his engravings and of his designs for Wedgwood, was also out of sympathy with the Revolution.

If literature and philosophy could be so interpreted, it is only to be expected that Greek history would provide anti-democratic lessons for those who were anxious to find them. John Gillies, whose two-volume study appeared in 1786, expressed some admiration for Athens and its democracy but also pointed out 'the evils inherent in every form of Republican policy', an interpretation which was fittingly embellished by a dedication to George III (see No. 22). In his view, Britain had a more stable and desirable system because of the emphasis it placed on the 'lawful dominion of hereditary Kings'. There are times when his account of Athenian society seems to be directed at the political reformers of his own age. Gillies' history was soon translated into French and German but it was overshadowed by the larger achievement of William Mitford (1744–1827) whose history appeared in five volumes between 1784 and 1810. If Gillies preferred the stability of constitutional monarchy to the turbulence of democracy, Mitford earned the title of 'the Tory historian of Greece'. Byron, who did not approve of his habit of 'praising tyrants', granted him the ambivalent virtues of 'learning, labour, research, wrath, and partiality'.[60] Mitford was certainly partial. The Athenian people he caricatured as a 'complex Nero' while in Macedon he discovered 'that popular attachment to the constitution and to the reigning family, the firmest support of political arrangement'. What Coleridge saw as his 'zeal against democratic government'[61] became more attractive to many readers as the French Revolution took its troubled course: the parallel between Athens and revolutionary France could be used to potent effect.

Greek history, it would seem, was by no means a simple advertisement for the virtues of democracy. The historical record was ambiguous and, as with every other aspect of Greek civilization, a great deal depended on the eye of the interpreter. If Gillies and Mitford interpreted the history of Greek democracy as a terrible warning, more radical thinkers were eager to seize on its happier aspects. It is ironical that while Mitford employed Athens as a grim illustration of what was to be avoided, Thomas Paine used the same example to illuminate the value of democracy: 'We see more to admire, and less to condemn, in that great, extraordinary people, than in anything which history affords.'[62]

Yet the English concern with Greek liberty was centred not so much on the rights of man as on a sympathetic identification with the struggle to break free from Turkish rule. English travellers tended to lament the decline of Greek fortunes so vividly symbolized by the Turkish occupation of the Acropolis, where a mosque had been built inside the Parthenon, and to hope that one day the Greeks would regain their independence; there were many who considered this a distant possibility because the modern Greeks seemed to have sunk into an unattractive apathy. Although these feelings were often aroused by first-hand observation, the sympathetic impulse was frequently stimulated not by travel but by the reading of Greek history and literature and by a strong belief that Greece was the home not simply of democratic politics but of liberty itself. Not surprisingly, this theme can be detected at the height of the period of Philhellenism when, for example, a poem in the workers' newspaper *Black Dwarf* interprets Peterloo in terms of the struggle between Turks and Greeks: the crowds now become 'each helpless Greek' while the yeomanry are transformed into 'ye English Janizaries of the *north*' (1 December 1819). This attitude can be traced back throughout much of the eighteenth century. It appears in Samuel Johnson who was stirred by the philhellenic spirit when he revised his play *Irene* (produced in 1749) and developed the theme of conflict between Grecian liberty and Turkish tyranny. It is prominent in Thomson's *Liberty*, in Glover's *Leonidas* and in Collins's 'Ode to Liberty' but it can also be found in the poetry of Thomas Warton, of Gray and of Falconer, and in Sir William Young's *The Spirit of Athens* (1777). Glover's interest suggests some of the political complications of the subject: although he later composed *The Athenaid* (posthumously published in 1787) his fame was based on *Leonidas* (1737). This lengthy poem was directed against the administration of Sir Robert Walpole but its political message was linked with the celebration of the Spartan virtues and the endorsement of their value in the struggle for liberty. The emphasis is significant: although Athens was a regular focus of sympathetic interest, oligarchic Sparta was also much admired, not least because of its contribution to the struggle against the Persians. English supporters of the Greek claim for independence could hardly fail to be moved by the heroism of the Spartans: 'Of the three hundred give but three, / To make a new Thermopylae.'[63] Sometimes the equation was altered so that the French rather than the Turks were identified with the Persians. A revival of interest in *Leonidas* may be traced to the Napoleonic threat: there were new editions in 1798 and 1804, a broadsheet of 1803 entitled *The Briton's Prayer* (which was based on passages from Glover's poem) and a dramatized 'enlargement' of 1792.[64] Classical history still had its uses.

In England, of course, an admiration for Sparta never fuelled a revolution as it seems to have done in France but the Spartan example remained very attractive, especially to the Whigs. This is probably symptomatic: the British tendency was to identify not with democratic Athens but with Greece as a whole in its struggle for liberty in which the Spartans had played a celebrated part. The positive values which could be deduced from the Greek example were elevated and rather generalized in their application. Perhaps the finest example is provided by an anecdote concerning the Earl of Granville told by Robert Wood in his book on Homer:

Being directed to wait upon his Lordship, a few days before he died, with the preliminary articles of the Treaty of Paris, I found him so languid, that I proposed postponing my business for another time; but he insisted that I should stay, saying, it could not prolong his life, to neglect his duty; and repeating the following passage, out of Sarpedon's speech [*Iliad*, xii.310–28], he dwelled with particular emphasis on the third line, which recalled to his mind the distinguishing part he had taken in public affairs ... His Lordship repeated the last word [let us go] several times with a calm and determinate resignation; and after a serious pause of some minutes, he desired to hear the treaty read ...

Homer, it would seem could offer lessons in morality which raised him far above the status of the vigorous recorder of a primitive society and the celebrator of its heroes. It was precisely this quality of moral grandeur which caused William Pitt to recommend to his nephew the study of Homer (significantly coupled with Virgil):

You cannot read them too much: they are not only the two greatest poets, but they contain the finest lessons for your age to imbibe: lessons of honour, courage, disinterestedness, love of truth, command of temper, gentleness of behaviour, humanity, and in one word, virtue in its true signification. [65]

Such moral fervour might easily cause us to forget that, as we have seen, many writers were prepared to draw comparisons between the Homeric warriors and the American Indians which were not entirely flattering.

The contrast is emblematic. If Homer could be many things to many men, so too could the Greek example. The fascination of Romantic Hellenism is in its endless variety, in the scope which it offers for views which are often radically opposed. Throughout the eighteenth and in the early years of the nineteenth century the image of Greece was constantly refined, revised, refuted or reinterpreted: what we have briefly examined in this introduction is a complex and continuous process of redefinition. Greece provided a pretext for revolutionary politics and for rigid conservatism; it acted as an inhibiting example to writers and artists and as a liberating possibility; sometimes it stimulated, sometimes it provoked angry and dismissive reactions. Through all the changes, political and aesthetic, which mark this period of history, Greece remained a rich imaginative matrix either as an ideal toward which one might aspire or as a false example which must be repudiated: it was a mirror in which the age could see itself.

NOTES TO INTRODUCTION

1 *An Account of a late Voyage to Athens*, 1676, pp. 123–4.
2 Charles Perry, *A View of the Levant*, 1743, pp. 504–5.
3 II. lxxiii (ll. 693–6).
4 *A Journey into Greece*, 1682, p. 347. For the close connections between travel and scientific enquiry, see R. W. Frantz, *The English Traveller and the Movement of Ideas 1660–1732*, Lincoln, Nebr., 1934.
5 Shelley, *Hellas*, ll. 698–9.
6 'Extract of a Letter from an English Historical Painter at Rome', *Annals of the Fine Arts*, v (1820), 102–5.
7 *Byron's Letters and Journals*, ed. Leslie E. Marchand, 1973– , iv. 325. See pp. 58–9 below.
8 *The Works of Lord Byron: Letters and Journals*, ed. R. E. Prothero, 1898–1901, v. 551.
9 E. V. Lucas, *Charles Lamb and the Lloyds*, 1898, pp. 190, 183.
10 P.-A. Guys, *Voyage littéraire de la Grèce*, Paris, 1771, ii. 56. Like Mary Wortley Montagu, to whose letters he refers (ii. 79), Guys compares contemporary customs and dress to those described in Homer and other classical writers.
11 *Italian Journey [1786–1788]*, tr. W. H. Auden and Elizabeth Mayer, Penguin Books, Harmondsworth, 1970, p. 310.
12 *Byron's Letters and Journals*, ed. Marchand, viii.21–2. The phrase about 'authenticity' comes from Thomas Campbell's comment on the *Oriental Eclogues* of Collins; Bryant's book is obliquely referred to in *Don Juan*, IV.ci. For Troy, see SPENCER (*Fair Greece, Sad Relic*), pp. 203–5 and SPENCER ('Robert Wood and the Problem of Troy in the Eighteenth Century'), CLARKE, pp. 183–5.

13   *Essay upon Literature*, 1726, pp. 118, 117; the final quotation is cited by Ian Watt, *The Rise of the Novel*, 1957, p. 242, a study to which I am much indebted in this survey.

14   i.19.

15   *Lettre sur les occupations de l'Académie française*, v, pp. 107, 50.

16   *L'Iliade d'Homère*, Paris, 1711, i.xxvi.

17   FOERSTER, pp. 9–10.

18   MANUEL, p. 16.

19   Hugh Honour, *The New Golden Land: European Images of America from the Discoveries to the Present Time*, 1976, p. 277.

20   *Moeurs des sauvages amériquains*, Paris, ii.428. See Margaret T. Hodgen, *Early Anthropology in the Sixteenth and Seventeenth Centuries*, Philadelphia, Pa., 1964.

21   Cf. 'I have known the poet blamed for the insolent and abusive language which he puts into the mouths of his heroes, both in their assemblies and in the heat of battle: I then cast my eyes on children who approach much nearer to nature than ourselves, on the vulgar always in a state of childhood, on savages who are always the vulgar; and have observed in all these, that their anger constantly expresses itself in insolence and outrage, previous to producing any other effect.' Jean-Jacques Barthélemy, *Les Voyages du jeune Anacharsis en Grèce*, Paris, 1788; English. tr. by W. Beaumont, 2nd ed. 1794, i.109.

22   *Lady Blessington's Conversations of Lord Byron*, ed. Ernest J. Lovell, Jr., Princeton, N.J., 1969, p.141.

23   See No. 21; *Correspondence*, ed. T. Wright, 1904, ii.404.

24   See *Essay Supplementary to the Preface, The Prose Works of William Wordsworth*, ed. W. J. B. Owen and J. Smyser, Oxford, 1974, ii.73–4; Coleridge, *Biographia Literaria*, ed. George Watson, 1975, p. 22n.; Southey, review of *Works of the English Poets, Quarterly Review*, xii (1814) which includes this judgement: 'The astronomy in these lines would not appear more extraordinary to Dr. Herschell than the imagery to every person who has observed moonlight scenes' (87). For a detailed account of Romantic reactions to Pope, see Upali Amarasinghe, *Dryden and Pope in the Early Nineteenth Century*, Cambridge, 1962.

25   *Sketches of the History of Man*, Edinburgh, 1778, i.366n., cited by FOERSTER, p. 44n.

26   *The Letters of Charles and Mary Anne Lamb,* ed. Edwin W. Marrs, Jr., Ithaca, Cal., and London, 1975– , iii.17.

27   *The Letters of Philip Dormer Stanhope*, ed. Bonamy Dobrée, 1932, iv.1306, 1610.

28   See No. 29; Lamb, *Letters,* ed. Marrs, ii.82; *The Letters of John Keats*, 1814–21, ed. H. E. Rollins, Cambridge, Mass., 1958, ii.308, 326; see Timothy WEBB (*The Violet in the Crucible*), pp. 137–40;

Geoffrey Keynes, *Blake Studies*, Oxford, 1971, p. 161; Godwin quoted in *Shelley Memorials*, 3rd. ed. 1875, p. 47.

29 *Essay upon Literature,* pp. 115–16.

30 BUSH (*Mythology*), p.32.

31 Cited in James Sutherland, *A Preface to Eighteenth Century Poetry* [1949], repr. 1966, p. 142. Cf. Pluche's comment in MANUEL, p. 5.

32 *Letters,* ed. Dobreé, ii. 362.

33 *Biographia Literaria,* p. 10.

34 *Biographia Literaria,* p. 4.

35 'To the Muses'.

36 *A Tour thro' the Whole Island of Great Britain,* ed. G. D. H. Cole, 1927, i.173.

37 *The Lounger,* 37 (10 October 1785) cited in Sutherland, *A Preface,* p. 143.

38 Cited in MANUEL, p. 52.

39 *Collected Letters,* ii.865–6.

40 i.39ff.

41 'Pastoral Poesy', ll. 13–14.

42 By Milton's time the idea was commonplace (see *Paradise Regained,* iv. 336 ff.). In his later years, Blake claimed that Greek art derived from the Cherubim of Solomon's temple (*Complete Writings,* ed. G. Keynes, 1966, pp. 565, 775).

43 *Excursion,* iv.718–62, 847–87; vi.52–57; *Prelude,* viii.312ff. (1805–6), 173ff. (1850). See also *Excursion,* vii.728–40.

44 iv.718–62.

45 Preface of 1815, *Prose Works,* iii.34.

46 *Coleridge's Miscellaneous Criticism,* ed. Thomas Middleton Raysor, 1936, p. 148. Cf. Schlegel, pp. 214–15 below.

47 Cited in CLARKE, p. 116n.

48 KUHN, p. 1094.

49 Preface to *Foliage, Literary Criticism,* ed. L. H. and C. W. Houtchens, Columbia University Press, New York and London, 1956, p. 130.

50 *Don Juan,* XI.1x.

51 *Miscellaneous Criticism,* p. 148.

52 *Literary Criticism,* p. 135.

53 *Shelley's Prose,* ed. David Lee Clark, Albuquerque, N. Mex., corr. ed., 1966, p. 219 (corrected). See, in particular, Peacock's 'Sir Calidore' (1818) and Hunt's Preface to *Foliage* (1818). For further discussion, see WEBB (*The Violet in the Crucible*), chapter II.

54 *Shelley's Prose,* p. 274.

55 William Sharp, *The Life and Letters of Joseph Severn,* 1892, p. 29.

56 *Letters,* ed. Dobrée, iii.1155.

57 See John Nichols, *Literary Anecdotes of the Eighteenth Century,* 1812–15, iv. 585.

58 *Selected Letters of Samuel Richardson*, ed. John Carroll, Oxford, 1964, p. 134 (?late 1749).
59 *Complete Writings*, ed. Geoffrey Keynes, 1966, p. 778.
60 Note to *Don Juan*, XII.19.
61 *Miscellaneous Criticism*, pp. 146–7.
62 *The Rights of Man* [1792], Everyman ed., 1915, p. 177.
63 'The Isles of Greece', *Don Juan*, III. 86, stanza 7.
64 RAWSON, pp. 357–8.
65 *Correspondence of William Pitt, Earl of Chatham*, 1838, i.62–3.

1   *From*
**FRANÇOIS DE SALIGNAC
DE LA MOTHE FÉNELON**
Les Avantures de Télémaque
(1699; tr. John Hawkesworth 1768)

Fénelon (1651–1715), Archbishop of Cambrai, was originally known to his contemporaries as a *philosophe* and controversialist. *Télémaque* is a Homeric imitation, a strongly didactic work based loosely on the travels of the son of Odysseus, which combines elements of epic, romance and even Greek tragedy with the morality of an educational treatise. Behind it lies the Renaissance tradition of princely courtesy books as much as the example of Homer. Fénelon was fond of giving advice and he found an ideal platform in his position as tutor to the Duke of Burgundy, son of the Dauphin. *Télémaque* was probably composed in 1694 but it was not published till 1699, when it went through twenty editions within a year; it made a great impact both on the court and on the wider reading public, which readily interpreted it as a satire on the excesses of Louis XIV and his courtiers.

In fact, *Télémaque* was an attempt to bring morality back into politics, to emphasize the importance of duty rather than self-indulgence and to rediscover the virtues of simplicity. Under the guidance of Minerva (disguised as the elderly Mentor), Telemachus goes in search of his father; his travels become an educational progress, in which he learns not only how to be a good man but how to be a good ruler, under the stern but kindly tutelage of Minerva. The passage from Book One illustrates this process; in rejecting the advice of Calypso, Telemachus rides above the solicitations of sensual pleasure and learns to prefer the calmer and superior attractions of restraint and virtue. At times Minerva (Wisdom) takes on a positive and religious colouring which reminds one both that Fénelon was an Archbishop and that for him self-control and reason involved far more than a mere exercise of the negative faculties. Behind such allegorical interpretations of the *Odyssey* there was a long tradition, including the fathers of the Church, the Neo-Platonists, and, predominantly, Virgil, whose *Aeneid* imbues the travels of the hero with such *gravitas* and so strong a sense of moral duty.[1] A later and much more complex reading of the Calypso adventure can be found in Thomas Taylor's interpretation of the *Odyssey* (see No. 23).

One of the most striking features of *Télémaque* is its use of the idealized landscape: Fénelon was deliberately setting up a contrast between the luxury and corruption of the Baroque age and the simplicity and virtue of the golden age. This does not involve the celebration of the noble savage or the abandonment of restraint and order (in fact, Fénelon disapproved of the brutality of the Homeric heroes); rather, it is the recognition of the value of true civilization based on the simplicity of nature as opposed to the hypocritical and elaborately ostentatious charade with which civilization is generally identified. So Fénelon can write: '. . . it is no wonder that we are pleased with such natural descriptions as we find in the *Odyssey*. This simplicity of manners seems to recall the golden age. I am more pleased with honest Eumeus [the swineherd] than with the polite heroes of *Clelia* or *Cleopatra*.'[2] This is the moral thrust behind the account of Apollo's sojourn on earth and behind Adoam's description of the good society in Beetica.[3] Such idealizations may be hard for the modern reader to accept but they had much to do with the success of Fénelon in the eighteenth century.[4] His admirers included Jean Terrasson, who stated with some extravagance: 'Le *Télémaque* est le plus beau poème qui existe parce qu'il est le plus moral, le plus philosophique'; Richard Steele, who claimed with greater sobriety: 'The Story of

Telemachus is formed altogether in the Spirit of *Homer*, and will give an unlearned Reader a Notion of that great Poet's Manner of Writing more than any Translation of him can possibly do'; Pope, whose translation of Homer he undoubtedly influenced; and Henry Fielding, who cited *Télémaque* as one of the structural models for *Joseph Andrews*.[5] *Télémaque* had a number of successors, including Andrew Ramsay's *Les Voyages de Cyrus* (1727) and Barthélemy's *Les Voyages du jeune Anacharsis en Grèce* (begun in 1757, published in 1788; see No. 24).

There were numerous translations, including at least two in verse (see Chronology). The version cited here is by John Hawkesworth (1715?–1773). Hawkesworth was a miscellaneous writer, who edited and contributed to *The Adventurer* (see No. 10) and who had adapted Southerne's *Oroonoko*. Five years after the translation of *Télémaque*, Hawkesworth published *A New Voyage Round the World*, a book compiled from the journals of Captain Cook and the naturalists Banks and Solander who had accompanied him on his first voyage. Comparison of the original accounts with Hawkesworth's version reveals that he tended to romanticize the Tahitians, emphasizing their virtues and excusing their faults.[6] For another account of Tahiti and its relation to Romantic Hellenism, see No. 20.

NOTES

1 For interpretations of the *Odyssey*, see STANFORD, and D. C. Allen, *Mysteriously Meant*, Baltimore and London, 1970, especially Ch. iv.

2 *Lettre sur les occupations de l'Académie française*, v, 'Projet de la poétique'.

3 Books II and VIII. See also book XXIII.

4 Cf. Salomon Gessner on the idealized landscapes of Claude and the Poussins, HONOUR, p. 167. On the *locus amoenus*, see E. R. Curtius, *European Literature and the Latin Middle Ages*, 1953, chapter x.

5 Antoine Adam, *Histoire de la littérature française au XVIIᵉ siècle*, Paris, 1962, v.175; *The Tatler*, No. 156; Author's Preface to *Joseph Andrews*.

6 See B. SMITH, pp. 22–4, 28–9.

When they arrived at the entrance of the grotto, *Telemachus* was surprized to discover, under the appearance of rural simplicity, whatever could captivate the sight: there was, indeed, neither gold nor silver, nor marble; no decorated columns, no paintings, no statues were to be seen; but the grotto consisted of several vaults cut in the rock; the roof of it was embellished with shells and pebbles; and the want of tapestry was supplied by the luxuriance of a young vine, which extended its branches equally on every side: here the heat of the sun was tempered by the freshness of the breeze; the rivulets, that, with soothing murmurs, wandered through meadows of intermingled violets and amaranth, formed innumerable baths that were pure and transparent as crystal; the verdant carpet which nature had spread round the grotto, was adorned with a thousand flowers; and, at a small distance, there was a wood of those trees that, in every season, unfold new blossoms, which diffuse ambrosial fragrance, and ripen into golden fruit: in this wood, which was impervious to the rays of the sun, and heightened the beauty of the adjacent meadows by an agreeable opposition of light and shade, nothing was to be heard but the melody of birds, or the fall of water, which, precipitated from the summit of a rock, was dashed into foam below, where forming a small rivulet it fled in haste over the meadow.

The grotto of *Calypso* was situated on the declivity of an hill, and commanded a prospect of the sea, sometimes smooth peaceful and limpid, sometimes swelling into mountains, and breaking with idle rage against the shore. At another view, a river was discovered, in which were many islands, surrounded with limes that were covered with flowers, and poplars that raised their heads to the clouds: the streams which formed these islands, seemed to stray through the fields with a kind of sportful wantonness; some rolled along in translucent waves, with a tumultuous rapidity; some glided away in silence, with a motion that was scarce perceptible; and others, after a long circuit, turned back as if they wished to issue again from their source, and were unwilling to quit the paradise through which they flowed: the distant hills and mountains hid their summits in the blue vapours that hovered over them, and diversified the horizon with cloudy figures that were equally pleasing and romantic: the mountains that were less remote were covered with vines, the branches of which were interwoven with each other, and hung down in festoons; the grapes, which surpassed in lustre the richest purple, were too exuberant to be concealed by the foliage, and the branches bowed under the weight of the fruit: the fig, the olive, the pomgranate, and other trees without number, overspread the plain; so that the whole country had the appearance of a garden, infinitely varied and without bounds.

The Goddess having displayed this profusion of beauty to *Telemachus*, dismissed him: 'Go now, said she, and refresh yourself, and change your apparel which is wet: I will afterwards see you again, and relate such things, as shall not amuse your ear only but affect your heart.' She then caused him to enter, with his friend, into the most secret recess of a grotto adjoining to her own: here the nymphs had already kindled a fire with some billets of cedar which perfumed the place, and had left change of apparel for the new guests. *Telemachus* perceiving that a tunic of the finest wool whiter than snow, and a purple robe richly embroidered with gold, were intended for him, contemplated the magnificence of his dress with a pleasure, to which young minds are easily betrayed.

Mentor perceived his weakness, and reproved it: 'Are these then, said he, O *Telemachus*, such thoughts as become the son of *Ulysses*? Be rather studious to appropriate the character of thy father, and to surmount the persecutions of fortune. The youth, who, like a woman, loves to adorn his person, has renounced all claim both to wisdom and to glory: glory is due to those only who dare to associate with pain, and have trampled pleasure under their feet.'

Telemachus answered with a sigh; 'May the Gods destroy me, rather than suffer me to be enslaved by voluptuous effeminacy! No, the son of *Ulysses* shall never be seduced by the charms of enervating and inglorious ease. But how gracious is Heaven, to have directed us, destitute and shipwrecked, to this Goddess, or this mortal, who has loaded us with benefits!' 'Fear rather, replied *Mentor*, lest her wiles should overwhelm thee with ruin: fear her deceitful blandishments, more than the rocks on which thou hast suffered shipwreck; for shipwreck and death are less dreadful, than those pleasures by which virtue is subverted. Believe not the tales which she shall relate: the presumption of youth hopes all things from itself, and, however impotent, believes it has power over every event; it dreams of security in the midst of danger, and listens to subtilty without suspicion. Beware of the seducing eloquence of *Calypso*; that mischief which, like a serpent, is concealed by the flowers under which it approaches; dread the latent poison! Trust not thyself, but confide implicitly in my counsel.'

From **Book 2**

[After a disagreement with Jupiter] 'Apollo, divested of his rays, was compelled to become a shepherd, and kept the flocks of Admetus king of Thessaly.

'While he was thus disgraced and in exile, he used to sooth his mind with music, under the shade of some elms that flourished upon the borders of a limpid stream. This drew about him all the neighbouring shepherds, whose life till then had been rude and brutal, whose knowledge had been confined to the management of their sheep, and whose country had the appearance of a desert. To these savages, Apollo, varying the subject of his song, taught all the arts, by which existence is improved into felicity. Sometimes he celebrated the flowers which improve the graces of Spring, the fragrance which she diffuses, and the verdure that rises under her feet: sometimes the delightful evenings of Summer, her zephyrs that refresh mankind, and her dews that allay the thirst of the earth: nor were the golden fruits of Autumn forgotten, with which she rewards the labour of the husbandman; nor the chearful idleness of Winter, who piles his fires till they emulate the sun, and invites the youth to dancing and festivity: he described also the gloomy forests with which the mountains are overshadowed, and the rivers that wind with a pleasing intricacy through the luxuriant meadows of the valley. Thus were the shepherds of Thessaly made acquainted with the happiness that is to be found in a rural life, by those to whom nature is not bountiful in vain: their pipes now rendered them more happy than kings; and those uncorrupted pleasures which fly from the palace were invited to the cottage. The shepherdesses were followed by the sports, the smiles and the graces, and adorned by simplicity and innocence: every day was devoted to joy; and nothing was to be heard, but the chirping of birds, the whispers of the zephyrs that sported among the branches of the trees, the murmurs of water falling from a rock, or the songs with which the muses inspired the shepherds who followed Apollo: they were taught also to conquer in the race, and to shoot with the bow. The Gods themselves became jealous of their happiness; they now thought the obscurity of a shepherd better than the splendour of a Deity, and recalled Apollo to Olympus.

'By this story, my son, be thou instructed: thou art now in the same state with that of Apollo in his exile; like him, therefore, fertilize an uncultivated soil, and call plenty to a desart; teach these rustics the power of music, soften the obdurate heart to sensibility, and captivate the savage with the charms of virtue. Let them taste the pleasures of innocence and retirement; and heighten this felicity with the transporting knowledge, that it is not dependent upon the caprice of fortune. The day approaches, my son, the day approaches, in which the pains and cares that surround a throne, will teach thee to remember these wilds with regret.'

2 *From*
ALEXANDER POPE
Preface to *The Iliad of Homer*
(1715; variously revised;
text based on the subscribers' quarto edition
together with the poet's revisions)

Alexander Pope (1688–1744) issued his proposals for a translation of the *Iliad* in 1713, though he had previously tried his hand at several passages from Homer, including the celebrated *Episode of Sarpedon*. The first volume of the *Iliad* appeared in 1715 and the fifth and sixth in 1720. The Preface is important not only as a guide to Pope's own practice as a translator but because of what it reveals about early eighteenth-century attitudes to Homer, to epic poetry and to translation, and because of its influence on subsequent readers and translators.

Pope's admiration for Homer is based on an excited though clear-eyed appreciation of his 'unequal'd Fire and Rapture'; his critical faculty detected absurdities and imperfections but his poetic intuition enabled him to 'admire even while we disapprove'. Pope responds to Homer as to a force of nature: Augustan notions of correctness and decorum are abandoned in the face of poetry which is so forcible 'that no Man of a true Poetical Spirit is Master of himself while he reads him'.[1] This irresistible force, this *vivida vis animi*, is identified with the invention, which is the defining characteristic of genius; here Pope seems to be asserting the validity of the imaginative powers in opposition to philosophers such as Locke who gave priority to the rational faculties. Homer is the greatest and most convincing example of the creative process of mind; Pope's account of his achievement is 'a paean to the supremacy of imagination and a testimony to its indivisibility from judgement'.[2] In keeping with this, Pope's own translation subscribes to the supremacy of poetic intuition over the retarding anxieties of scholarship. Pope prepared carefully for his great undertaking and he laboriously consulted commentators, geographers, poets and critics ancient and modern, as well as his predecessors in the art of translation (Chapman, Ogilby, Hobbes, Dryden, Anne Dacier and others); yet, in spite of this, and in spite of the careful and often illuminating annotation with which he buttressed his own translation, his intention was to transcend the fortifications of scholarship and to give wing to the invention.

The contrast between nature and correctness gives rise to a significant image in the Preface: Homer's work is compared to 'a wild Paradise' as opposed to 'an uniform and bounded Walk of Art'. This contrast is particularly instructive and at first, perhaps, surprising both because of Pope's own delight in gardens and because one of his first translations from Homer was the description of the gardens of Alcinous from Book Seven of the *Odyssey* which he included in an early essay on gardens: '. . . Close to the gates a spacious garden lies, / From storms defended, and inclement skies'. Yet, in spite of this interest, and in spite of his admiration for Fénelon's *Télémaque* (see No. 1) with its evocation of the peaceful simplicity of a golden age, it was the wildness and sublimity of the *Iliad* which first attracted Pope to attempt a full-scale translation. [3] The terms of the contrast may perhaps be traced back to Addison, who informed readers of the *Spectator* in 1712 that

Reading the *Iliad* is like travelling through a Country uninhabited, where the Fancy is entertained with a thousand Savage Prospects of vast Desarts, wide uncultivated Marshes, huge Forests, mis-shapen Rocks and Precipices. On the contrary, the *Aeneid* is like a well-ordered Garden, where it is impossible to find out any part unadorned, or to cast our Eyes upon a single Spot, that does not produce some beautiful Plant or Flower. [4]

Variations on this theme can be traced throughout the eighteenth century and into the Romantic period: in this book, examples can be found in Blackwell, Warton and Cowper, among others. It is a peculiar irony that for Cowper and the Romantics, Pope himself came to be associated with the garden and the walk of art: the neat fencing of the heroic couplet gave to his version of Homer an air of sophisticated restraint and a narrowness of perspective which failed to evoke the exuberant energies and the wide vistas of the original. Similarly, critics were to find fault with Pope for his failure to achieve that very simplicity which he selects as one of those features of the Homeric style which the translator must endeavour to reproduce.

The Bible provides Pope with a justification and an analogy to this Homeric simplicity towards which he aspired. Addison had already noticed the parallel: just as Solomon finds a resemblance between the nose of his beloved and 'the Tower of *Libanon* which looketh toward *Damascus*', so Homer compares the angry Odysseus to 'a Piece of Flesh broiled on the Coals'.[5] Mme Dacier found similar justifications for the apparently shocking in Homer. In spite of sharing these views, Pope could rarely bring himself to translate the 'low' without attempting to 'heighten the Expression' so that the subject matter grows 'great in the Poet's Hands'. A good example can be found in Book 17 of the *Iliad* where Menelaus is compared to a fly. The note comments: '... our present Idea of the Fly is indeed very low, as taken from the Littleness and Insignificancy of this Creature. However, since there is really no Meanness in it, there ought to be none in expressing it; and I have done my best in the Translation to keep up the Dignity of my Author'. For further criticism of Pope's translation, see Cowper's essay (No. 21) with my accompanying introduction. See also pp. 15–16, 141–3.

NOTES

1 Cf. *The Correspondence of Alexander Pope*, ed. George Sherburn, Oxford, 1956, i.43–5 (to Ralph Bridges, 5 April 1708).

2 Maynard Mack, Introduction to *The Iliad of Homer, The Poems of Alexander Pope*, London and New Haven, Conn., 1967, vii.xlvii.

3 Mme Dacier took issue: 'So far from the *Iliad* being an untended wilderness it is the best laid out and most symmetrical garden that ever was. M. Le Nôtre, who led the world in this particular art, never achieved a more consummate regularity in his gardens than did Homer in his poetry' (HONOUR, p.64).

4 *The Spectator*, ed. Donald F. Bond, Oxford, 1965, iii.564.

5 *The Spectator*, ii.127–8 (3 September 1711); the reference is to *Odyssey*, xx.25–30.

Homer is universally allow'd to have had the greatest Invention of any Writer whatever. The Praise of Judgment *Virgil* has justly contested with him, and others may have their Pretensions as to particular Excellencies; but his Invention remains yet unrival'd. Nor is it a Wonder if he has ever been acknowledg'd the greatest of Poets, who most excell'd in That which is the very Foundation of Poetry. It is the Invention that in different degrees distinguishes all great Genius's: The utmost Stretch of human Study, Learning, and Industry, which master every thing besides, can never attain to this. It furnishes Art with all her Materials, and without it Judgment itself can at best but *steal wisely*: For Art is only like a prudent Steward that lives on managing the Riches of Nature. Whatever Praises may be given to Works of Judgment, there is not even a single Beauty in them to which the Invention must not contribute. As in the most regular Gardens, Art can only reduce the beauties of Nature to more regularity, and such a Figure, which the common Eye may better take in, and is therefore more entertain'd with. And perhaps the reason why common Criticks are inclin'd to prefer a judicious and methodical Genius to a great and fruitful one, is, because they find it easier for themselves to pursue their Observations through an uniform and bounded Walk of Art, than to comprehend the vast and various Extent of Nature.

Our Author's Work is a wild Paradise, where if we cannot see all the Beauties so distinctly as in an order'd Garden, it is only because the Number of them is infinitely greater. 'Tis like a copious Nursery which contains the Seeds and first Productions of every kind, out of which those who follow'd him have but selected some particular Plants, each according to his Fancy, to cultivate and beautify. If some things are too luxuriant, it is owing to the Richness of the Soil; and if others are not arriv'd to Perfection or Maturity, it is only because they are over-run and opprest by those of a stronger Nature.

It is to the Strength of this amazing Invention we are to

attribute that unequal'd Fire and Rapture, which is so forcible in *Homer*, that no Man of a true Poetical Spirit is Master of himself while he reads him.[1] What he writes is of the most animated Nature imaginable; every thing moves, every thing lives, and is put in Action. If a Council be call'd, or a Battle fought, you are not coldly inform'd of what was said or done as from a third Person; the Reader is hurry'd out of himself by the Force of the Poet's Imagination, and turns in one place to a Hearer, in another to a Spectator. The Course of his Verses resembles that of the Army he describes,

Οἱ δ' ἄρ' ἴσαν, ὡς εἴ τε πυρὶ Χθὼν πᾶσα νέμοιτο.

They pour along like a Fire that sweeps the whole Earth before it.[2] 'Tis however remarkable that his Fancy, which is every where vigorous, is not discover'd immediately at the beginning of his Poem in its fullest Splendor: It grows in the Progress both upon himself and others, and becomes on Fire like a Chariot-Wheel, by its own Rapidity. Exact Disposition, just Thought, correct Elocution, polish'd Numbers, may have been found in a thousand; but this Poetical *Fire*, this *Vivida vis animi*,[3] in a very few. Even in Works where all those are imperfect or neglected, this can over-power Criticism, and make us admire even while we disapprove. Nay, where this appears, tho' attended with Absurdities, it brightens all the Rubbish about it, 'till we see nothing but its own Splendor. This *Fire* is discern'd in *Virgil*, but discern'd as through a Glass, reflected from *Homer*, more shining than fierce, but every where equal and constant. In *Lucan* and *Statius*,[4] it bursts out in sudden, short, and interrupted Flashes: In *Milton*, it glows like a Furnace kept up to an uncommon ardour by the Force of Art: In *Shakespear*, it strikes before we are aware, like an accidental Fire from Heaven: But in *Homer*, and in him only, it burns every where clearly, and every where irresistibly.

I shall here endeavour to show, how this vast *Invention* exerts itself in a manner superior to that of any Poet, thro' all the main constituent Parts of his Work, as it is the great and peculiar Characteristick which distinguishes him from all other Authors.

This strong and ruling Faculty was like a powerful Star, which in the Violence of its Course, drew all things within its *Vortex*. It seem'd not enough to have taken in the whole Circle of Arts, and the whole Compass of Nature to supply his maxims and reflections; all the inward Passions and Affections of Mankind to furnish his Characters, and all the outward Forms and Images of Things for his Descriptions: but wanting yet an ampler Sphere to expatiate in, he open'd a new and boundless Walk for his Imagination, and created a World for himself in the Invention of *Fable*. That which *Aristotle*[5] calls the *Soul of Poetry*, was first breath'd into it by *Homer*. I shall begin with considering him in this Part, as it is naturally the first, and I speak of it both as it means the Design of a Poem, and as it is taken for Fiction . . . .

Having now spoken of the Beauties and Defects of the Original, it remains to treat of the Translation, with the same View to the chief Characteristic. As far as that is seen in the main Parts of the Poem, such as the *Fable, Manners,* and *Sentiments,* no Translator can prejudice it but by wilful Omissions or Contractions. As it also breaks out in every particular *Image, Description,* and *Simile*; who ever lessens or too much softens those, takes off from this chief Character. It is the first grand Duty of an Interpreter to give his Author entire and unmaim'd; and for the rest, the *Diction* and *Versification* only are his proper Province; since these must be his own, but the others he is to take as he finds them.

It should then be consider'd what Methods may afford some Equivalent in our Language for the Graces of these in the *Greek*. It is certain no literal Translation can be just to an excellent Original in a superior Language: but it is a great Mistake to imagine (as many have done) that a rash Paraphrase can make amends for this general Defect; which

49

is no less in danger to lose the Spirit of an Ancient, by
deviating into the modern Manners of Expression. If there be
sometimes a *Darkness*, there is often a *Light* in Antiquity,
which nothing better preserves than a Version almost literal. I
know no Liberties one ought to take, but those which are
necessary for transfusing the Spirit of the Original, and
supporting the Poetical Style of the Translation: and I will
venture to say, there have not been more Men misled in
former times by a servile dull Adherence to the Letter, than
have been deluded in ours by a chimerical insolent Hope of
raising and improving their Author. It is not to be doubted
that the *Fire* of the Poem is what a Translator should
principally regard, as it is most likely to expire in his
managing: However it is his safest way to be content with
preserving this to his utmost in the Whole, without
endeavouring to be more than he finds his Author is, in any
particular Place. 'Tis a great Secret in Writing to know when
to be plain, and when poetical and figurative; and it is what
Homer will teach us if we will but follow modestly in his
Footsteps. Where his Diction is bold and lofty, let us raise
ours as high as we can; but where his is plain and humble, we
ought not to be deterr'd from imitating him by the fear of
incurring the Censure of a meer *English* Critick. Nothing that
belongs to *Homer* seems to have been more commonly
mistaken than the just Pitch of his Style: Some of his
Translators having swell'd into Fustian in a proud Confidence
of the *Sublime*; others sunk into Flatness in a cold and
timorous Notion of *Simplicity*. Methinks I see these different
Followers of *Homer*, some sweating and straining after him
by violent Leaps and Bounds, (the certain Signs of false
Mettle) others slowly and servilely creeping in his Train, while
the Poet himself is all the time proceeding with an unaffected
and equal Majesty before them. However of the two
Extreams one could sooner pardon Frenzy than Frigidity: No
Author is to be envy'd for such Commendations as he may
gain by that Character of Style, which his Friends must agree

together to call *Simplicity*, and the rest of the World will call *Dulness*. There is a *graceful* and *dignify'd* Simplicity, as well as a *bald* and *sordid* one, which differ as much from each other as the Air of a *plain* Man from that of a *Sloven*: 'Tis one thing to be tricked up, and another not to be dress'd at all. Simplicity is the Mean between Ostentation and Rusticity.

This pure and noble Simplicity is no where in such Perfection as in the *Scripture* and our Author. One may affirm with all respect to the inspired Writings, that the *Divine Spirit* made use of no other Words but what were intelligible and common to Men at that Time, and in that Part of the World; and as *Homer* is the Author nearest to those, his Style must of course bear a greater Resemblance to the sacred Books than that of any other Writer. This Consideration (together with what has been observ'd of the Parity of some of his Thoughts) may methinks induce a Translator on the one hand to give into several of those general Phrases and Manners of Expression, which have attained a Veneration even in our Language from being used in the *Old Testament*; as on the other, to avoid those which have been appropriated to the Divinity, and in a manner consign'd to Mystery and Religion.

For a farther Preservation of this Air of Simplicity, a particular Care should be taken to express with all Plainness those *Moral Sentences* and *Proverbial Speeches* which are so numerous in this Poet. They have something Venerable, and as I may say *Oracular*, in that unadorn'd Gravity and Shortness with which they are deliver'd: a Grace which would be utterly lost by endeavouring to give them what we call a more ingenious (that is a more modern) Turn in the Paraphrase.

Perhaps the Mixture of some *Græcisms* and old Words after the manner of *Milton*, if done without too much Affectation, might not have an ill Effect in a Version of this particular Work, which most of any other seems to require a venerable *Antique* Cast. But certainly the use of *modern*

Terms of *War* and *Government*, such as *Platoon, Campagne, Junto*, or the like (into which some of his Translators have fallen) cannot be allowable; those only excepted, without which it is impossible to treat the Subjects in any living Language ...

That which in my Opinion ought to be the Endeavour of any one who translates *Homer* is above all things to keep alive that Spirit and Fire which makes his chief Character. In particular Places, where the Sense can bear any Doubt, to follow the strongest and most Poetical, as most agreeing with that Character. To copy him in all the Variations of his Style, and the different Modulations of his Numbers. To preserve in the more active or descriptive Parts, a Warmth and Elevation; in the more sedate or narrative, a Plainness and Solemnity; in the Speeches a Fulness and Perspicuity; in the Sentences a Shortness and Gravity. Not to neglect even the little Figures and Turns on the Words, nor sometimes the very Cast of the Periods. Neither to omit or confound any Rites or Customs of Antiquity. Perhaps too he ought to include the whole in a shorter Compass, than has hitherto been done by any Translator who has tolerably preserved either the Sense or Poetry. What I would farther recommend to him, is to study his Author rather from his own Text than from any Commentaries, how learned soever, or whatever Figure they may make in the Estimation of the World. To consider him attentively in Comparison with *Virgil* above all the Ancients, and with *Milton* above all the Moderns. Next these the Archbishop of *Cambray*'s *Telemachus*[6] may give him the truest Idea of the Spirit and Turn of our Author, and *Bossu*'s admirable Treatise of the Epic Poem[7] the justest Notion of his Design and Conduct. But after all, with whatever Judgment and Study a Man may proceed, or with whatever Happiness he may perform such a Work; he must hope to please but a few, those only who have at once a Taste of Poetry, and competent Learning. For to satisfy such as want either, is not in the Nature of this Undertaking; since a meer Modern Wit can like nothing that is not *Modern*, and a Pedant nothing that is not *Greek*.

3   *From*
LADY MARY WORTLEY MONTAGU
Letter to Alexander Pope
1 April 1717 (published 1763)

Mary Wortley Montagu (1689–1762) accompanied her husband when he was appointed Ambassador to the Sublime Porte in 1716. She stayed in Turkey till June 1718, when she returned by sea. The two letters extracted here are important not only for their liveliness and their detailed observation but because they are informed by the recognition that Homer can be better understood when he is acknowledged as the product of a particular environment. This is one of the first significant collisions between the idealized notion of Homer and of Greek literature in general and the realities of Greek life. Not only can Mary Wortley Montagu corroborate Homer's descriptions of everyday life from first-hand observation but her travels also reveal to her the exactness of his geography: 'Almost every Epithet he gives to a Mountain or plain is still just for it' (see Robert Wood's development of this point in No. 16). The importance of these observations was not lost on her friend and correspondent Alexander Pope, who told her: 'I make not the least question but you could give me great Eclaircissements upon many passages in Homer since you have been enlightened by the same Sun that inspired the Father of Poetry. You are now glowing under the Climate that animated him; you may see his Images rising more boldly about you, in the very Scenes of his story and action; you may lay the immortal work on some broken column of a Hero's Sepulcher, and read the Fall of Troy in the Shade of a Trojan Ruin'. [1] In another letter, Pope lamented with courtly modesty: '. . . it is never to be repaird, the loss that Homer has sustained, for want of my translating him in Asia'. [2]

Mary Wortley Montagu's taste is fairly typical of her period but she also displays an openness of mind which gives her letters much of their characteristic flavour. In particular, we see her testing her notions on pastoral, on the proper subject-matter of poetry and on poetic diction. These spirited letters are very much the product of the Augustan period yet they look forward to the Romantics. The literary touchstones are Ovid and Virgil but the general inclination of interest is away from Roman literature to Greek, a trend which was to become more evident as the century progressed. Mary Wortley Montagu was by no means the first literary traveller (Addison had recently toured Italy after refreshing his knowledge of the poetic tradition) but her attention and response to the romantic associations of place was to have many successors, of whom the most celebrated was Byron in *Childe Harold*. Later visitors to Troy (or whichever site they identified as Priam's city) were often more extravagant in their postures but this early attempt to relate the Trojan landscape to the *Iliad* remains an interesting index of a growing sense of the significance of place.

It is also interesting that towards the end of the first letter she includes a literal translation of some Turkish verses, the style of which she identifies as 'the Sublime, that is, a stile proper for Poetry, and which is the exact scripture stile'. These verses lead her to an important observation: 'Monsieur Boileau has very justly observ'd, we are never to judge of the Elevation of an Expression in an Ancient Author by the sound it carrys with us, which may be extremely fine with them, at the same time it looks low or uncouth to us. You [Pope] are so well acquainted with Homer, you cannot but have observ'd the same thing, and you must have the same Indulgence for all Oriental Poetry.' Pope had struggled with this problem, not always successfully, because Augustan theories of decorum made it difficult to accommodate the unvarnished particularity of some of Homer's imagery. The interest of Mary Wortley Montagu's observation is in the conjunction between the style of Homer and the Bible: the same comparison had recently been made by Anne Dacier who had written of Homer 'son style est le mesme que celuy qui regne dans les livres des anciens Hebreux',[3] by Addison, and by Pope himself who had said in his Preface that the *Iliad* was 'very much in the language of Scripture, and in the Spirit of the Orientals'. Longinus, who did much to influence eighteenth-century attitudes, made a brief but telling comparison between Homer and Genesis[4] and the parallel became commonplace in the second half of the century.

NOTES

1 *The Correspondence of Alexander Pope*, ed. George Sherburn, Oxford, 1956, i.407.
2 *Ibid.*, i.493.
3 *L'Iliade d'Homère*, Paris, 1711, i.431.
4 Longinus ix.8. *On the Sublime* (1st century A.D.) was translated by John Pulteney from Boileau's French version in 1680; further English versions included those by L. Welsted (1712) and by William Smith (1739; 4th ed. 1770). See S. H. Monk, *The Sublime*, Ann Arbor, Mich., 1960, especially Chapter 1.

I dare say You expect at least something very new in this Letter after I have gone a Journey not undertaken by any Christian of some 100 years . . .

I am at this present writeing in a House situate on the banks of the Hebrus, which runs under my Chamber Window. My Garden is full of Tall Cypress Trees, upon the branches of which several Couple of true Turtles are saying soft things to one another from Morning till night. How naturally do boughs and vows come into my head at this minute! And must not you confess to my praise that tis more than an ordinary Discretion that can resist the wicked Suggestions of Poetry in a place where Truth for once furnishes all the Ideas of Pastorall? The Summer is allready far advanc'd in this part of the World, and for some miles round Adrianople the whole ground is laid out in Gardens, and the Banks of the River set with Rows of Fruit trees, under which all the most considerable Turks divert them selves every Evening; not with walking, that is not one of their Pleasures, but a set party of 'em chuse out a green spot where the Shade is very thick, and there they spread a carpet on which they sit drinking their Coffée and generally attended by some slave with a fine voice or that plays on some instrument. Every 20 paces you may see one of these little companys listening to the dashing of the river, and this taste is so universal that the very Gardiners are not without it. I have often seen them and their children siting on the banks and playing on a rural Instrument perfectly answering the description of the Ancient Fistula,[1] being compos'd of unequal reeds, with a simple but agreable softness in the Sound. Mr. Adison might here make the Experiment he speaks of in his travells, there not being one instrument of music among the Greek or Roman statues that is not to be found in the hands of the people of this country.[2] The young Lads gennerally divert themselves with makeing Girlands for their favourite Lambs, which I have often seen painted and adorn'd with flowers, lying at their feet while they sung or play'd. It is not that they ever read Romances, but these are the Ancient Amusements here, and as natural to them as Cudgel playing and football to our British Swains, the softness and warmth of the Climate forbiding all rough Exercises, which were never so much as heard of amongst 'em, and naturally inspiring a Lazyness and aversion to Labour, which the great Plenty indulges. These Gardiners are the only happy race of Country people in Turkey. They furnish all the City with Fruit and herbs, and seem to live very easily. They are most of 'em Greeks and have little Houses in the midst of their Gardens where their Wives and daughters take a Liberty not permitted in the Town: I mean, to go unvail'd. These Wenches are very neat and handsome, and pass their time at their Looms under the shade of their Trees. I no longer look upon Theocritus as a Romantic Writer; he has only given a plain image of the Way of Life amongst the Peasants of his Country, which before oppresion had reduc'd them to want, were I suppose all employ'd as the better sort of 'em are now. I don't doubt had he been born a Briton his Idylliums had been fill'd with Descriptions of Thrashing and churning, both which are unknown here, the Corn being all trod out by Oxen, and Butter (I speak it with sorrow) unheard of.

I read over your Homer[3] here with an infinite Pleasure, and find several little passages explain'd that I did not before entirely comprehend the Beauty of, many of the customs and much of the dress then in fashion being yet retain'd; and I don't wonder to find more remains here of an Age so distant than is to be found in any other Country, the Turks not takeing that pains to introduce their own Manners as has been generally practis'd by other nations that imagine themselves more polite. It would be too tedious to you to point out all the passages that relate to the present ¬ustoms, but I can assure you that the Princesses and great Ladys pass their time at their Looms embroidering Veils and Robes, surrounded by their Maids, which are allways very numerous, in the same Manner as we find Andromache and Helen describ'd. [4] The description of the belt of Menelaus exactly ressembles those that are now worn by the great Men, fasten'd before with broad Golden Clasps and embrodier'd round with rich work. [5] The Snowy Veil that Helen throws over her face is still fashionable; [6] and I never see (as I do very often) halfe a dozen old Bashaws with their reverend Beards siting basking in the Sun, but I recollect Good King Priam and his Councillors. Their manner of danceing is certainly the same that Diana is sung to have danc'd by Eurotas. [7] The great Lady still Leads the dance and is follow'd by a troop of young Girls who imitate her steps, and if she sings, make up the Chorus. The Tunes are extreme Gay and Lively, yet with something in 'em wonderfull soft. The steps are vary'd according to the Pleasure of her that leads the dance, but allways in exact time and infinitly more Agreable than any of our Dances, at least in my Opinion. I sometimes make one in the Train, but am not skilfull enough to lead. These are Grecian Dances, the Turkish being very different.

I should have told you in the first place that the Eastern Manners give a great light into many scripture passages that appear odd to us, their Phrases being commonly what we should call Scripture Language. The vulgar Turk is very different from what is spoke at Court or amongst the people of figure, who allways mix so much Arabic and Persian in their discourse that it may very well be call'd another Language; and 'tis as ridiculous to make use of the expressions commonly us'd, in speaking to a Great Man or a Lady, as it would be to talk broad Yorkshire or Sommerset shire in the drawing-room. Besides this distinction they have what they call the Sublime, that is, a stile proper for Poetry, and which is the exact scripture stile ...

4 From
LADY MARY WORTLEY MONTAGU
Letter to the Abbé Conti
31 July 1718 (published 1763)

All that is now left of Troy is the ground on which it stood, for I am firmly perswaded whatever pieces of Antiquity may be found round it are much more modern ... However, there is some pleasure in seeing the valley where I imagin'd the famous Duel of Menelaus and Paris had been fought,[1] and where the greatest city in the world was situate; and tis certainly the noblest Situation that can be found for the head of a great Empire ... North of the promontory of Sigæum, we saw that of Rhœteum, fam'd for the sepulchre of Ajax. While I view'd these celebrated Fields and Rivers, I admir'd the exact Geography of Homer, whom I had in my hand. Allmost every Epithet he gives to a Mountain or plain is still just for it, and I spent several hours in as agreable Cogitations as ever Don Quixote had on Mount Montesinos.[2] We saild that night to the shore where tis vulgarly reported Troy stood and I took the pains of rising at 2 in the morning to view cooly those Ruins which are commonly shew'd to strangers and which the Turks call eski-Stamboul, i.e. old Constantinople.[3] For that reason, as well as some others, I conjecture them to be the remains of that city begun by Constantine. I hir'd an Ass (the only voiture to be had there) that I might go some miles into the Country and take a tour round the Ancient Walls, which are of a vast extent. We found the remains of a castle on a Hill and another in a valley, several broken Pillars, and 2 pedestals from which I took these Latin Inscriptions . . .

Passing the strait between the Island of Andros and Achaia (now Libadia) we saw the Promontory of Sunium (now call'd Cape Colonna), where are yet standing the vast pillars of a Temple of Minerva. [4] This venerable sight made me think with double regret on a Beautifull Temple of Thesus, which I am assur'd was allmost entire at Athens till the last Campaign in the Morea, that the Turks fill'd it with Powder and it was accidentally blown up. [5] You may beleive I had a great mind to land on the fam'd Peloponessus, thô it were only to look on the Rivers of Asopus, Peneus, Inachus, and Eurotas, the Feilds of Arcadia and other Scenes of ancient Mythology. But instead of demy Gods and heros, I was credibly inform'd 'tis now over run by Robbers, and that I should run a great risque of falling into their hands by undertakeing such a Journey through a desart country . . . We came that evening in sight of Candia . . . I will pass by all the other Islands with this general refflection, that 'tis impossible to imagine any thing more agreable than this Journey would have been between 2 and 3,000 years since, when, after drinking a dish of tea with Sapho, I might have gone the same evening to visit the temple of Homer in Chios, and have pass'd this voyage in takeing plans of magnificent Temples, delineateing the miracles of Statuarys and converseing with the most polite and most gay of humankind. Alas! Art is extinct here. The wonders of Nature alone remain . . .

5 From
CHARLES CRAWFORD
A Dissertation on the Phaedon
(1733)

Charles Crawford, fellow-commoner of Queens' College, Cambridge, was not in any sense a notable figure; he is included here because his book on the *Phaedo* provides a simple-minded but striking illustration of the main prejudices which depressed the reputation of Plato in the eighteenth century. In particular, he takes a gloating pleasure in indicting Plato for homosexuality; it was this charge which Shelley felt it necessary to answer in his 'Discourse on the Manners of the Antient Greeks Relative to the Subject of Love' which was intended to facilitate a more sympathetic response to Plato's *Symposium* by placing it in its social and cultural context. There were others who criticized Plato not because they thought him immoral but because they felt that his notion of love was unrealistic. Chambers's *Cyclopaedia* provides a robustly self-satisfied example of this attitude: 'The world has a long time laughed at Plato's notion of love and friendship. In effect, they appear arrant chimeras, contrary to the intentions of nature, and inconsistent with the great law of self-preservation; which love and friendship are both ultimately resolvable into.'[1] Likewise, Byron asserted physiological reality in *Don Juan*: 'Oh Plato! Plato! you ... have been, / At best, no better than a go-between' (I.cxvi; for seventeenth-century analogies, see William Cartwright, 'No Platonique Love' and John Cleveland, 'The Antiplatonick'). See Nos. 18, 23, 25 and 34.

NOTE

1   *Cyclopaedia* by Ephraim Chambers (d. 1740) with a supplement by Abraham Rees, 1781.

[Preface]

I am of opinion that the credit which Plato has acquired in the world is the greatest satire upon the understanding of mankind. We scarce ever hear him spoken of but by the appellation of the divine, the immortal, or the god-like Plato.[1] Nay some have carried their admiration to such a pitch of extravagance, as to say that he was particularly and supernaturally inspired.—Amongst the Fanatics of this stamp we may reckon some of the Fathers, and the learned Monsieur Dacier, who wrote his Life, and translated some part of his works. [2]—Notwithstanding this, he was, to speak after a very celebrated writer, the most wild and inconsistent author that ever wrote, who instead of a rational system of philosophy, raised by the observation of the phænomena of Nature, constructed a fantastic hypothetical one of imagination, and corrupted the true springs of knowledge. His disciples, many of whom were men of learning and ability, contracted the errors of their master; they implanted them into those of their own time, and succeeding ages have adopted the infatuation. He laid a flimsey foundation for science, upon which the latter Platonicians have raised a superstructure that is altogether grotesque and uncouth. —There cannot be a greater instance of the blind partiality of mankind for this philosopher, than the distinguishing that friendship or affection, which has nothing sensual in it, by the appellation of *Platonic Love,* when he was as much addicted to a certain unnatural inclination, as any man of that sort who ever disgraced a human form.—We have the strongest evidence of his being guilty of this crime that history can furnish us with. [3] It is asserted by several, and denied by none ... His *Master-Misses* are said to have been without number.—How then must the bosom of every generous young man burn with indignation at the contempt, which was expressed by this unnatural philosopher, for that sex which ought to be the objects of his most fervent admiration! ...

—The man who prefers the love of boys to that of women, seems to me to have been cursed with as black a soul as he who would prefer deformity to beauty, idiotism to genius, filth to cleanliness, darkness to light, confusion to order, or hell to heaven . . .

6 From
THOMAS BLACKWELL
An Enquiry into the Life and Writings of Homer
(1735; second edition 1736)

Blackwell (1701–1757) became professor of Greek at Marischal College, Aberdeen when he was only twenty-four. His study of Homer which was first published anonymously was successful and influential, though it was not without its critics.[1] He started from the rather rigidly mechanistic premise that the poet is more or less entirely the product of external factors, a mimetic recorder rather than an individual genius. It followed that some authors are more privileged than others since certain kinds of society are especially propitious for the production of literature. For example, Congreve and Pope both produced accurate pictures of English society as they knew it but they were unlucky to live in an age in which natural and simple manners had been overlaid by the polished veneer of 'civilization' and in which poets were obliged to *unlearn* our daily way of Life'. In contrast, Homer lived in a society which was ideally suited to the needs of epic poetry. Throughout his book Blackwell emphasizes the 'naturalness' of the Greek way of life in Homer's time, which he compares unfavourably with the more 'civilized' behaviour of later and more sophisticated societies. Of course, his main concern is to isolate those factors which help to produce epic poetry not to make a comparison of the values of ancient and modern societies; yet one can detect in his language an unmistakable attraction towards the uncomplicated simplicities of the primitive. Blackwell speaks of his contemporaries with the vigorous contempt of a man who prefers the energetic to the polite. He acknowledges that the literature of his own hot-house society lacks the vigour of Homer's language which has many 'strong beautiful Expressions' and which exhibits 'a sufficient Quantity of its [language's] *Original, amazing, metaphoric* Tincture'. Yet he also recognizes that Homer's society was often brutal and violent and that it lacked the stability provided by cities and settled possessions. It seems that there is an unfortunate but necessary connection between violence and the incidence of epic poetry.

Blackwell's book is notable for its evocation of the life of a bard as Blackwell imagined it. As a bard, Homer was in a particularly privileged position: he mixed with all classes of society from kings to beggars, he observed the circumstances of trade and navigation, of war and peace. He was able to travel extensively both throughout Greece and abroad: he had first-hand knowledge of the plain of Troy and it seems likely that he had visited Egypt where he improved his knowledge of science and of theology. Homer was also fortunate in the time of his birth. Had he been born much sooner, 'he could have seen nothing but Nakedness and Barbarity'; had he come much later, he would have experienced either times of peace or a general state of warfare. As it was, he found Greek society at the one point in its development which was ideally suited for the creation of epic poetry.

Blackwell's book exerted considerable influence on the Scottish critics and in particular on Lord Monboddo, James Beattie, William Duff and James Macpherson, who were stimulated by his theories concerning primitive civilizations.[2] Monboddo's predilection for the ancient and the primitive was a celebrated feature of intellectual life (see Peacock's kindly satire in *Melincourt*) while Macpherson's simulation of epic in the Ossian prose-poems helped to shape German ideas of the primitive, which had already been influenced by Blackwell's theories.

NOTES

1   For contemporary reactions, see FOERSTER, pp.124–6.
2   See FOERSTER, pp. 41 f.

He [Homer] saw Towns taken and plundered, the Men put to
the Sword, and the Women made Slaves: He beheld their
despairing Faces, and suppliant Postures; heard their
Moanings o'er their murdered Husbands, and Prayers for
their Infants to the Victor.

On the other hand, he might view Cities blessed with
Peace, spirited by Liberty, flourishing in Trade, and
increasing in Wealth. He was not engaged in Affairs himself,
to draw off his Attention; but he wander'd through the
various Scenes, and observed them at leisure. Nor was it the
least instructive Sight, to see a *Colony* led out, a City
founded, the Foundations of Order and Policy laid, with all
the Provisions for the Security of the People: Such Scenes
afford *extended* Views, and natural ones too, as they are the
immediate Effect of the great Parent of Invention, *Necessity*,
in its young and untaught Essays.

The Importance of this good Fortune will best appear, if we
reflect on the Pleasure which arises from a Representation of
natural and *simple Manners*: It is irresistible and inchanting;
they best shew human Wants and Feelings; they give us back
the Emotions of an *artless* Mind, and the plain Methods we
fall upon to indulge them: Goodness and Honesty have their
Share in the Delight; for we begin to love the Men, and wou'd
rather have to do with them, than with more refined but
double Characters. Thus the various Works necessary for
building a House, or a Ship; for planting a Field, or forging a
Weapon, if described with an Eye to the Sentiments and
Attention of the Man so employed, give us great Pleasure,
because we feel the same. Innocence, we say, is beautiful; and
the Sketches of it, wherever they are truly hit off, never fail to
charm: Witness the few Strokes of that nature in Mr.
Dryden's *Conquest* of *Mexico*, and the *Inchanted Island*.[1]

Accordingly, we find *Homer* describing very minutely the
Houses, Tables, and Way of Living of the Ancients; and we

read these Descriptions with pleasure. But on the contrary, when we consider our own Customs, we find that our first Business, when we sit down to poetize in the higher Strains, is to *unlearn* our daily way of Life; to forget our manner of Sleeping, Eating, and Diversions: We are obliged to adopt a Set of *more natural* Manners, which however are foreign to us; and must be like Plants raised up in Hot-Beds or Green-Houses, in comparison of those which grow in Soils fitted by Nature for such Productions. Nay, so far are we from enriching Poetry with *new* Images drawn from Nature, that we find it difficult to understand the *old*. We live within Doors, cover'd, as it were, from *Nature's Face*; and passing our Days supinely ignorant of her Beauties. We are apt to think the Similies taken from her *low*, and the ancient Manners *mean*, or absurd. But let us be ingenuous, *My Lord*,[2] and confess, that while the Moderns admire nothing but Pomp, and can think nothing *Great* or *Beautiful*, but what is the Produce of Wealth, they exclude themselves from the pleasantest and most natural Images that adorned the old Poetry. *State* and *Form* disguise Man; and Wealth and Luxury disguise Nature. Their Effects in Writing are answerable: A Lord-Mayor's Show, or grand Procession of any kind, is not very delicious Reading, if described minutely, and at length; and great Ceremony is at least equally tiresome in a Poem, as in ordinary Conversation.

It has been an old Complaint, that we love to disguise every thing, and most of all *Ourselves*. All our Titles and Distinctions have been represented as Coverings, and Additions of Grandeur to what Nature gave us. Happy indeed for the best of Ends, I mean the publick Tranquillity and good Order; but incapable of giving delight in Fiction or Poetry.

By this time, your Lordship sees I am in the case of a noble Historian;[3] who having related the constant Superiority his *Greeks* had over the Inhabitants of the *Assyrian* Vales, concludes "That it has not been given by the Gods, to one and the same Country, to produce rich Crops and warlike Men:" Neither indeed does it seem to be given to one and the same Kingdom, to be throughly civilized, and afford proper Subjects for Poetry.

The *Marvellous* and *Wonderful* is the Nerve of the Epic Strain: But what marvellous Things happen in a well-ordered State? We can hardly be surprized; We know the Springs and Method of acting; Every thing happens in *Order*, and according to Custom or Law. But in a wide uncultivated Country, not under a regular Government, or split into many, whose Inhabitants live scattered, and ignorant of Laws and Discipline; In such a Country, the Manners are *simple*, and Accidents will happen every Day: Exposition and Loss of Infants; Encounters; Escapes; Rescues; and every other thing that can inflame the human Passions while acting, or awake them when described, and recalled by Imitation.

These are not to be found in a well-governed State, except it be during the Time of a *Civil War*, when it ceases to be so: and yet, with all the Disorder and Misery that attends that last of Ills, the Period while it rages is a fitter Subject for an Epic Poem, than the most glorious Campaign that ever was made in *Flanders*. Even the Things that give the greatest Lustre in a regular Government; the greatest Honours and highest Trusts, will scarcely bear *Poetry*: The *Muse* refuses to bestow her Embellishments on a *Duke*'s Patent, or a *General*'s Commission. They can neither raise our Wonder, nor gain our Heart: For Peace, Harmony and good Order, which make the Happiness of a People, are the *Bane* of a Poem that subsists by Wonder and Surprize.

To be convinced of this, we need only suppose that the *Greeks*, at the time of the *Trojan* War, had been a Nation eminent for Loyalty and Discipline: that Commissions in due Form had been issued out, Regiments raised, Arms and Horses bought up, and a compleat Army set on foot. Let us suppose that all Success had attended them in their Expedition; that every Officer had vied with another in Bravery against the Foe, and in Submission to his General: That in consequence of these Preparations, and of this good Order, they had at first Onset routed the *Trojans*, and driven them into the Town: Suppose this, and think,—What will become of the glorious *Iliad*? The Wrath of *Achilles*, the Wisdom of *Nestor*, the Bravery of *Diomedes*, and the Craft of *Ulysses* will vanish in a moment. But Matters are managed quite otherwise;

> Seditione, Dolis, Scelere atque Libidine & Ira,
> Iliacos intra Muros peccatur, & extra.[4]

It is thus that a People's Felicity clips the Wings of their Verse: It affords few Materials for Admiration or Pity; and tho' the Pleasure arising from the sublimer kinds of Writing, may make us regret the Silence of the Muses, yet I am persuaded your Lordship will join in the Wish, *That we may never be a proper Subject of an* Heroic Poem . . .

From   **Section 4**

In effect, *Arms* at that time was the honoured Profession, and a *publick Spirit* the courted Character: There was a Necessity for them both. The *Man* who had bravely defended his City, enlarged its Dominion, or died in its Cause, was revered like a God: Love of Liberty, and Contempt of Death, with their noblest Consequences, Honour, Probity, and Temperance, were *Realities*. There was, as I said, a *Necessity* for those Virtues: No Safety to Life or Fortune without them: For while every State, that is to say, almost every City was envied by its warlike and encroaching Neighbour, there was no choice, but either resolutely to defend itself by dint of Arms, or shamefully submit to Oppression and Slavery. And no wonder if the Man who learns these Virtues from *Necessity*, and the Things themselves, knows them better than Schools and Systems can instruct him; and that the Representations of such genuine Characters bear the Marks of *Truth*, and far outshine those taken from counterfeit Worth, or fainter Patterns.

Thus we find, that the *Fortunes*, the *Manners*, and the *Language* of a People are all linked together, and necessarily influence one another. Men take their Sentiments from their Fortunes; if they are low, it is their constant Concern *how to mend them*; if they are easy, *how to enjoy them*: And according to this Bent, they turn both their Conduct and their Conversation; and assume the Language, Air, and Garb peculiar to the *Manner* of the different Characters.

In most of the *Greek* Cities, *Policy* and *Laws* were but just a forming, when *Homer* came into the World. The first Sketches of them were extremely *simple*; taking their Rise from the Exigencies of the rude Way of Life then prevailing. The great Law of *Hospitality* made the chief Part of the Institution: To violate a Stranger, who had taken Sanctuary under your *Roof*, had participated of your *Table*, or sat down by your *Fire*, was made the highest, and most detestable Impiety. The rest were of a piece; generally Prohibitions from Violence, or such Regulations of Manners as we should think unnecessary or barbarous. The Tribes were but beginning to live secure within the Walls of their new-fenced Towns, and had as yet neither Time nor Skill to frame a Domestick Policy, or Municipal Laws; and far less to think of publick Methods of training up their Citizens: *They lived naturally,* and were governed by the *natural Poise* of the Passions, as it is settled in every human Breast. This made them speak and act, without other Restraint than their own native Apprehensions of *Good* and *Evil, Just* and *Unjust*, each as he was prompted from *within*. "These Manners afford the most *natural* Pictures, and proper Words to paint them."

They have a peculiar Effect upon the Language, not only as they are natural, but as they are ingenuous and *good*. While a Nation continues simple and sincere, whatever they say receives a *Weight* from *Truth*: Their Sentiments are strong and honest; which always produce *fit Words* to express them: Their Passions are sound and genuine, not adulterated or disguised, and break out in their own artless Phrase and unaffected Stile. They are not accustomed to the *Prattle*, and little pretty *Forms* that enervate a polished Speech: nor are they over-run with *Quibble* and *Sheer-Wit*, which makes its Appearance late in every Country, and in *Greece* came long after the *Trojan* Times. And *this* I take to be the reason, "Why most Nations are so delighted with their ancient Poets:" [5] Before they are polished into Flattery and refined into Falsehood, we feel the *Force* of their *Words*, and the *Truth* of their *Thoughts*.

In common Life, no doubt, the witty facetious Man is now the preferable Character: But he is only a *middling* Person, and no *Hero*; bearing a Personage for which there is hardly an Inch of room in an *Epic Poem*. To be witty in a Matter of Consequence, where the Risque is high, and the Execution requires *Caution* or *Boldness*, is *Impertinence* and *Buffoonry* . . .

From Section 8

It is, I think, generally allowed that *Homer* took his Characters from *Nature* or *real Life*; and if so, the Picture of the ΑΟΙΔΟΣ [6] is his *own*. He does indeed omit no opportunity to *do honour* to the Profession, nor even to mention it. He has painted every Circumstance of it, draws Similies from it, tells its effects upon the Hearers, and of all the Wooers who had been devouring *Ulysses*' Estate in his absence, he spares not one, save *Phemius* the *Bard*, and a ΚΗΡΥΞ, or *Publick Servant*. [7]

Few people have conceived a just Opinion of this Profession, or entered into its *Dignity*. The Reason of which I take to be, That we have no modern Character like it: For I should be unwilling to admit the *Irish* or *Highland Rüners*[8] to a share of the Honour; tho' their Business, which is to entertain a Company with the Recital of some Adventure, resembles a part of the other. The *Trovadores* or *Troubadours* of *Provence*, the earliest of the Moderns who discovered any Vein for Poetry, have a better Claim. They sung their Verses to the Harp, or other Instrument they cou'd use, and attained to a just *Cadence* and *Return* of Verse in their *Stanza's*; but had neither Manners nor Language for great Attempts.

This ignorance of an ancient Character has made some ingenious Men, and Admirers of *Homer*, take pains to vindicate him from it, as a mean and contemptible Calling; or at least to dissemble and slur it over. It was indeed no Life of Wealth or Power, but of great *Ease* and much *Honour*. The ΑΟΙΔΟΙ were welcome to Kings and Courts; were necessary at Feasts and Sacrifices; and were highly reverenced by the People . . .

It will easily be granted, that Men pinched in their *Living*, and forced to have their Thoughts ever upon the stretch for Subsistence, cannot have room for rapturous Views, and poetick Strains. [9] The same Reason excludes all Men of *Business,* who are thoroughly so, from the Society of the *Muses.*

Now if we were to sit down and contrive, *what kind* of Life is the least obnoxious to these Inconveniences, we shall find none so free from *Care, Business,* or *Want*, as that of a *Bard*. It is exactly the easy, independent State, that is unawed by *Laws*, and the *Regards* that molest us in Communities; that knows no Duties or Obligations but those of Hospitality and Humanity: that subjects the Mind to no Tincture of Discipline, but lays it open to all the *natural Sensations*, with which the various Parts of the Universe affect a *sagacious, perceptive, mimicking Creature.*

As this Condition is in itself of the utmost Importance to a *Poet*, the Consequences of it are almost equally happy: The ΑΟΙΔΟΙ, or *Bards*, were under a necessity of frequent Travelling, and every now and then exercising their *Vein* upon the greatest Subjects. In this Situation did *Homer* begin to wander over *Greece*, carrying with him those *Qualities* that procured him a *Welcome* wherever he came. I have already shewn what a noble Scene for Travelling the *Grecian Cities* and young Commonwealths then afforded. *Homer* staid so long in each of them, as was necessary *to see*, but not to be *moulded* into their Manners. The *Order* of a Town, and the *Forms* brought into the common City-life, elude the Passions, and abate their Force by turning them upon little Objects. But he neither led a Town nor Country-Life; and in this respect was truly a *Citizen of the Universe* ...

The next Advantage of *Homer's* Profession, was the *Access* it gave him into the Houses and Company of the *Greatest Men*. The Effects of it appear in every Line of his Works; not only in his Characters of them, and Accounts of their Actions; but the more *familiar* Part of Life; their manner of Conversing and method of Entertaining, are accurately and minutely painted. He knows their Rarities and *Plate*, and can hold forth the Neatness and Elegance of their *Bijouterie*. He has nicely inspected the Trinkets their Ladies wore; their *Bracelets, Buckles,* and *Necklaces*, whose Prettinesses he sometimes talks of with great Taste and Exactness ... In a word, there is scarce a Circumstance in *Oeconomy* but what he has somewhere described, or made it evident that he knew.

Nor cou'd it be otherwise, if we consider the daily Life of the ΑΟΙΔΟΙ. The Manner was, when a *Bard* came to a House, he was first welcomed by the Master, and after he had been entertained according to the ancient Mode; that is, after he had bathed, eaten, and drunk some ΜΕΛΙΗΔΕΑ ΟΙΝΟΝ , *heart-chearing Wine*, he was called upon to entertain the Family in his turn: He then tuned his *Lyre*, and raised his *Voice*, and sung to the listening Crowd some Adventure of the *Gods*, or some Performance of *Men*.

Many Advantages accrue from hence to the *Poet*: He is under a happy Necessity of making no *fanciful Conceits*, or profound Verses in an uncommon Language: But if he would succeed, he must entertain his wondering Audience in a simple, intelligible Stile. He might indeed tell wonderful Stories of strange Performances, and Places strange: but they must be *plainly* told, and with a constant eye to *natural Manners* and *human Passions*: He needed not keep strictly to them; *that* wou'd raise no Admiration; but with an Analogy or Likeness, such as the Tenour and Circumstance of the *tender* or *woeful* Tale wou'd bear.

Here too was abundance of Opportunities not only of *judging* what was amiss, what was true or false in his *Song*; but of *helping it*. While he was personating a *Hero*; while his Fancy was warming, and his Words flowing; when he had fully entered into the *Measure*, was struck with the *Rhythmus*, and seized with the *Sound*; like a Torrent, he wou'd fill up the Hollows of the Work; the boldest Metaphors and glowing Figures wou'd come rushing upon him, and cast a *Fire* and *Grace* into the Composition, which no Criticism can ever supply.

As to the *Audience*, I might shew the Good-fortune of our Poet in that particular, by reminding your Lordship of the Monitor of the younger *Gracchus*, or the *Slave* who directed and check'd the most fluent Orator of *Augustus*' Court;[10] but *Moliere's old Woman* comes nearest our Purpose. It was by her Ear and Taste that that celebrated Comedian tried the success of his Comic Scenes, and as they affected her more or less, so he judged of their Force and Failures. Thus the most approved Writer among the Moderns makes choice of a Circumstance for his Rule that *Homer* was obliged to regard in every Performance.

The more we consider its Influence upon Poetry, the stronger and wider it appears: To this Necessity of pleasing his Audience, I wou'd ascribe that *just Measure* of *Probability and Wonder* which runs thro' the greatest part of his Works. The People must be entertained: that is, they must be kept at *a gaze*, and at the same time must comprehend the Dangers, and feel the Passions of the Description. The

Adventure must be such as they can understand; and the Method in which it is brought about, must surprize their Imagination, draw forth their Attention, and win their Heart. This at once accounts for the Stories which *Homer* tells, improbable indeed in themselves, and yet bearing such a *Resemblance* to Nature and Truth ... For his Poems were made to be *recited,* or sung to a *Company*; and not read in private, or perused in a Book, which few were then capable of doing: and I will venture to affirm, that whoever reads not *Homer* in *this View* loses a great Part of the Delight he might receive from the Poet.

His stile, properly so called, cannot be understood in any other light; nor can the *Strain*, and *Manner* of his Work be felt and relished unless we put ourselves in the place of his Audience, and imagine it coming from the Mouth of a *Rhapsodist*: Neither to say the truth, is there any thing but *this* situation, that will fully account for all his Heroes telling miraculous Tales as well as himself, and sometimes in the *Heat of a Battle*. But when we remember his *Profession*, and his common *Audience*, we see the Necessity of *Stories*, and of such as he usually tells. It was not the Inhabitants of a *great luxurious City* he had to entertain with unnatural Flights, and lewd Fancies; but the martial Race of a wide and free Country, who willingly listen to the Prowess of their Ancestors, and Atchievements of their Kings.

It wou'd be tedious to insist upon every particular in the Life of a *Rhapsodist*; but there are two Advantages more which deserve our notice. The first is the *Habit* which the Poet must acquire by singing *extempory Strains*. We have daily proofs of the power of *Practice* in every Art and Employment. An Inclination indulged turns to a *Habit*, and that, when cultivated, rises to an *Ease* and *Mastery* in the Profession. It immediately affects our Speech and Conversation; as we daily see in *Lawyers, Seamen*, and most Sets of Men who converse with ease and fluency in their *own* Stile, tho' they are often puzzled when forced to affect another. To what heights such a *Genius* as *Homer's* might rise by constant Culture, is hard to tell; *Eustathius* says, "That he breathed nothing but *Verse*; and was so possess'd with the *Heroic Muse*, as to speak in *Numbers* with more ease than others in *Prose*."

The second Peculiarity which attends a *Stroling Life* is, *great Returns of Mirth and Humour*. After suffering Cold and Fatigue, a flood of Joy comes impetuous upon a Man when he is refreshed, and begins to grow warm. His Heart dilates, his Spirits flow, and if there is any *Vein of Humour* or Thought within him, it will certainly break loose, and be set a running. The *poetick,* and most kinds of Strolers, are commonly Men of great Health; of the quickest and truest Feelings: They are obliged to no exhausting Labour, to stiffen their Bodies and depress their Minds. Their Life is the likest to the plentiful State of the *Golden Age*; without Care or Ambition, full of Variety and Change, and constantly giving or receiving the most natural and elegant Pleasures . . .

From **Section 12**

I cannot pretend to determine the precise time he tarried in each Country; how soon he left *Ionia*, or how frequently he returned to it. A great part of his Life he spent in *Chios*, whose Inhabitants were *Ionians* as well as those of the other Islands in the *Archipelago*. It is accordingly certain, that his Language and Manners are principally *Ionic*, tho' all the Dialects of *Greece* are employed in his Poetry, and give proof that he has visited the principal Nations, and learned the Peculiarities of their Speech. His *own*, no doubt, has been formed, where he spent his Youth; and afterwards, by wandering up and down in *Asia* and *Greece*, he hath attained that easy familiar manner of speaking of them, for which he is admired. This is a Blessing so rare in a Poet's Lot, to be as it were a *Native of both Countries*, that it will be worth while to take a View of some of its Consequences.

The first which presents itself, is *That he* must have been acquainted with the *Field of Action*, the *Plains of Troy*. It was this enabled him to describe it so minutely; and give it that Air of Veracity it bears from those *natural Incidents* he has thrown into his Narration. He had them, not by Reading or Speculation, but from the *Places themselves*, and the Prospects that arise from the Culture and Disposition of the Grounds. *Who* but the Man that had wandered over that delightful Plain, that had viewed the Bendings of the Coast, and every Corner of the Fields, could have described or feigned the genuine *Marks* of it: The *Tomb* of *Dardanus*, the *Springs* of *Scamander*, the *Banks* of *Simoïs*, the *Beach Tree*, with many other Circumstances that distinguish the *Environs*, and enrich his Landskip? Other Writers, before they relate an Action that happened in any place, first *describe that Place*, be it a Grove, or Rock, or River, or the Declivity of a Mountain. These they *feign* according to the strength of their Fancy, and then they *apply them.*[11] *Homer* mentions his Places with an appearance of Certainty, *as already subsisting*, and already *known*: He does it almost in the manner of an *Historian*, and leaves you to pick up a more particular Knowledge of them from the Circumstances of the Action to which they belong . . .

The Characteristick of *Homer*'s Hero is *violent Passion*; his *honoratus Achilles* must be '*Impiger, iracundus, inexorabilis, acer*':[12] Paint him, says *Horace*, '*Forward, and fierce, of unrelenting Wrath.*' Nay so great was his *Impotence* of Mind, that when the young *Antilochus* brought him the dismal News of *Patroclus*'s Death, he was forced to hold the Hands of the distracted Hero, lest he should have attempted to cut his own Throat. It is true, we are apt to make *allowances* for this Excess of Passion: We think of the *ill Usage* he met with: Our *eye* is turned upon his unbounded *Courage* and superior Strength, and we are willing to *bear* with his haughty Spirit:

But what shall we say to the *Prince* of the *Grecian* Powers, who was to think for them all, and lead their Armies; their Stay and Confidence, the stately *Agamemnon*? How is he tossed and agitated between *Anger, Love*, and *Dread* of a Miscarriage? He is not ashamed to own his Passion for a *Captive Maid*, in face of the whole Army: He tells them plainly "that he likes her much better than his Lady, the beautiful *Clytemnestra*, of the prime *Grecian* Nobility."[13] He is besides, now and then, a little *covetous*; and tortur'd with *Fear* to such a degree, that his Teeth chatter, and his Knees strike one against another; He groans and weeps, and rends his Hair; and is in such *piteous plight*, that if we were not well assured of his personal Bravery, we should take him for a downright *Coward*.

But *Virgil* durst make no such Condescension to Nature, nor represent the *human Frailties* in their genuine Light. His Characters are all *formed* and *regulated*; and except that his *Hero* is sometimes, as Don *Quixote* says of his *Amadis, algo lloron, a little apt to weep*; excepting *that*, and the Cave-Adventure, [14] he behaves in every other respect with all the Dignity and Reserve of a *Roman Senator*.

Here the Force of the *Model* appears, and the Power of *publick Manners. Virgil's* Poem was to be read by a People deeply disciplin'd; whose early Necessities had taught them *political Forms*, and from being a Company of *Banditti*, had *forced* them into publick Virtue. These Forms had time to take root in the Minds and Manners of the Nation; and *Constancy, Severity*, and *Truth*, was become a *Roman* Character. Even when the Substance was gone, when Luxury and high Ambition had stript them of their original Integrity, they were still forced to feign and dissemble: They put on a *Shew* of Virtue; and tho' they were really vicious, and knew themselves to be so, yet they could not bear a *professed Ruffian*, nor an *avowed Profligate*: They became nicely sensible of Reputation, and what they called a Man's *Fortune*; not in our Sense of the Word, but that *Fate*, which as they imagin'd, attends every Man, and over-rules all human Enterprizes. For this reason they did not love that any *Accident*, which had frighted or put them in disorder, should be known. They thought it diminished their Authority, and made them *look little* in the Eyes of the People; and therefore concealed their Passions, and the Events that raised them. Thus they *disunited* things from their Appearances, and by that means disguised their *Humanity*.

But the *natural Greek*, in *Homer*'s days, covered none of his Sentiments. He frankly owned the Pleasures of *Love* and *Wine*; he told how voraciously he *eat* when he was hungry, and how horribly he was *frighted* when he saw an approaching Danger: He look'd upon no means as base to escape it; and was not at all ashamed to relate the *Trick* or *Fetch* that had brought him off: While the *haughty Roman*, who scorn'd to owe his Life to any thing but his Virtue and Fortitude, despised accidental Escapes, and fortuitous Relief in Perils; and snuffed at the *Suppleness* and *Levity of Mind* necessary to put them in practice.

7   From
JOHN DYER
The Ruins of Rome. A Poem
(1740)

John Dyer (1699–1758) is best known as the author of *Grongar Hill* (1727). *The Ruins of Rome* is not, in itself, an example of Romantic Hellenism but it is included here because it illustrates several trends of sensibility which were to be important in the literature stimulated by the Greek landscape. Dyer among the ruins of Rome bears a close similarity to English travellers and poets at Troy, Athens, Corinth, Ephesus, Mycenae and many other sites which were famous in classical antiquity. His poem belongs to a tradition which can be traced back in English to Spenser's *The Ruines of Time*; in its turn it looks forward to Goldsmith,

Wordsworth, Shelley and many others. See Laurence Goldstein, *Ruins and Empire: the Evolution of a Theme in Augustan and Romantic Literature*, Pittsburgh, 1977, MACAULAY and Nos. 11 and 33. The notes are Dyer's own and are given at the end of the extract.

O'er which in distant View
Th'*Etruscan* Mountains swell, with Ruins crown'd
Of antient Towns; and blue Soracte spires,
Wrapping his sides in Tempests. Eastward hence,
Nigh where the *Cestian Pyramid* divides [1]
The mould'ring Wall, behold yon Fabric huge
Whose dust the solemn Antiquarian turns,
And thence, in broken Sculptures cast abroad,
Like *Sybil*'s leaves, collects the Builder's Name
Rejoic'd, and the green Medals frequent found
Doom *Caracalla* to perpetual Fame:
The stately Pines, that spread their branches wide
In the dun Ruins of its ample Halls, [2]
Appear but Tufts; as may whate'er is High
Sink in Comparison, minute and vile.
    These, and unnumber'd, yet their brows uplift,
Rent of their Graces; as *Brittania*'s Oaks
On *Merlin*'s Mount or *Snowden*'s rugged sides,
Stand in the Clouds, their branches scatter'd round,
After the tempest; *Mausoleums, Cirques,
Naumachias*, Forums; *Trajan*'s *Column* Tall,
From whose low base the Sculptures wind aloft,
And lead, through various Toils, up the rough Steep,
It's Hero to the Skies: And his dark *Tow'r*, [3]
Whose execrable hand the City fir'd,
And, while the dreadful Conflagration blaz'd,
Play'd to the Flames; and *Phoebus' letter'd Dome*; [4]
And the rough Reliques of *Carinae*'s Street,
Where now the Shepherd to his nibbling sheep

Sits piping with his oaten reed; as erst
There pip'd the Shepherd to his nibbling sheep,
When th'humble Roof *Anchises'* Son explor'd
Of good *Evander*, wealth-despising King,
Amid the Thickets: so revolves the Scene;
So Time ordains, who rolls the things of Pride
From Dust again to Dust: Behold that Heap
Of mouldring Urns (their Ashes blown away,
Dust of the Mighty) the same Story tell;
And at it's Base, from whence the Serpent glides
Down the green desert Street, yon hoary Monk
Laments the same, the Vision as he views,
The Solitary, Silent, Solemn Scene,
Where Caesars, Heroes, Peasants, Hermits lie,
Blended in dust together; where the Slave
Rests from his Labours; where th'insulting Proud
Resigns his Pow'r; The Miser drops his Hoard;
Where Human Folly sleeps.—There is a Mood,
(I sing not to the vacant and the young)
There is a kindly Mood of Melancholy,
That wings the Soul and points her to the skies;
When Tribulation cloaths the child of Man,
When Age descends with sorrow to the grave,
'Tis sweetly-soothing Sympathy to Pain,
A gently-wak'ning Call to Health and Ease,
How musical! When all-devouring Time,
Here sitting on his Throne of Ruins hoar,
With Winds and Tempests sweeps his various Lyre,
How sweet thy Diapason, Melancholy!
  Cool Ev'ning comes; the setting Sun displays
His visible great Round between yon Tow'rs,
As through two shady Cliffs; away my Muse,
Though yet the Prospect pleases, ever new
In vast Variety, and yet delight
The many figur'd Sculptures of the path
Half beauteous, half effac'd; the Traveller

Such antique Marbles to his native Land
Oft hence conveys; and ev'ry realm and state
With *Rome*'s august Remains, Heroes and Gods,
Deck their long Galleries and winding Groves;
Yet miss we not th'innumerable Thefts,
Yet still profuse of graces teems the Waste.

   Suffice it Now *th'Esquilian Mount* to reach
With weary Wing, and seek the sacred Rests
Of *Maro*'s *humble Tenement*; a low
Plain Wall remains; a little sun-gilt Heap,
Grotesque and Wild: the Gourd and Olive brown
Weave the light Roof; the Gourd and Olive fan
Their am'rous foliage, mingling with the Vine,
Who drops her purple Clusters through the Green.
Here let me lie, with pleasing fancy sooth'd . . .

NOTES

1   *The Tomb of Cestius*, partly within and partly without the Walls.
2   *The Baths of Caracalla*, a vast Ruin.
3   *Nero*'s.
4   The *Palatin* Library.

8 *From*
JOSEPH SPENCE

Polymetis: or, an Enquiry concerning the Agreement between
the Works of the Roman Poets, and the Remains of
the Antient Artists
(1747; second edition 1755)

Spence (1699–1768) was the author of *Anecdotes*, and both
Professor of Modern History and Professor of Poetry at Oxford.
Polymetis was a popular handbook whose heavily documented text

was enriched by numerous illustrations mainly from statues, gems and vases; this conjunction of the literary and the visual was based on the premise that 'Scarce any thing can be good in a poetical description; which would appear absurd, if represented in a statue, or picture'. This coincided well with the taste of many of Spence's contemporaries; his interest in the picturesque would have been well satisfied by Pope's transmogrification of Homer into (among other things) a landscape painter with an eighteenth-century sense of order and perspective (see p. 136).

However, his book was founded on several false premises, the most fundamental of which according to Thomas Gray was that 'he professes to neglect the Greek Writers, who could have given him more Instruction on the very Heads he professes to treat, than all the others put together'.[1] The first extract reveals that this weighting was deliberate; Spence is not concerned with those Greek deities who were not 'naturalized in Rome', just as he excludes the gods of the underworld from the calm precincts of the garden in which *Polymetis* is set.

Secondly, as Lessing pointed out in *Laokoon* (1766), Spence's approach was both simple-minded and erroneous: 'to attempt to establish such illustrations by finding design in what was mere accident, and especially to attribute to the poet in every trifle a reference to this statue or that painting, is to render him a very equivocal service', with the result that Spence's book 'is altogether intolerable to any reader of taste'.[2] More crucially still, Spence was misled by the Horatian adage *ut pictura poesis* into the false assumption that there was little essential difference between the modes of poetry and the plastic arts.

In spite of these shortcomings, Spence is included here because of his popularity and influence—'it was such men as Spence who during the eighteenth century kept alive the attractive aspects of myth and bequeathed them to the romantic writers of the nineteenth century'.[3] Keats certainly made use of *Polymetis* and it may have encouraged him to conceive his mythological scenes in terms which were influenced by painting and sculpture.[4] Spence also provides an instructive contrast with later writers on art such as Winckelmann, who knew his book and with whose description of the *Apollo Belvedere* the second extract should be compared (see pp. 128–9). Spence's tone is much less intense than that of

Winckelmann. His handbook was designed to treat a serious subject with urbanity and 'to take off some of the sullenness, and severity, that has generally been thrown over the studies of Criticism, and Antiquities'. Yet, although the prose is sufficiently clear and unassuming and the opening chapter in particular captures something of the relaxed intimacy which Spence was aiming for, *Polymetis* also conveys a strongly didactic flavour. Perhaps this is not altogether surprising: Spence had been tutor and companion to the Earl of Middlesex, John Morley Trevor and the Earl of Lincoln on their Grand Tours of France and Italy (1730–3, 1737–8, 1739–42).[5]

NOTES

1 *Correspondence of Thomas Gray*, ed. P. Toynbee and L. Whibley, Oxford, 1935, i.268–70.
2 Tr. by W. A. Steel, Everyman edition, London and New York, 1930, p. 34.
3 FELDMAN and RICHARDSON, p. 132.
4 See Ian Jack, *Keats and the Mirror of Art*, Oxford, 1967.
5 See Joseph Spence, *Letters from the Grand Tour*, ed. Slava Klima, Montreal and London, 1975.

From   Book 1, Dialogue 1
The General Design of the Work

Polymetis, who is as well known for his taste in the polite arts, as for his superiour talents in affairs of state, took two or three of his friends with him the last summer to his villa near the town; to breathe fresh air, and relax themselves after the business of a long session. It was customary with the old Greeks and Romans, to talk over points of philosophy at their tables. Polymetis kept up this good old custom at his house; ...nd the part of the entertainment that was generally the most agreeable to his friends, consisted in the discourses he gave then. on learning, or on the polite arts; of which he was extreamly fond. They came thither always with some expectation of it; and seldom left his table without being pleased, and perhaps improved, by their treat.

At present the party consisted only of himself, Philander, and Mysagetes; two persons equally friends to Polymetis; tho' very different in their own tempers: This, of a gayer turn; the other of a serious one . . .

They came early to the villa: and sat down to their tea, in the library; which looks directly upon the gardens, that were just then finished and brought to their present perfection. You see, says Polymetis, I have followed the taste in fashion (which, as it happens, is certainly the best taste too) of making my gardens rather wild than regular. Their general air, I hope, has nothing stiff and unnatural in it; and the lower part, in particular, joins in with the view of the country, as if it made a part of it. Indeed the mode has allowed me to have as many temples as I could wish, in such a space of ground: but I would not have you imagine that they are temples only for shew; I have found out a use for them, which you might not think of. The statues I got formerly from Italy, and which used to croud up all my house, are placed in them . . .

The deities of the Romans (says Polymetis) were so numerous, that they might well complain of wanting a Nomenclatour to help them to remember all their names. Their vulgar religion, as indeed that of the heathens in general, was a sort of Manicheism. [1] Whatever was able to do good or to do harm to man, was immediately looked on as a superiour power; which, in their language, was the same as a deity. It was hence that they had such a multitude of gods, that their temples were better peopled with statues, than their cities with men. It is a perfect mob of deities, if you look upon them all together: but they are reducible enough to order; and fall into fewer classes, than one would at first imagine. I have reduced them to six; and considering their vast number, it was no little trouble to bring them into that compass . . .

What a pity it is, says Mysagetes smiling, that you should

not get a Hell to adorn your garden with, and make the work compleat? Why seriously, replied Polymetis, I have thought even of that. One might have contrived a deep wood, toward the bottom of the hill, which should have led you through a narrow walk (growing every step darker and darker, as more thickened with yew and cypress) down to a vast, rough horrid cave: in which such a gloomy light let in from above, as falls about the middle of the grotto of Pausilipo,[2] might have half shewn you and half concealed the dismal deities and inhabitants of the lower world. But had this been proper for a garden that does not belong to Benedictins or Carthusians, it might however be very well spared in my present design. My collection, you know, consists wholly of antiques: and there are so few antient statues that any way relate to the subterraneous world, that I should have been at some loss for the most proper furniture for such a repository; had I been ever so fond of introducing it. As to what other remains there are of this kind, tho' you do not meet with them in my garden, I may perhaps find another place more convenient to shew you some of them; if you should be fond of such terrible sights. So that on the whole, I think I have done right in contenting myself here with the temples of the heavens, and the four elementary ones, which you see under it: in which are all the figures I have of the imaginary beings that belong to either of them; disposed each according to his rank and character.

The statues are placed in niches made for them; and ornamented with copies of such antient relievo's or pictures as relate to them. In their pedestals, I have contrived drawers, to put in the medals, gems, prints and drawings, I have been so long getting together: such under each, as have any reference to the deity they are placed under: much in the manner as the books of the Sibyls were kept by Augustus in the base of the Palatine Apollo.[3] And thus I have disposed of all my collection, with somewhat more of regularity and order, than is generally observed in much better collections than I am master of.

You, Philander, know that my principal view in making this collection was to compare the descriptions and expressions in the Roman poets that any way relate to the imaginary beings, with the works that remain to us of the old artists; and to please myself with the mutual lights they might give each to the other. I have often thought when in Italy, and at Rome in particular, that they enjoy there the convenience of a sort of cotemporary comments on Virgil and Horace, in the nobler remains of the antient statuaries and painters. When you look on the old pictures or sculptures, you look on the works of men who thought much in the same train with the old poets. There was generally the greatest union in their designs: and where they are engaged on the same subjects, they must be the best explainers of one another. As we lie so far north from this last great seat of empire, we are placed out of the reach of consulting these finer remains of antiquity so much, and so frequently, as one could wish. The only way of supplying this defect to any degree among us, is by copies, prints, and drawings: and as I have long had this thought, my collection is at length grown very numerous; and indeed almost as full as I could desire it, as to the point which has all along been my particular aim.

I have always admired your collection, says Philander; but might not one who has no such collection, make a shift with father Montfaucon? [4] That father's work, replied Polymetis, is largely stockt with figures; and perhaps too largely, to be of service in the design we are talking of. We are much obliged to him for his industry: but his choice is rather too loose and unconfined. He has taken in all the different figures he could meet with; of whatever age, or country. You have, even in the better part of his collection, Tuscan gods mixt with Roman; old Gallick figures, with those of Syria: and the monsters of Egypt, with the deities of Athens. This must bring in a great deal of confusion, and strangely multiply the appearance and attributes of almost every deity. As you see them there, the descriptions of them in the Roman poets do not agree with the artists; nor the works of the artists with the poets. As my view was a more particular one, I found myself obliged to confine my collection to the deities as received in Italy; and even in such parts of Italy only, where they were uniformly received. This cuts off any figures that were not of the growth, or at least made free of Rome . . .

I am very glad, says Mysagetes, to hear that you have decimated your gods: for I should have been heartily vext to see a deity with a dog's, or a hawk's head, upon its shoulders: and could never have been brought to view a Squat-Jug[5] with the respect that may, perhaps, be due to whatever was formerly the divinity of a great and learned nation.

From **Book 2, Dialogue 8**

On their return to the Rotonda, Polymetis led his friends directly to the statue of Apollo; who stands so gracefully, in the act of shooting off his bow. They easily knew it to be a copy of the Apollo Belvedere. Among all the statues of the antients, (says Polymetis,) which the moderns have as yet discovered, there are about twenty that might be placed in the first class; each as the chief beauty, in its kind. For example, there is nothing in marble equal to the Venus of Medici, for softness and tenderness; as there is nothing so strong and nervous, as the Hercules Farnese. The face of the dying gladiator, is the most expressive of a human passion; and the air of the Apollo Belvedere, gives us an idea of something above human; more strongly, than any figure among the great numbers that remain to us. These are all therefore constantly reckoned in this superior class: and as the excellence of the Apollo Belvedere consists in the expression of something divine, whereas the rest excel only in things that are common to men; this statue may, perhaps justly enough, claim the preference, even in this distinguished class of the best remains of all antiquity.

Any one, who has been much used to see collections of antient statues, may remember that the first and chief thing by which he used to distinguish an Apollo, (at a distance, or in a croud of figures,) was the beauty of his face. He is handsomer than Mercury; and not so effeminate as Bacchus; his two chief rivals for beauty, among all the deities of his own sex. And it is remarkable, by the way, that the Roman poets, when they are speaking of the softer beauties or fine air of any prince, or hero, generally compare them to one or other of these three gods; and oftner to Apollo, than to either of the other. This most usual compliment of theirs is a very high one; for indeed nothing can be conceived finer than the face of Apollo. His features are all extremely beautiful, according to our common ideas of beauty; beside which, his face has sometimes an air of divinity diffused over it, (and particularly in the Apollo Belvedere,) of which we should have had no idea at all, without the help of the artist. He is always young and beardless; and his long beautiful hair, when unconfined, falls in natural easy waves, all down his shoulders; and sometimes over his breast. His stature is free and erect. His limbs, are exactly proportioned; with as much of softness in all of them, as is consistent with strength: and with a grace resulting from the whole, which is much more easily felt than described; and which indeed it would be very impertinent to pretend to describe, to any one who has seen the Apollo Belvedere.

If we have so high ideas of the beauty of Apollo from the statues we see of him; what ideas must the old Roman poets have had, who saw him so much oftner, both in marble and in colours; and who set their own imaginations to work, to form the finest notions of him that they could? It is hence that they speak so very highly of his beauty. Virgil calls him the Beautiful; and Tibullus, the Well-shaped God.[6] The latter of these poets has a full description of his person, which I must read to you; the rather, because I suspect it contains several strokes taken from some very celebrated pictures; which might be generally known and admired at Rome in his time, tho' they are lost to us . . . [7]

Nothing was looked upon as more essential to the beauty of any young person among the Romans, than a long fine head of hair. This is one of the distinguishing things, in the heads of Apollo in old gems; and is extremely well expressed in this description. One meets with it often too in the statues of this god; and particularly, in a very fine one, in the Great Duke's gallery . . . The Romans had a custom of cutting their hair short, at a certain age; and of keeping it forever after. This ceremony, (for they made a great ceremony of it,) was performed in their youth; when they were about seventeen, or eighteen: and this is one reason of their poets taking so much notice of the long hair of Apollo, and of their giving him so frequently the titles of Crinitus, and Intonsus. When they said he had always long hair, it was the same as if they had said he was always young. In seeing the collections of antient statues one is apt now and then to take a Bacchus for Apollo, on this very account: for Bacchus in the beauty of his face, and the length of his hair, comes nearest to Apollo of all the other deities; and they are often spoke of together by the poets, as distinguished from all the other gods, and as the only rivals for excellence, in this point of beauty.

There is one thing however which seems peculiar to Apollo; and of which we might have had as strong an idea from the painters of old, as we have of his fine hair from the statuaries, had the works of the former been so durable as those of the latter. All one can say of it now is, that there was probably, in the old pictures of Apollo, a certain brightness beaming from his eyes; and, perhaps, diffused all over his face; in the same manner, as the body of the principal figure is all luminous and resplendent, in the famous nativity by Correggio; and the transfiguration, by Raphael. What made me first suspect this, was the antient poets speaking so often of the brightness of Apollo's face, and the beaming splendour of his eyes ... [8]

As to his particular character, you see it is the Apollo Venator. [9] But tho' he presides over the chace, and seems actually engaged in it, he is dressed rather fine for his character. His hair is in some sort dressed; and collected together a little above his forehead. His Chlamys, [10] which is only fastened with a gem over his breast, falls loosely down his back, and is tossed over his arm. On his feet you see one sort of the fine buskins, which they used antiently for the chace. All the rest of his body is naked. In short he is, in every thing, just as Maximus Tyrius has described him: "The god, in the bloom of youth; almost all naked, tho' he has a Chlamys over his shoulders: holding his bow; and seeming not only going to move on, but to move on rapidly." [11]

9   From
JAMES STUART and NICHOLAS REVETT
Proposals for publishing an accurate description of the Antiquities of Athens

(1751; reprinted from the first edition of *Antiquities*, 1762)

James Stuart (1713–88), painter and architect, and Nicholas Revett (1720–1804), architect and draughtsman, played an important part in the history of English Hellenism with their publication in 1762 of the first volume of *The Antiquities of Athens*. Stuart and Revett met in Rome where, after a short visit to Naples in 1748, they conceived the plan of visiting Athens and making an accurate delineation of its monuments and buildings. This project arose out of a sense of dissatisfaction with previous accounts of Athens, which had all been provided by travellers who were 'too little conversant with Painting, Sculpture, and Architecture, to give us tolerable Ideas of what they saw'. They first prepared their *Proposals* in 1748; these were variously printed in London and Venice between 1751 and 1753. Stuart and Revett were much assisted by members of the Society of Dilettanti, to which they were eventually elected themselves. After a false start in 1750, they embarked again for Athens in the following year and remained there till 1753 when the disorders resulting from the death of Osman, Chief of the Black Eunuchs, 'compelled them to desist from their labours' (*Dictionary of National Biography*). The hazards referred to in the *Proposals* were, indeed, very real: on more than one occasion Stuart was nearly murdered. After leaving Attica, Stuart and Revett visited Smyrna and the islands of the Archipelago and returned to England early in 1755.

Although they received support and assistance from individual members of the Society of Dilettanti as well as from the Society as a whole, the first fruit of their labours did not appear till 1762. They were anticipated by four years by Julien Davide Le Roy, who had been in Rome when the *Proposals* first appeared and who had visited Greece in 1754. With the help of royal patronage and the backing of the French Academy, Le Roy published *Les Ruines des plus beaux monuments de la Grèce,* which included views and elevations of the most important buildings at Corinth, Athens, Delos and Sunium, and some charming engravings of life in the Levant; however, Le Roy had carried out his research too quickly and his book was full of errors and seriously deficient in its representation of Greek architecture. An English translation was published in 1759, a year which also saw the appearance of Richard Sayer's *Ruins of Athens and other valuable antiquities in Greece.* As soon as *The Antiquities of Athens* was published, it was clear that both of these books had been superseded, as had the work of the Irish artist Richard Dalton.

Stuart and Revett had initiated a new era in the study of classical art and antiquities. Unlike their predecessors, they had taken careful measurements which could satisfy both the architect and the archaeologist. Buildings were scrupulously reproduced by means of detailed plans and elevations and a technical commentary. Although the works in question were mainly minor and Hellenistic, the professional attention to detail and the attractive presentation of the volume ensured its success. Among those who subscribed were Reynolds, Garrick, Horace Walpole, Sterne, Benjamin Franklin, the Abbé Barthélemy and many members of the aristocracy. Yet of more than five hundred subscribers to the first volume, only four were architects and three builders: the initial impact of the *Antiquities of Athens* was on general taste rather than on architecture.[1] It gave added momentum to the growing interest in things Grecian of which it was itself a notable product; the Preface unequivocally declares a shift in allegiance from Rome to Athens. Stuart and Revett do not allow themselves much time for general commentary but the book conveys a strong admiration for Athens, 'once the most distinguished seat of Genius and Liberty', and an affectionate identification with its inhabitants.

Although this interest in the Athenians can be seen as a mark of Romantic Hellenism, it is important to recognize that the overall effect of the *Antiquities* was also in accordance with the principles of Neo-classicism. Enthusiasm for Greece was kept in check by the severely linear nature of the great majority of the illustrations, whose refrigerated style has much in common with the emphasis on outline of artists such as Flaxman, Cumberland and Blake. Eloquent and grumpy testimony to the innovatory power of Stuart and Revett is provided by Horace Walpole:

They who are industrious and correct, and wish to forget nothing, should go to Greece, where there is nothing left to be seen, but that ugly pigeon-house, the Temple of the Winds, that fly-cage, Demosthenes' Lanthorn, and one or two fragments of a portico, or a piece of a column crushed into a mud wall; and with such a morsel, and many quotations, a true classic antiquary can compose a whole folio and call it Ionian Antiquities! [2]

Although Walpole refers to *Ionian Antiquities* by name, his examples are taken from the first volume of the *Antiquities of Athens*. He was reacting against a shift in taste which was already powerfully in motion when he was writing: the Tower of the Winds was the model for the Pigeonhouse at Badger House, Shropshire (1780), the Radcliffe Observatory at Oxford (1773–94) and, at a later stage, for St Pancras New Church in London (1819–22), while Demosthenes' Lanthorn (more correctly known as the Choragic Monument of Lysicrates) was copied in numerous garden temples and funeral monuments.[3]

The movement was consolidated in 1789 with the appearance of the second volume, which included the major monuments of the Acropolis. By this time Revett had withdrawn from the project, piqued by the undue share of the credit generally given to Stuart. He had played a distinguished part in the production of *Ionian Antiquities* (see No. 28) and he had enjoyed some success as an architect (his most celebrated works including an island temple at West Wycombe Park and a church at Ayot St Lawrence which was heavily influenced by the Temple of Apollo at Delos). Stuart was already dead, after a more successful career than that of Revett; he had been painter to the Society of Dilettanti before he was succeeded by Reynolds and he had designed a number of buildings based on Greek models, including a Doric temple at Hagley Park in 1758–9 and a variety of buildings at Shugborough, among them a Doric temple, a Tower of the Winds, a 'Demosthenes' Lanthorn' and a triumphal arch (all *c*. 1764). A third volume of *Antiquities* was published in 1794 (see No. 17), a fourth in 1814 and a fifth in 1830. From conception to completion the project had taken eighty-two years but its impact continued to be felt for the greater part of the nineteenth century.

NOTES

1 Details from OSBORN, p. 288 and CROOK (*The Greek Revival*, 1972), p. 17.
2 *The Letters of Horace Walpole*, ed. Peter Cunningham, Edinburgh, 1906, ix. 349 (25 September 1791).
3 For illustrations, see CROOK (*The Greek Revival*, 1972).

There is perhaps no part of Europe, which more deservedly claims the attention and excites the curiosity of the Lovers of polite Literature, than the Territory of Attica, and Athens its capital City; whether we reflect on the Figure it makes in History, on account of the excellent Men it has produced in every Art, both of War and Peace; or whether we consider the Antiquities which are said to be still remaining there, Monuments of the good sense and elevated genius of the Athenians, and the most perfect Models of what is excellent in Sculpture and Architecture.

Many Authors have mentioned these Remains of Athenian Art as works of great magnificence and most exquisite taste; but their descriptions are so confused, and their measures, when they have given any, are so insufficient, that the most expert Architect could not, from all the Books that have been published on this subject, form a distinct Idea of any one Building these Authors have described. Their writings seem rather calculated to raise our Admiration, than to satisfy our Curiosity or improve our Taste.

Rome who borrowed her Arts, and frequently her Artificers from Greece, was adorned with magnificent Structures and excellent Sculptures: a considerable number of which have been published, in the Collections of Desgodetz, Palladio, Serlio, Santo Bartoli, [1] and other ingenious Men; and altho' many of the Originals which they have copied are since destroyed, yet the memory, and even the form of them, nay the Arts which produced them, seem secure from perishing; since the industry of those excellent Artists, has dispersed Representations of them through all the polite Nations of Europe.

But Athens the Mother of elegance and politeness, whose magnificence scarce yielded to that of Rome, and who for the beauties of a correct style must be allowed to surpass her; has been almost entirely neglected. So that unless exact copies of them be speedily made, all her beauteous Fabricks, her Temples, her Theatres, her Palaces, now in ruins, will drop into Oblivion; and Posterity will have to reproach us, that we have not left them a tolerable Idea of what was so excellent, and so much deserved our attention; but that we have suffered the perfection of an Art to perish, when it was perhaps in our power to have retrieved it.

The reason indeed, why those Antiquities have hitherto been thus neglected, is obvious. Greece, since the revival of the Arts, has been in the possession of Barbarians; and Artists capable of such a Work, have been able to satisfy their passion, whether it was for Fame or Profit, without risking themselves among such professed Enemies to the Arts as the Turks are. The ignorance and jealousy of that uncultivated people may, perhaps, render an undertaking of this sort, still somewhat dangerous.

Among the Travellers who have visited these Countries, some have been abundantly furnished with Literature, but they have all of them been too little conversant with Painting, Sculpture, and Architecture, to give us tolerable Ideas of what they saw. The Books therefore, in which their Travels are described, are not of such utility nor such entertainment to the Public, as a person acquainted with the practice of these Arts might have rendered them. For the best verbal descriptions cannot be supposed to convey so adequate an Idea, of the magnificence and elegance of Buildings; the fine form, expression, or proportion of Sculptures; the beauty and variety of a Country, or the exact Scene of any celebrated Action, as may be formed from drawings made on the spot, with diligence and fidelity, by the hand of an Artist.

We have therefore resolved to make a journey to Athens; and to publish at our return, such Remains of that famous City as we may be permitted to copy, and that appear to merit our attention; not doubting but a work of this kind, will meet with the approbation of all those Gentlemen who are lovers of the Arts; and assuring ourselves, that those Artists who aim at perfection, must be more pleased, and better instructed, the nearer they can approach the Fountain-Head of their Art; for so we may call those examples which the greatest Artists, and the best Ages of antiquity have left them.

We propose that each of the Antiquities which are to compose this Work, shall be treated of in the following manner. First a View of it will be given, faithfully exhibiting the present Appearance of that particular Building and of the circumjacent Country; to this will follow, Architectural Plans and Elevations, in which will be expressed the measure of every Moulding, as well as the general disposition and ordonnance of the whole Building; and lastly will be given, exact Delineations of the Statues and Basso-relievos with which those Buildings are decorated. These Sculptures we imagine will be extremely curious, as well on account of their workmanship, as of the subjects they represent. To these we propose adding some Maps and Charts, shewing the general situation and connection of the whole Work. All this perhaps may be conveniently distributed into three folio Volumes, after the following manner.

The first Volume may contain the Antiquities belonging to the Acropolis, or ancient fortress of Athens; the second those of the City; and the third, those which lye dispersed in different parts of the Athenian Territory: of all which the annexed Catalogue will give a more distinct Idea . . .

All the different Subjects we shall treat of, will be illustrated, with such explanations and descriptions as may serve to render the Prints intelligible; and this will be chiefly done, by pointing out the relation they may have to the doctrine of Vitruvius, [2] or to the accounts of them which Strabo, Pausanias [3] or other ancient writers have left us.

10 *From*
JOSEPH WARTON
Two essays from *The Adventurer*, Numbers 75 and 80
(24 July and 11 August, 1753; second edition 1754)

Joseph Warton (1722–1800), critic and poet, was the author of *Odes* (1744, 1746) and the translator of Virgil's *Eclogues* and *Georgics*. He and his brother Thomas (1728–90) are often associated with the early stirrings of Romanticism; certainly, they were both alert to important trends in literature which had been ignored or neglected. Thomas Warton's *Observations on Spenser's Faery Queen* (1754) marked a crucial shift of interest; Joseph's essays on the *Odyssey* were less influential but they divined an undercurrent in eighteenth-century taste which was to become increasingly significant. When Joseph wrote his essays, the *Iliad* had received much more attention than the *Odyssey*; indeed, its reputation was perhaps as high as it ever had been. Longinus, who exerted considerable influence on English criticism (see p. 55n.4), had preferred the *Iliad* to the *Odyssey*, which he regarded as the product of waning powers, comparing Homer to the setting sun. The *Iliad* was a poem of the public world, setting forth memorable examples of heroic behaviour (see for instance its influence on the Earl of Granville, Introduction, p. 31). Warton acknowledged its moral value but he reacted against its militarism and the bloodiness of its battle scenes; the *Odyssey,* he claimed, had greater moral value and was more relevant to the life of the common reader. In this claim he was not deviating from the long established belief that Homer was a great moral educator but his shift of attention from the public and heroic world to the domesticities of the *Odyssey* is symptomatic of an age which had produced the novels of Defoe and Richardson. Defoe had severely criticized both the unreality and the militaristic ethos of the classical epic, while Richardson (whose *Clarissa* had appeared as recently as 1747–8) was opposed to its false code of honour and its masculine brutality. Thirty years later Dr Johnson was to reveal that he preferred the story of the *Odyssey* to that of the *Aeneid* because 'The story of the *Odyssey* is interesting, as a great part of it is domestick'.[1] The taste was shared by Goethe and by Rousseau, whose *Émile* exclaims on being hospitably received in a country cottage, 'Je crois être au temps d'Homère'[2] with the advent of the Romantic period the *Iliad* was still admired but it was the *Odyssey* which did more to stimulate the poetic imagination.

Warton was much interested in pastoral, both as the translator of Virgil and as a critic who was in reaction against the predominantly urban vision of Pope. His championing of the *Odyssey* sets up a series of contrasts between pastoral simplicity and the refinements of the court and the drawing room. This polarity may be traced back at least as far as Fénelon whose *Télémaque*, also based on the *Odyssey,* was a reaction against the Baroque excesses of the court of Louis XIV (see No. 1). As the century progresses, good breeding, false complexion, stiff brocades, immeasurable hoops and French politesse tend to be associated not with the literature to which the *Odyssey* represents a fresh and natural alternative but with Pope's translations: Edward Young, for example, considered that Pope had put Homer in petticoats,[3] while William Cowper imagined Pope's Homer in a strait waistcoat (see No. 21). Much the same associations are evoked by Leigh Hunt in the Preface to *Foliage* which appeared as long afterwards as 1818. Though the emphases are different, the basic urge behind all these critiques is a desire for a closer contact with the natural and the uncomplicated, a return to a primeval or patriarchal simplicity, and the rediscovery of 'the very voice of nature and affection'.

NOTES

1 *Life,* 1 May 1783.
2 For Goethe, see *Italian Journey*, tr. W. H. Auden and Elizabeth Mayer, Harmondsworth, 1970, p. 310. For Rousseau, see *Émile ou de l'éducation*, [1762], Garnier, Paris, p. 525. Seeing a kitchen-garden, Émile is put in mind of the garden of Alcinous (*Odyssey*, vii. 112–32) which is so much criticized by people of taste for its simplicity and lack of sophistication. Rousseau comments that this is a royal garden 'dans lequel, à la honte de ce vieux rêveur d'Homère et des princes, de son temps, on ne voit ni treillages, ni statues, ni cascades, ni boulingrins [bowling greens]' (p. 534).
3 *Conjectures on Original Composition*, 1759, p. 59.

No. 75, Tuesday, July 24, 1753

——*Quid virtus & quid sapientia possit,*
Utile proposuit nobis exemplar Ulyssen.

HORACE.[1]

To shew what pious wisdom's pow'r can do,
The poet sets Ulysses in our view.

FRANCIS.

I have frequently wondered at the common practice of our instructors of youth, in making their pupils far more intimately acquainted with the *Iliad* than with the *Odyssey* of *Homer*. This absurd custom, which seems to arise from the supposed superiority of the former poem, has inclined me to make some reflections on the excellence of the latter; a task I am the more readily induced to undertake, as so little is performed in the dissertation prefixed by Broome[2] to POPE'S translation of this work, which one may venture to pronounce is confused defective and dull. Those who receive all their opinions in criticism from custom and authority, and never dare to consult the decisions of reason and the voice of nature and truth, must not accuse me of being affectedly paradoxical, if I endeavour to maintain that the *Odyssey* excells the *Iliad* in many respects; and that for several reasons young scholars should peruse it early and attentively.

The moral of this poem is more extensively useful than that of the *Iliad*; which, indeed, by displaying the dire effects of discord among rulers, may rectify the conduct of princes, and may be called the *Manual of Monarchs*: whereas the patience, the prudence, the wisdom, the temperance, and fortitude of *Ulysses*, afford a pattern, the utility of which is not confined within the compass of courts and palaces, but descends and diffuses its influence over common life and daily practice. If the fairest examples ought to be placed before us in an age prone to imitation, if patriotism be preferable to implacability, if an eager desire to return to one's country and family be more manly and noble than an eager desire to be revenged of an enemy, then should our eyes rather be fixed on *Ulysses* than *Achilles*. Unexperienced minds, too easily captivated with the fire and fury of a gallant general, are apt to prefer courage to constancy, and firmness to humanity. We do not behold the destroyers of peace and the murderers of mankind, with the detestation due to their crimes; because we have been inured almost from our infancy to listen to the praises that have been wantonly lavished on them by the most exquisite poetry: "The muses," to apply the words of an ancient Lyric, "have concealed and decorated the bloody sword with wreaths of myrtle." [3] Let the *Iliad* be ever ranked at the head of human compositions for its spirit and sublimity; but let not the milder, and, perhaps, more insinuating and attractive beauties of the *Odyssey* be despised and overlooked. In the one we are placed amidst the rage of storms and tempests:

And when in autumn Jove his fury pours,
And earth is loaden with incessant showers:
From their deep beds he bids the rivers rise,
And opens all the flood-gates of the skies.

POPE.

In the other, all is tranquil and sedate, and calmly delightful:

Stern winter smiles on that auspicious clime;
The fields are florid with unfading prime:
From the bleak pole no winds inclement blow,
Mold the round hail, or shake the fleecy snow:
But from the breezy deep, the Blest inhale
The fragrant murmurs of the western gale.

POPE.[4]

Accordingly, to distinguish the very different natures of these poems, it was anciently the practice of those who publickly recited them, to represent the *Iliad*, in allusion to the bloodshed it described, in a robe of scarlet; and the *Odyssey*, on account of the voyages it relates, in an azure vestment.

The predominant passion of *Ulysses* being the love of his country, for the sake of which he even refuses immortality, the poet has taken every occasion to display it in the liveliest and most striking colours. The first time we behold the hero, we find him disconsolately sitting on the solitary shore, sighing to return to Ithaca, weeping incessantly, and still casting his eyes upon the sea.[5] "While a goddess," says Minerva at the very beginning of the poem, "by her power and her allurements detains him from Ithaca, he is dying with desire to see even so much as the smoke arise from his much-loved island: tarda fluunt ingrataque tempora!"[6] While the luxurious Phæacians were enjoying a delicious banquet, he attended not to their mirth and music, for the time approached when he was to return to Ithaca: they had prepared a ship for him to set sail in the very next morning; and the thoughts of his approaching happiness having engrossed all his soul, "He sate, and ey'd the sun, and wish'd the night."

To represent his impatience more strongly, the poet adds a most expressive simile, suited to the simplicity of ancient times: "The setting of the sun," says he, "was as welcome and grateful to *Ulysses*, as it is to a well-laboured plowman, who earnestly waits for its decline, that he may return to his supper, while his weary knees are painful to him as he walks along." [8]"Notwithstanding all the pleasures and endearments I received from Calypso, yet," says our hero, "I perpetually bedewed with my tears the garments which this immortal beauty gave to me." [9] We are presented in every page with fresh instances of this love of his country, and his whole behaviour convinces us,

ὣς οὐδὲν γλύκιον ἧς πατρίδος, οὐδὲ τοκήων. [10]

This generous sentiment runs like a golden vein throughout the whole poem.

If this animating example were duly and deeply inculcated, how strong an impression would it necessarily make upon the yielding minds of youth, when melted and mollified by the warmth of such exalted poetry!

Nor is the *Odyssey* less excellent and useful, in the amiable pictures it affords of private affections and domestic tendernesses,

> and all the charities
> Of father, son, and brother

MILTON.[11]

When *Ulysses* descends into the infernal regions, it is finely contrived that he should meet his aged mother *Anticlea*. After his first sorrow and surprize, he eagerly inquires into the causes of her death, and adds, "Doth my father yet live? does my son possess my dominions, or does he groan under the tyranny of some usurper who thinks I shall never return? Is my wife still constant to my bed? or hath some noble Grecian married her?"—These questions are the very voice of nature and affection. *Anticlea* answers, that "she herself died with grief for the loss of *Ulysses*; that *Laertes* languishes away life in solitude and sorrow for him; and that *Penelope* perpetually and inconsolably bewails his absence, and sighs for his return." [12]

When the hero, disguised like a stranger, has the first interview with his father, whom he finds diverting his cares with rural amusements in his little garden, he informs him that he had seen his son in his travels, but now despairs of beholding him again. Upon this the sorrow of *Laertes* is inexpressible: *Ulysses* can counterfeit no longer, but exclaims ardently,

> I, I am he! O father rise! behold
> Thy son! [13]

And the discovery of himself to *Telemachus*, in the sixteenth book, in a speech of short and broken exclamations, is equally tender and pathetic. [14]

The duties of universal benevolence, of charity, and of hospitality, that unknown and unpractised virtue, are perpetually inculcated with more emphasis and elegance than in any ancient philosopher, and I wish I could not add than in any modern. *Ulysses* meets with a friendly reception in all the various nations to which he is driven; who declare their inviolable obligations to protect and cherish the stranger and the wanderer. Above all, how amiable is the behaviour of *Eumeus* to his unknown master, who asks for his charity. "It is not lawful for me," says the δῖος ὑφορβὸς, "I dare not despise any stranger or indigent man, even if he were much meaner than thou appearest to be; for the poor and strangers are sent to us by *Jupiter*!" [15] "Keep," says *Epictetus*, "continually in thy memory, what *Eumeus* speaks in *Homer* to the disguised *Ulysses*." [16] I am sensible, that many superficial French critics have endeavoured to ridicule all that passes at the lodge of *Eumeus*, as coarse and indelicate, and below the dignity of epic poetry: but let them attend to the following observation of the greatest genius of their nation: "Since it is delightful," says *Fenelon* "in one of *Titian*'s landscapes to see the goats climbing up a hanging rock, or to behold in one of *Teniers*'s pieces a country feast and rustic dances; it is no wonder, that we are pleased with such natural descriptions as we find in the *Odyssey*. This simplicity of manners seems to recall the golden age. I am more pleased with honest *Eumeus*, than with the polite heroes of Clelia or Cleopatra". [17]

The moral precepts with which every page of the *Odyssey* is pregnant, are equally noble. *Plato*'s wish is here accomplished; for we behold *Virtue* personally appearing to the sons of men, in her most awful and most alluring charms. [18]

The remaining reasons, why the *Odyssey* is equal if not superior to the *Iliad*, and why it is a poem most peculiarly proper for the perusal of youth; are, because the great variety of events and scenes it contains, interest and engage the attention more than the *Iliad*; because characters and images drawn from familiar life, are more useful to the generality of readers, and are also more difficult to be drawn; and because the conduct of this poem, considered as the most perfect of Epopees, is more artful and judicious than that of the other. The discussion of these beauties will make the subject of some ensuing paper.

No. 80. Saturday, August 11, 1753

There are not wanting persons so dull and insensible, as to deter students from reading books of this kind, which, they say, are poetical, and pernicious to the purity of morals: but I am of the opinion, that they are not only worthy to be read by the instructors of youth in their schools, but that the old and experienced should again and again peruse them.

ERASMUS.

Greatness, novelty, and beauty, are usually and justly reckoned the three principal sources of the pleasures that strike the imagination. If the *Iliad* be allowed to abound in objects that may be referred to the first species, yet the *Odyssey* may boast a greater number of images that are beautiful and uncommon. The vast variety of scenes perpetually shifting before us, the train of unexpected events, and the many sudden turns of fortune in this diversified poem, must more deeply engage the reader, and keep his attention more alive and active, than the martial uniformity of the *Iliad*. The continual glare of a single colour that unchangeably predominates throughout a whole piece, is apt to dazzle and disgust the eye of the beholder. I will not, indeed, presume to say with *Voltaire*, that among the greatest admirers of antiquity, there is scarce one to be found, who could ever read the *Iliad* with that eagerness and rapture, which a woman feels when she peruses the novel of *Zayde*;[1] but will, however, venture to affirm that the *Speciosa Miracula*[2] of the *Odyssey*, are better calculated to excite our curiosity and wonder, and to allure us forward with unextinguished impatience to the catastrophe, than the perpetual tumult and terror that reign through the *Iliad*.

The boundless exuberance of his imagination, his unwearied spirit and fire, has enabled *Homer* to diversify the descriptions of his battles with many circumstances of great variety: sometimes by specifying the different characters, ages, professions, or nations, of his dying heroes; sometimes by describing different kinds of wounds and deaths; and sometimes by tender and pathetic strokes, which remind the reader, of the aged parent who is fondly expecting the return of his son just murdered, of the desolate condition of the widows who will now be enslaved, and of the children that will be dashed against the stones. But notwithstanding this delicate art and address in the poet, the subject remains the same; and from this sameness, it will I fear grow tedious and insipid to impartial readers: these small modifications and adjuncts, are not sufficiently efficacious, to give the grace of novelty to repetition, and to make tautology delightful: the battles are, indeed, nobly and variously painted, yet still they are only battles. [3] But when we accompany *Ulysses* through the manifold perils he underwent by sea and land, and visit with him the strange nations to which the anger of Neptune has driven him, all whose manners and customs are described in the most lively and picturesque terms; when we survey the wondrous monsters he encountred and escaped,

> *Antiphaten, Scyllamque, & cum Cyclope Charybdin:*
> Antiphates his hideous feast devour,
> Charybdis bark and Polyphemus roar. [4]   FRANCIS.

When we see him refuse the charms of Calypso, and the cup of Circe; when we descend with him into hell, and hear him converse with all the glorious heroes that assisted at the Trojan war; when after struggling with ten thousand difficulties unforeseen and almost unsurmountable, he is at last restored to the peaceable possession of his kingdom and his queen; when such objects as these are displayed, so new and so interesting; when all the descriptions, incidents, scenes and persons, differ so widely from each other; then it is that poetry becomes "a perpetual feast of nectared sweets,"[5] and a feast of such an exalted nature as to produce neither satiety or disgust.

But besides its variety, the *Odyssey* is the most amusing and entertaining of all other poems, on account of the pictures it preserves to us of ancient manners customs laws and politics, and of the domestic life of the heroic ages. The more any nation becomes polished, the more the genuine feelings of nature are disguised, and their manners are consequently less adapted to bear a faithful description. Good-breeding is founded on the dissimulation or suppression of such sentiments, as may probably provoke or offend those with whom we converse. The little forms and ceremonies which have been introduced into civil life by the moderns, are not suited to the dignity and simplicity of the *Epic Muse*. The coronation feast of an European monarch would not shine half so much in poetry, as the simple supper prepared for *Ulysses* at the Phæacian court; the gardens of *Alcinous* are much fitter for description than those of Versailles;[6] and *Nausicaa*, descending to the river to wash her garments, and dancing afterwards upon the banks with her fellow-virgins, like Diana amidst her nymphs, "Tho' all are fair, she shines above the rest"[7] is a far more graceful figure, than the most glittering lady in the drawing-room, with a complexion plaistered to repair the vigils of cards, and a shape violated by a stiff brocade and an immeasurable hoop. The compliment also which *Ulysses* pays to this innocent unadorned beauty, especially when he compares her to a young palm-tree of Delos,[8] contains more gallantry and elegance, than the most applauded sonnet of the politest French marquis that ever rhymed. However indelicate I may be esteemed, I freely confess I had rather sit in the grotto of *Calypso*, than in the most pompous saloon of *Louis XV*. The tea and the card tables can be introduced with propriety and success only in the mock-heroic, as they have been very happily in the Rape of the Lock; but the present modes of life must be forgotten when we attempt any thing in the serious or sublime poetry; for heroism disdains the luxurious refinements, the false delicacy and state of modern ages. The primeval, I was about to say, patriarchal simplicity of manners displayed in the *Odyssey*, is a perpetual source of true poetry, is inexpressibly pleasing to all who are uncorrupted by the business and the vanities of life, and may therefore prove equally instructive and captivating to younger readers.

It seems to be a tenet universally received among common critics, as certain and indisputable, that images and characters of peaceful and domestic life are not so difficult to be drawn, as pictures of war and fury. I own myself of a quite contrary opinion; and think the description of Andromache parting with Hector in the *Iliad*, and the tender circumstance of the child Astyanax starting back from his father's helmet and clinging to the bosom of his nurse, are as great efforts of the imagination of *Homer*, as the dreadful picture of Achilles fighting with the rivers, or dragging the carcass of Hector at his chariot-wheels: [9] the behaviour of *Hecuba*, when she points to the breast that had suckled her dear *Hector*, is as finely conceived as the most gallant exploits of *Diomede* and *Ajax*: the *Natural* is as strong an evidence of true genius, as the *Sublime*. It is in such images the *Odyssey* abounds; the superior utility of which, as they more nearly concern and more strongly affect us, need not be pointed out. Let *Longinus* admire the majesty of Neptune whirling his chariot over the deep, surrounded by sea monsters that gambolled before their king; the description of the dog Argus, creeping to the feet of his master, whom he alone knew in his disguise, and expiring with joy for his return, [10] is so inexpressibly pathetic, that it equals if not exceeds any of the magnificent and bolder images, which that excellent critic hath produced in his treatise on the sublime. He justly commends the prayer of Ajax, who when he was surrounded with a thick darkness that prevented the display of his prowess, begs of Jupiter only to remove the clouds that involved him; "and then," says he, "destroy me if thou wilt in the daylight". [11] But surely the reflections which *Ulysses* makes to Amphinomus, the most virtuous of the suitors, concerning the misery and vanity of man, will be found to deserve equal commendations, if we consider their propriety solemnity and truth. Our hero, in the disguise of a beggar, had just been spurned at and ridiculed by the rest of the riotous lovers, but is kindly relieved by Amphinomus, whose behaviour is finely contrasted to the brutality of his brethren. Upon which *Ulysses* says, "Hear me, O Amphinomus! and ponder the words I shall speak unto thee. Of all creatures that breathe or creep upon the earth, the most weak and impotent is man. For he never thinks that evil shall befall him at another season, while the Gods bestow on him strength and happiness. But when the immortal Gods afflict him with adversity, he bears it with unwillingness and repining. Such is the mind of the inhabitants of earth, that it changes as Jupiter sends happiness or misery. I once numbered myself among the happy, and elated with prosperity and pride, and relying on my family and friends, committed many acts of injustice. But let no man be proud or unjust, but receive whatever gifts the Gods bestow on him with humility and silence." [12] I chose to translate this sententious passage as literally as possible, to preserve the air of its venerable simplicity and striking solemnity. If we recollect the speaker, and the occasion of the speech, we cannot fail of being deeply affected. Can we, therefore, forbear giving our assent to the truth of the title which *Alcidamas*, according to *Aristotle* in his rhetoric, bestows on the *Odyssey*; who calls it "a beautiful mirror of human life." [13]

Homer, in the *Iliad*, resembles the river Nile, when it descends in a cataract that deafens and astonishes the neighbouring inhabitants. In the *Odyssey*, he is still like the same Nile, when its genial inundations gently diffuse fertility and fatness over the peaceful plains of Egypt.

11 From
ROBERT WOOD
The Ruins of Palmyra,
otherwise Tedmor, in the Desart
(1753)

Robert Wood (1717?–1771), who later became a politician (see Introduction, p. 31), travelled widely as a young man in Greece and the Near East. After spending the winter of 1749–50 at Rome, he embarked in 1750 on an expedition together with James 'Jamaica' Dawkins, a young and wealthy member of the Society of Dilettanti who had been involved in sponsoring the expedition of Stuart and Revett (whom Wood and Dawkins were later to meet at Athens in 1751). The party included John Bouverie (who died in Magnesia) and an Italian artist called Borra. The range of their travels is detailed by Wood in his preface; it included a visit to Sigeum and the mouth of the Scamander (see Mary Wortley Montagu's visit in No. 4) which ultimately stimulated Wood to write his most famous book, the *Essay on the Original Genius of Homer* (1767), which was first published as an introduction to *A Comparative View of the antient and present state of the Troade*.

On his return to England, Wood published *The Ruins of Palmyra* (1753) and *The Ruins of Balbec* (1757). *The Ruins of Palmyra* was important because for the ruined city of the imagination it substituted fifty-seven plates accompanied by detailed descriptions and measurements of the ruins and antiquities. Horace Walpole was delighted: 'The pomp of the buildings has not a nobler air, than the simplicity of the narration ... '[1] Gavin Hamilton celebrated by painting the 'Discovery of Palmyra by Wood and Dawkins' (1758); *discovery* somewhat inflates the significance of the occasion and the travellers are accorded a certain additional *gravitas* by their appearance in Roman togas.[2] However, this exaggeration indicated a genuine excitement and, together with *The Ruins of Balbec,* Wood's pioneering study of Palmyra certainly helped to set a fashion. Under Wood's influence, Julien Davide Le Roy hastily produced *Les Ruines des plus beaux monuments de la Grèce* (1758). More importantly, the way was now opened for lavish and important studies such as Robert Adam's *The Palace of the Emperor Diocletian, at Spalatro, in*

Dalmatia (1764), Chandler, Pars and Revett's *Ionian Antiquities* (first volume, 1769) and Charles Cameron's *The Baths of the Romans* (1772). *The Ruins* also exerted considerable influence on architectural design and particularly on ornamentation. It was the direct inspiration for a number of striking designs, most notably for the ceiling by Robert Adam at Osterley Park House in the drawing room which Walpole regarded as 'worthy of Eve before the Fall'. Jean-Jacques Barthélemy (see No. 24) was also inspired by an inscription in the book to attempt to produce his own Palmyrene alphabet.

The text of *The Ruins of Palmyra* is a brief but important contribution to the literature of ruins; like his contemporary Gibbon, Wood found that his historical imagination was stimulated by the architectural fragments of the past. Like John Dyer (see No. 7) and like so many poets and travellers in Greece, he experienced a nostalgic regret for the departed glories of the past: 'How much is it to be regretted that we do not know more of a country, which has left such monuments of its magnificence? Where Zenobia was queen, and where Longinus was first Minister?' Like travellers and ambassadors from Sir Thomas Roe (*c.* 1581–1644) to Lord Elgin, he also felt a proprietary right towards any marbles which he wished to acquire; it is only the 'avarice or superstition' of the local inhabitants which sometimes stand in his way.[3] Finally, his introductory note is also important because it recognizes the importance of place and the significance of poetical geography. This theme takes us back to Mary Wortley Montagu but it looks forward, even more significantly, to his own epoch-making study of Homer (see No. 16).

Palmyra was the setting and occasion for Volney's *Les Ruines*, which profoundly influenced the young Shelley, and the subject of a youthful poem by Peacock (1806; revised 1812). See Nos. 7 and 33.

NOTES

1 *Anecdotes of Painting*, Strawberry Hill, 1762, pp. xiii–xiv.
   For other reactions and reviews, see WIEBENSON, pp. 92–7.
2 See IRWIN, plate 17. For Wood's contribution as an explorer

and archaeologist, see Iain Browning, *Palmyra,* 1979.
3 See the story told in the note to *Childe Harold*, II. xii.

From **Preface**

... We passed the winter together at Rome, and employed most of that time in refreshing our memories with regard to the antient history and geography of the countries we proposed to see.

We met our ship at Naples in the spring. She brought from London a library, consisting chiefly of all the Greek historians and poets, some books of antiquities, and the best voyage writers, what mathematical instruments we thought necessary, and such things as might be proper presents for the Turkish Grandees, or others, to whom, in the course of our voyages we should be obliged to address our selves.

We visited most of the islands of the Archipelago, part of Greece in Europe; the Asiatick and European coasts of the Hellespont, Propontis and Bosphorus, as far as the Black-sea, most of the inland parts of Asia Minor, Syria, Phoenicia, Palestine and Egypt.

The various countries we went through, furnish, no doubt, much entertainment of different sorts. But however we might each of us have some favourite curiosity to indulge, what enjoyed our greatest attention was rather their antient than present state.

It is impossible to consider with indifference those countries which gave birth to letters and arts, where soldiers, orators, philosophers, poets and artists have shewn the boldest and happiest flights of genius, and done the greatest honour to human nature.

Circumstances of climate and situation, otherwise trivial, become interesting from that connection with great men, and great actions, which history and poetry have given them: The life of Miltiades or Leonidas could never be read with so much pleasure, as on the plains of Marathon[1] or at the streights of Thermopylae; the Iliad has new beauties on the banks of the Scamander; and the Odyssey is most pleasing in the countries where Ulysses travelled and Homer sung.

The particular pleasure, it is true, which an imagination warmed upon the spot receives from those scenes of heroic actions, the traveller only can feel, nor is it to be communicated by description. But classical ground not only makes us always relish the poet, or historian more, but sometimes helps us to understand them better. Where we thought the present face of the country was the best comment on an antient author, we made our draftsman take a view, or make a plan of it. This sort of entertainment we extended to poetical geography, and spent a fortnight with great pleasure, in making a map of the Scamandrian plain, with Homer in our hands.

Inscriptions we copied as they fell in our way, and carried off the marbles whenever it was possible; for the avarice or superstition of the inhabitants made that task difficult and sometimes impracticable . . .

12   *From*
JOHANN JOACHIM WINCKELMANN
Gedancken über die Nachahmung der griechischen Wercke in der Mahlerey und Bildhauer-Kunst
(1755; tr. Henry Fuseli as *The Imitation of the Painting and Sculpture of the Greeks*, 1765)

Winckelmann (1717–68) was the son of a Prussian cobbler; renouncing Lutheranism he became an abbé and librarian to Cardinals Archinto (1755–8) and Albani (from 1758) at Rome. The rest of his life centred on Rome, though he made a number of expeditions to classical sites such as those at Paestum, Pompeii and Herculaneum. In 1763 he was appointed prefect of antiquities at the Vatican. In 1768 he was murdered at an inn in Trieste after a visit to Germany and Austria.

Winckelmann exercized a profound influence on the taste of his age; his writings played a large part in shifting the emphasis from Rome to Greece. A number of eighteenth-century travellers had been to Asia Minor and Greece and some had recorded their travels (for details, see Chronology). Admiration for Greek art was also in evidence before Winckelmann—for example, in Le Roy and Caylus (whose illustrated books helped to create a predilection for things Grecian), in Shaftesbury, in Thomson's poem *Liberty* and even in Hogarth; but the taste remained largely conventional and uninspired. Winckelmann's informed yet rhapsodic account of Greek art and of sculpture in particular had the advantage of building on these beginnings yet it can truly be said that he was responsible for opening the eyes of a generation. Hegel expressed this well: 'Winckelmann, by contemplation of the ideal works of the ancients, received a sort of inspiration, through which he opened a new sense for the study of art. He is to be regarded as one of those who, in the sphere of art, have known how to initiate a new organ for the human spirit.' (This quotation is cited by Walter Pater in his essay on Winckelmann (1867); Pater's own work, notably his prose poem on the *Mona Lisa*, demonstrates that the reverberations of Winckelmann's influence could still be felt a century later.)

If Hegel's assessment suggests a process which is closer to religious meditation than to the more laborious pursuits of scholarship, that is entirely appropriate to Winckelmann's methods. From his studies in the collection at Dresden and in the libraries and galleries at Rome he acquired a reservoir of knowledge which informed his writings on the history of art; yet his works are notable not for scholarship but for poetic intuition and an inspired ability to appreciate and identify with the statues he is describing. His responses to the *Torso Belvedere,* the *Apollo Belvedere* and the *Laocoön* (see Nos. 13–15) do not represent the detached analysis of the art historian or the cultured poise of the connoisseur; they are ecstatic outpourings of the spirit which arise from an intensity of contemplation.

Behind these passages (whose ardour is certainly not dampened in Fuseli's translations) lies the tradition of the *ecphrasis*, the extended description as practised by a number of classical writers on works of art. Winckelmann's classical predecessors found it hard to rise above the technical or the merely descriptive; so did his immediate predecessors and contemporaries until he showed them the way. His response to the *Apollo Belvedere* makes a revealing contrast to the terse appraisal of the Jonathan Richardsons, senior and junior, who describe the statue in their celebrated *An Account of the Statues . . . Italy and . . . France* (1722). Another revealing contrast is afforded by Joseph Spence, who devotes a detailed analysis in his *Polymetis* (1747) to the subject of Apollo in art and literature (see No. 8); here the scholarly apparatus and the elaborate accumulation of footnotes obstructs and precludes any true freshness of response.[1] Winckelmann has a scholar's knowledge of his subject and an educated eye for the details of technique but he empathizes and he is highly subjective. In the case of the *Torso* (which had left its mark on Michelangelo's Sistine Chapel and which was a favourite with Rubens) it even seems that his imagination is stimulated to greater activity by the fragmentary condition of the statue. As he put it in the *History of Art*:

. . . we . . . have, as it were, nothing but a shadowy outline of the object of our wishes, but that very indistinctness only awakens a more earnest longing for what we have lost, and we study the copies of the originals more attentively than we should have studied the originals themselves, if we had been in full possession of them.

The habit was catching: inspired by Winckelmann, Goethe recorded that 'The Apollo Belvedere has . . . swept me off my feet' and took a connoisseur's delight in the marble's capacity to suggest the 'bloom of eternal youth'.[2] Many others were touched by Winckelmann's enthusiasm: it is amusing and instructive to see the historian John Gillies melting into rapturous admiration of the *Apollo*, the relatively staid banker-poet Samuel Rogers composing an ecstatic address to the *Torso,* and the poet Thomas Campbell capitulating before the marble charms of the *Apollo* on a visit to the Louvre (see No. 32). The responses may be as conventional as those of James Thomson (in *Liberty*) but the breathless rapture must owe something to Winckelmann.

Winckelmann's theory of art is derived from several fundamental principles which inform most of his criticism. Firstly, under the influence of Shaftesbury and Montesquieu, he believed in the importance of environment. The characteristics of Greek art are attributed both to the benevolent climate and to the democratic nature of Greek institutions: Winckelmann's view of Greek society is admiring and idealized. Secondly, Winckelmann held that, if art is a product of the environment, political as well as physical, it also represents in itself an important influence on morality. This view he shared with Shaftesbury and with his fellow-countryman Lessing.[3] One result of this attitude is that Winckelmann tends to ignore the more frivolous or light-hearted manifestations of Greek art which appealed, for example, to interior designers such as Robert Adam.

Thirdly, like many neo-classicists, Winckelmann subscribed to a belief in the superiority of art to nature. He pays keen-eyed homage to the anatomical accuracy of Greek sculpture and to its technical excellence but his deepest admiration is evoked by his desire for an ideal beauty which goes beyond the merely sensual and in which the particulars are subsumed in a greater unity. The characteristics of this beauty are *eine edle Einfalt und eine stille Grösse* (a noble simplicity and a calm grandeur). Simplicity involves the transcendence of individual detail and of realistic specificity: 'According to this idea, beauty should be like the best kind of water, drawn from the spring itself; the less taste it has, the more healthful it is considered, because free from all foreign admixture.' Simplicity is associated with contour, the 'characteristic distinction of the ancients', which 'unites or circumscribes every part of the most perfect Nature'. This predilection for outline Winckelmann shared with other believers in the neo-classical virtues; within a short time it was to be celebrated and pursued by English artists such as Flaxman, Blake and Cumberland. The emphasis on serenity is perhaps the keynote of Winckelmann's theory of art. Its most celebrated examples are the descriptions of the *Niobe*, which exhibits 'an equilibrium of feeling' by uniting the anguish of death with the highest beauty, and the *Laocoön* (see No. 15). In the case of the *Laocoön* in particular it is hard to agree with Winckelmann's judgement but, whether right or wrong, his criteria became vastly influential and helped to create an image of Greek civilization which was not seriously challenged till Nietzsche recognized that 'Our classicists lack a genuine pleasure in the violent and powerful aspects of the ancient world,' and turned his attention to the Dionysiac. [4]

In spite of his originality, Winckelmann's view of Greek art was conditioned by the preconceptions of his time and, while both the substance and the tone of his appreciations was freshly individual, his choice of subjects usually conformed to the canons of neo-classical taste. This tendency was strengthened by his reluctance to visit Greece (he rejected at least six opportunities to do so) and by the fact that most of the statues which he was able to examine at first-hand were Greco-Roman copies which avoided individualized expressions. The *Apollo Belvedere* had long been admired by the time Winckelmann described it. It still retained this pre-eminence in the early nineteenth century: its translation to Paris was celebrated as one of the triumphs of Napoleon, it evoked three impassioned stanzas from that fashionable traveller, Childe Harold and it was one of the standards by which the Parliamentary Select Committee attempted to establish the artistic and financial value of the Elgin Marbles in 1816. Yet the Elgins established new criteria and their admirers became dissatisfied with the *Apollo*. Haydon wrote of 'the hard, marbly, puffed figure' while Flaxman 'told Hamilton . . . that the Apollo in comparison with the Theseus was a dancing master'.[5] Hazlitt, whose distaste for sculpture was modified by his admiration for the Marbles, condemned the *Apollo* and its 'supercilious air' in terms which reveal that he associated it both with the French (who had displayed it in the Louvre) and with the classicism of the eighteenth century: 'The Apollo Belvedere is positively bad, a theatrical coxcomb, and ill-made; I mean compared with the Theseus.'[6]

Winckelmann was not without his critics. Haydon described him as a 'useless rhapsodist', while Fuseli attacked him in his Royal Academy lectures for his 'frigid reveries and Platonic dreams on beauty'.[7] Yet it was largely this poetic quality in Winckelmann and his exceptional ability to empathize both with the ancient Greeks and with their works of art which won him so great an influence. Whatever the contradictions, the inconsistencies or the scholarly limitations of his work, Winckelmann made a significant contribution to the European imagination. As Goethe told Eckermann:

One notices that Winckelmann is feeling his way. Yet in doing so he follows a certain direction, and there is something great about it. He is like Columbus who had in his mind a notion of the New World before he actually discovered it. By reading Winckelmann one does not learn anything but one becomes somebody.[8]

1 Cf. *Crito: or, a Dialogue on Beauty*, 1752, pp. 11, 29.
2 *Italian Journey*, tr. W. H. Auden and Elizabeth Mayer, Penguin Books, Harmondsworth, 1970, pp. 136, 152 (see p. 131 and n.).
3 'As beautiful men produced beautiful statues, so the latter reacted upon the former and the state became indebted to beautiful statues for beautiful men' (cited in LARRABEE, p. 184).
4 Translated by William Arrowsmith, *Arion*, ii, No. 2 (1963), p. 19.
5 *The Diary of Benjamin Robert Haydon*, ed. Willard Bissell Pope, Cambridge, Mass., 1960, i.247 (see 487), ii.15.
6 *The Complete Works of William Hazlitt*, ed. P. P. Howe, 1930–4, xviii.113, x.222. Cf. 'The limbs have too much an appearance of . . . balancing and answering to one another, like the rhymes in verse. The Elgin Marbles are harmonious, flowing, varied prose' (x.169). For further reactions, see pp. 219–26.
7 *Lectures on Painting*, 1820, p.xi.
8 Tr. by L. D. Ettlinger, 'Winckelmann', THE AGE OF NEO-CLASSICISM, p.xxxiv.

From **Chapter I: Nature**

To the Greek climate we owe the production of *Taste*, and from thence it spread at length over all the politer world. Every invention, communicated by foreigners to that nation, was but the seed of what it became afterwards, changing both its nature and size in a country, chosen, as *Plato* says,[1] by Minerva, to be inhabited by the Greeks, as productive of every kind of genius.

But this *Taste* was not only original among the Greeks, but seemed also quite peculiar to their country: it seldom went abroad without loss, and was long ere it imparted its kind influences to more distant climes. It was, doubtless, a stranger to the northern zones, when Painting and Sculpture, those offsprings of Greece, were despised there to such a degree, that the most valuable pieces of *Correggio* served only for blinds to the windows of the royal stables at Stockholm.

There is but one way for the moderns to become great, and

perhaps unequalled; I mean, by imitating the antients. And what we are told of *Homer*, that whoever understands him well, admires him, we find no less true in matters concerning the antient, especially the Greek arts. But then we must be as familiar with them as with a friend, to find Laocoon as inimitable as *Homer*. By such intimacy our judgment will be that of *Nicomachus*: *Take these eyes*, replied he to some paltry critick, censuring the Helen of Zeuxis, *Take my eyes, and she will appear a goddess*.

With such eyes *Michael Angelo*, *Raphael*, and *Poussin*, considered the performances of the antients. They imbibed taste at its source; and *Raphael* particularly in its native country. We know, that he sent young artists to Greece, to copy there, for his use, the remains of antiquity.

An antient Roman statue, compared to a Greek one, will generally appear like *Virgil*'s Diana amidst her Oreads, in comparison of the Nausicaa of *Homer*, whom he imitated.[2]

Laocoon was the standard of the Roman artists, as well as ours; and the rules of *Polycletus* [3] became the rules of art.

I need not put the reader in mind of the negligences to be met with in the most celebrated antient performances: the Dolphin at the feet of the Medicean Venus, with the children, and the Parerga of the Diomedes by *Dioscorides*, being commonly known. The reverse of the best Egyptian and Syrian coins seldom equals the head, in point of workmanship. Great artists are wisely negligent, and even their errors instruct. Behold their works as *Lucian* bids you behold the Zeus of *Phidias*; *Zeus himself, not his footstool*.

It is not only *Nature* which the votaries of the Greeks find in their works, but still more, something superior to nature; ideal beauties, brain-born images, as *Proclus* says.[4]

The most beautiful body of ours would perhaps be as much inferior to the most beautiful Greek one, as Iphicles was to his brother Hercules. The forms of the Greeks, prepared to beauty, by the influence of the mildest and purest sky, became perfectly elegant by their early exercises. Take a Spartan youth, sprung from heroes, undistorted by swaddling-cloths; whose bed, from his seventh year, was the earth, familiar with wrestling and swimming from his infancy; and compare him with one of our young Sybarits, and then decide which of the two would be deemed worthy, by an artist, to serve for the model of a Theseus, and Achilles, or even a Bacchus. The latter would produce a Theseus fed on roses, the former a Theseus fed on flesh, to borrow the expression of *Euphranor*.[5]

The grand games were always a very strong incentive for every Greek youth to exercise himself. Whoever aspired to the honours of these was obliged, by the laws, to submit to a trial of ten months at Elis, the general rendezvous; and there the first rewards were commonly won by youths, as *Pindar* tells us. *To be like the God-like Diagoras*, was the fondest wish of every youth. [6]

Behold the swift Indian outstripping in pursuit the hart: how briskly his juices circulate! how flexible, how elastic his nerves and muscles! how easy his whole frame! Thus *Homer* draws his heroes, and his Achilles he eminently marks for "being swift of foot". [7]

By these exercises the bodies of the Greeks got the great and manly Contour observed in their statues, without any bloated corpulency. The young Spartans were bound to appear every tenth day naked before the Ephori,[8] who, when they perceived any inclinable to fatness, ordered them a scantier diet; nay, it was one of *Pythagoras*'s precepts, to beware of growing too corpulent; and, perhaps for the same reason, youths aspiring to wrestling-games were, in the remoter ages of Greece, during their trial, confined to a milk diet.

They were particularly cautious in avoiding every deforming custom; and *Alcibiades*, when a boy, refusing to learn to play on the flute, for fear of its discomposing his features, was followed by all the youth of Athens.[9]

In their dress they were professed followers of nature. No modern stiffening habit, no squeezing stays hindered Nature from forming easy beauty; the fair knew no anxiety about their attire, and from their loose and short habits the Spartan girls got the epithet of Phaenomirides.

We know what pains they took to have handsome children, but want to be acquainted with their methods: for certainly *Quillet*, in his Callipaedy, [10] falls short of their numerous expedients. They even attempted changing blue eyes to black ones, and games of beauty were exhibited at Elis, the rewards consisting of arms consecrated to the temple of Minerva. How could they miss of competent and learned judges, when, as *Aristotle* tells us, [11] the Greek youths were taught drawing expressly for that purpose? From their fine complexion, which, though mingled with a vast deal of foreign blood, is still preserved in most of the Greek islands, and from the still enticing beauty of the fair sex, especially at Chios; we may easily form an idea of the beauty of the former inhabitants, who boasted of being Aborigines, nay, more antient than the moon.

And are not there several modern nations, among whom beauty is too common to give any title to pre-eminence? Such are unanimously accounted the Georgians and the Kabardinski in the Crim[ea].

Those diseases which are destructive of beauty, were moreover unknown to the Greeks. There is not the least hint of the small-pox, in the writings of their physicians; and *Homer*, whose portraits are always so truly drawn, mentions not one pitted face. Venereal plagues, and their daughter the English malady, [12] had not yet names.

And must we not then, considering every advantage which nature bestows, or art teaches, for forming, preserving, and improving beauty, enjoyed and applied by the Grecians; must we not then confess, there is the strongest probability that the beauty of their persons excelled all we can have an idea of ?

Art claims liberty: in vain would nature produce her noblest offsprings, in a country where rigid laws would choak her progressive growth, as in Egypt, that pretended parent of sciences and arts: but in Greece, where, from their earliest youth, the happy inhabitants were devoted to mirth and pleasure, where narrow-spirited formality never restrained the liberty of manners, the artist enjoyed nature without a veil.

The Gymnasies, where, sheltered by public modesty, the youths exercised themselves naked, were the schools of art. These the philosopher frequented, as well as the artist. *Socrates* for the instruction of a Charmides, Autolycus, Lysis; *Phidias* for the improvement of his art by their beauty. Here he studied the elasticity of the muscles, the ever varying motions of the frame, the outlines of fair forms, or the Contour left by the young wrestler on the sand. Here beautiful nakedness appeared with such a liveliness of expression, such truth and variety of situations, such a noble air of the body, as it would be ridiculous to look for in any hired model of our academies.

Truth springs from the feelings of the heart. What shadow of it therefore can the modern artist hope for, by relying upon a vile model, whose soul is either too base to feel, or too stupid to express the passions, the sentiment his object claims? unhappy he! if experience and fancy fail him.

The beginning of many of *Plato*'s dialogues, supposed to have been held in the Gymnasies, cannot raise our admiration of the generous souls of the Athenian youth, without giving us, at the same time, a strong presumption of a suitable nobleness in their outward carriage and bodily exercises.

The fairest youths danced undressed on the theatre; and *Sophocles*, the great *Sophocles*, when young, was the first who dared to entertain his fellow-citizens in this manner.[13] *Phryne* went to bathe at the Eleusinian games, exposed to the eyes of all Greece, and rising from the water became the model of Venus Anadyomene.[14] During certain solemnities the young Spartan maidens danced naked before the young men: strange this may seem, but will appear more probable, when we consider that the christians of the primitive church, both men and women, were dipped together in the same font.

Then every solemnity, every festival, afforded the artist opportunity to familiarize himself with all the beauties of Nature.

In the most happy times of their freedom, the humanity of the Greeks abhorred bloody games, which even in the Ionick Asia had ceased long before, if, as some guess, they had once been usual there. *Antiochus Epiphanes*, by ordering shews of Roman gladiators, first presented them with such unhappy victims; and custom and time, weakening the pangs of sympathizing humanity, changed even these games into schools of art. There *Ctesias* studied his dying gladiator, in whom you might descry "how much life was still left in him".[15]

These frequent occasions of observing Nature, taught the Greeks to go on still farther. They began to form certain general ideas of beauty, with regard to the proportions of the inferiour parts, as well as of the whole frame: these they raised above the reach of mortality, according to the superiour model of some ideal nature.

Thus *Raphael* formed his Galatea, as we learn by his letter to Count Baltazar Castiglione, where he says, "Beauty being so seldom found among the fair, I avail myself of a certain ideal image". [16]

From   Chapter IV: Expression

The last and most eminent characteristic of the Greek works is a noble simplicity and sedate grandeur in Gesture and Expression. As the bottom of the sea lies peaceful beneath a foaming surface, a great soul lies sedate beneath the strife of passions in Greek figures.

'Tis in the face of Laocoon [that] this soul shines with full lustre, not confined however to the face, amidst the most violent sufferings. Pangs piercing every muscle, every labouring nerve; pangs which we almost feel ourselves, while we consider—not the face, nor the most expressive parts—only the belly contracted by excruciating pains: these however, I say, exert not themselves with violence, either in the face or gesture. He pierces not heaven, like the Laocoon of *Virgil*; his mouth is rather opened to discharge an anxious overloaded groan, as *Sadolet*[17] says; the struggling body and the supporting mind exert themselves with equal strength, nay balance all the frame.

Laocoon suffers, but suffers like the Philoctetes of *Sophocles*: we weeping feel his pains, but wish for the hero's strength to support his misery.

The Expression of so great a soul is beyond the force of mere nature. It was in his own mind the artist was to search for the strength of spirit with which he marked his marble. Greece enjoyed artists and philosophers in the same persons; and the wisdom of more than one *Metrodorus*[18] directed art, and inspired its figures with more than common souls.

Had Laocoon been covered with a garb becoming an ancient sacrificer, his sufferings would have lost one half of their Expression. *Bernini* pretended to perceive the first effects of the operating venom in the numbness of one of the thighs.

Every action or gesture in Greek figures, not stamped with this character of sage dignity, but too violent, too passionate, was called "Parenthyrsos."[19]

For, the more tranquillity reigns in a body, the fitter it is to draw the true character of the soul; which, in every excessive gesture, seems to rush from her proper centre, and being hurried away by extremes becomes unnatural. Wound up to the highest pitch of passion, she may force herself upon the duller eye; but the true sphere of her action is simplicity and calmness. In Laocoon sufferings alone had been Parenthyrsos; the artist therefore, in order to reconcile the significative and ennobling qualities of his soul, put him into a posture, allowing for the sufferings that were necessary, the next to a state of tranquillity: a tranquillity however that is characteristical: the soul will be herself—this individual—not the soul of mankind; sedate, but active; calm, but not indifferent or drowsy.

What a contrast! how diametrically opposite to this is the taste of our modern artists, especially the young ones! on nothing do they bestow their approbation, but contorsions and strange postures, inspired with boldness; this they pretend is done with spirit, with *Franchezza*.[20] Contrast is the darling of their ideal; in it they fancy every perfection. They fill their performances with comet-like excentric souls, despising every thing but an Ajax or a Capaneus.[21]

Arts have their infancy as well as men; they begin, as well as the artist, with froth and bombast: in such buskins the muse of Aeschilus stalks, and part of the diction in his Agamemnon is more loaded with hyperboles than all Heraclitus's nonsense.[22] Perhaps the primitive Greek painters drew in the same manner that their first good tragedian thought in.

In all human actions flutter and rashness precede, sedateness and solidity follow: but time only can discover, and the judicious will admire these only: they are the characteristics of great masters; violent passions run away with their disciples.

The sages in the art know the difficulties hid under that air of easiness:

> *ut sibi quivis*
> *Speret idem, sudet multum, frustraque laboret*
> *Ausus idem.* Horace[23]

La Fage, though an eminent designer, was not able to attain the purity of ancient taste.[24] Every thing is animated in his works; they demand, and at the same time dissipate, your attention, like a company striving to talk all at once.

13   *From*
JOHANN JOACHIM WINCKELMANN
Beschreibung des Torso im Belvedere zu Rom
(*Description of the Torso Belvedere in Rome*)
(1759; tr. Henry Fuseli, 1765)

Διὸς γόνον αἰγιόχοιο

Homer *Iliad* [1]

Reader, I now lead thee to that celebrated trunk of Hercules, of whose exalted beauties every praise falls short; I introduce thee to a performance the sublimest in its kind, and the most perfect offspring of art among those that have escaped the havock of time. But how shall I describe a statue destitute of all those parts which nature makes the chief standard of beauty, and the interpreters of the soul? As of a mighty oak, that, felled by the axe, has lost all its lofty branches, nothing remains but the trunk: thus mangled is the figure of our hero, without head, arms, breast, or legs.

The first look perhaps will shew thee nothing but a huge deformed block; but if thou art able to penetrate the mysteries of art, attention will open all her glories to thine eye; thou shalt see Alcides the hero transfused into the marble.

Where the poet ceased, the artist began; they leave him as soon as, matched with the goddess of eternal youth, he mixes with the gods, but the artist shows us his deified form, and, as it were, an immortal frame, in which humanity is only left to make visible that strength and ease, by which the hero had become conqueror of the world.

In the mighty outlines of this body I see the unsubdued force of him who crushed the giants in the Phlegræan plains, whilst the undulating contour reminds me, at the same time, of that elastic flexibility, that winged haste, from which all the various transformations of Achelous could not escape.[2]

There appears in every part of this body, as in so many pictures, every particular feat of the hero. As from the usefulness of the different parts of a building, we judge of the judicious plan of the architect; so here, from the harmonious variety of powers which the artist stamped on every different part, we may form an idea of his extensive views.

I cannot behold the few remains of the shoulders, without remembering, that their expanded strength, like two mountains, was said to have supported the zodiac. With what grandeur does the chest rise! how magnificent is its vaulted orb! Such was the chest on which Antæus and Geryon, though three-bodied, were crushed; no chest of an Olympian Pancratiast;[3] no chest of a Spartan victor, though sprung from heroes, could rise with such magnificence.

Ask those who know the height of mortal beauty, if they have ever seen a side comparable to his left one? The elasticity of the muscles is admirably balanced between rest and motion: by them the body must have been enabled to execute whatever it attempted. As when, from the first movings of the sea, a gentle horror glides over its smooth surface, and, undulating as they rise, the waves play, absorbed in each other and again refunded: thus waving, thus softly undulating, flows each muscle into the next, and a third, that rises between them, dissolves itself amidst their gentle conflict, and, as it were, escapes our eye.

Fain would I stop here, to fix in our fancy a permanent idea of this side—but there are no limits to with-hold the communication of still emerging beauties. Consider the thighs, whose fulness informs us that the hero never tottered, was never forced to stoop.

At this moment my soul flies over all the numerous tracts of earth which Hercules wanderered over, nor rests till arrived at the goal of his career, the monumental pillars where his foot reposed.—Such is the power of the thighs, whose never-wearied vigour, and more than human length, bore the hero through a hundred nations to immortality.—But a glance on the back revokes my rambling fancy; there new wonders arise. I look like one, who, after having admired the august front of a temple, is conducted to its top, where he is surprised at a dome, which his eyes can hardly command.

Here I see the chief system of the bones, the origin of the muscles, the cause of their motion and situation, and their assemblage, as if I beheld from the top of a mountain a country, over which nature has poured her various beauties; as smiling hills here softly descend into the lower vale, and there rise again, now confined and now enlarged: with such a pleasing variety here likewise arise hills of muscles, circumscribed by inferior ones, which, like the windings of Mæander, sensibly affect us, even before they strike the eye.

If you think it inconceivable how any part of the body but the head can be endowed with the power of thought; then learn here how the creative hand of the artist could animate matter. The back bending, as with intense meditation, gives me the idea of a head busied with the chearful remembrance of its astonishing atchievements; and with it, as it rises majestic and sage before my awed eye, all the other destroyed parts present themselves before me. An effusion of images pours from what is left, and immediately supplies the waste.

The might of the shoulders describes to me those arms, that strangled the lion on Cithæron's top, bound Cerberus, and dragged him from his post. The thighs and knees show me those legs, that knew no rest, and unfatigued outstripped and catched the brazen-footed stag.

By a mysterious art, our mind, through all these feats of the hero's force, is led to the perfections of his soul; a monument which you in vain look for among the poets; they sing the power of his arms alone. But here, not even a hint is left of violence or lascivious love; from the calm repose of the parts, the grand and settled soul appears; the man who became the emblem of virtue; who, from his love of justice alone, faced every obvious danger; who restored security to the earth, and peace to its inhabitants.

126

This eminent and noble form of perfect nature is, we might say, wrapt up in immortality—of which the shape is but the recipient; a higher spirit seems to have occupied the place of the mortal parts; 'tis no longer that frame which still has monsters to face, and fiends to subdue; 'tis that, which, on Oëta's brow, purified from the dregs of mortality, has recovered its primitive splendor, the likeness of his supreme father.

Thus perfect neither Hylas saw him, nor Iolas: 'twas Hebe, goddess of immortal youth, that received him thus, to bestow on his godlike essence her never-fading bloom. In her arms he partook of the ambrosia of the gods; of which his body, void of the grosser nourishments of man, seems replete, not overstocked.

O could I see this image in that primitive grandeur, that beauty with which it appeared to the artist—to say what he thought—what we should think; my great part after his were then to describe it! But wishes are vain; and as Psyche saw the fatal charms of her lover, only to bewail his flight; so I see only the shadow of this Hercules, to bewail him irreparably lost. [4]

Him art bemoans with me: for this work, which she might have opposed to the greatest discoveries of wit or meditation, and proud of whose superior merits she might even now, as in her golden days, have looked down on the homages of mankind; this very work, and perhaps the last, which the united strength of her forces produced—this work she sees now cruelly mangled, and, with many hundred others, almost destroyed.—But from these melancholy reflections her Genius turns, to teach us, from what remains, the ways that lead to perfection.

14 From
JOHANN JOACHIM WINCKELMANN
Beschreibung des Apollo im Belvedere
(*Description of the Apollo Belvedere*)
(1759; tr. Henry Fuseli, 1765)

[So said Phoebus,] the long-haired god who shoots afar and began to walk upon the wide-pathed earth; and all the goddesses were amazed at him.[1]

Of all the works that escaped the havock of time, the statue of *Apollo* in *Belvedere*, is the sublimest idea of art. To frame him the artist took no more of matter than what was necessary to make the God appear; such organs human nature knows not, such attitudes no mortal: an eternal spring, like that of *Elysium*, blends the grandeur of man with the charms of youth, and rosy beauty wantons all down the godlike system. Roam over the realms of incorporeal grace, invoke angelic nature to conceive his perfection; here sick decay, and human flaws dwell not, blood palpitates not here: an empyrean mind, like a flood of light, pours through the whole and marks the outline. He returns from *Python*,[2] whom his mighty stride attained, he bent his bow, the serpent fell; but heedless of the victim, his all-sufficient look as it were, measures immensity. Contempt shakes his lips, whilst indignation swells the nostrils and rises to the brow. Yet there peace dwells in blest tranquillity, and the smiles that beam in his eye seem to invite the love-sick muses. In no remains of antient art appears the father of gods and men whom *Homer* drew, with such majesty as here in the face of his son. A brow of Jupiter, big with the goddess of wisdom; eyebrows, whose nod rules fate; eyes of the queen of Heaven; that mouth which taught *Climene*[3] pleasure! his liquid hair waves here in ringlets like tendrils kissed by zephyrs, is there gathered in knots by the enamoured graces. He seems to enter a council of gods, who rise in awful haste. Wrapt in astonishment I forget what's round me; and to add dignity to contemplation, fancy myself more than man; my breast dilates to adore that which swells with the spirit of prophecy, *Delos* rises before me, the *Lycian* groves, *Dodona* nod! [4] but my strength forsakes me, art only can describe what art created: what I wrote of thee, stupendous image, I lay at thy feet, like the wreaths of those who could not reach the head of the divinities they came to worship!

The figure called the *Borghese Gladiator* appears by the shape of the letters on the inscription to be the most ancient of all the statues now at *Rome*, that are marked with an artist's name. *Agasias* of *Ephesus* lives only in this work. The *Torso* and *Apollo* are pure ideas, as *Laocoon* a compound of nature and ideal beauty; but the *Gladiator* is a beauty of nature only, unassisted by fancy; his charms are those of full-grown life: the former are like epics soaring from probability beyond truth into the marvellous; this resembles history which contains truth only, but truth dressed in elegance of thought, and polished by expression: the face manifestly characterises an individual, it is that of vigorous manhood stampt with the marks of restlessness and labour; *Vivos ducent de marmore vultus*. Virgil.[5] These two statues, probably, made part of the plunder from the temple of *Delos* ransacked for the palaces of *Nero* by a set of ruffians headed by one *Secundus Carinas*; for they were both discovered at *Antium*, now *Nettuno*, the birth-place of that emperor. Both have exercised the whims of conjecture; *Apollo*, notwithstanding the expression of the face and the calm majesty predominant in his air, is called a hunting Apollo by Mr. *Spence*;[6] and the Gladiator, though his eager and projected attitude directly oppose that of him who throws, what the vulgar call, a quoit, has been stiled a *Discobolus* by Stosch.[7]

15   From
JOHANN JOACHIM WINCHELMANN
Geschichte der Kunst des Alterthums
(History of Ancient Art)
(1764; tr. G. H. Lodge, 1849, 1881)

See introduction to No. 12; see also Nos. 13–14

From   **Book V Chapter 1**
The Conformation and Beauty of the
Male Deities and Heroes

Ideal beauty, however, exists not only in the spring-time of
life, and in youthful or female figures, but also in manhood, to
which the ancient artists, in the statues of their deities,
imparted the joyousness and freshness of youth. In Jupiter,
Neptune, and an Indian Bacchus, the beard and venerable
head-hair are the sole marks of age; it is not denoted either by
wrinkles, projecting cheek-bones, or hollow temples. The
cheeks are less full than in youthful divinities, and the
forehead is usually more rounded. This conformation is in
keeping with their admirable conception of the divine nature,
which neither suffers change from time, nor passes through
gradations of age, and in regard to which we must think of
existence without succession. Such elevated ideas of the
godhead ought to be peculiar to our artists, rather than to the
ancients; yet, in most of the figures of the Eternal
Father—according to the Italian manner of speaking of the
Deity—we see an aged man, with a bald head. Even Jupiter
himself is represented by the scholars of Raphael, in the *Feast
of the Gods*, in the Farnesina, with the hair of the head, as
well as of the beard, snow-white.

The Laocoön is the finest of all the statues which have
received their last finish from the chisel, and here, in
particular, an observant eye can discover with what masterly
address and skilful boldness the chisel has been managed, in
order not to impair, by polishing, the effect of those traits
which most evince the knowledge of the artist. Though the
outer skin of this statue when compared with a smooth and
polished surface appears somewhat rough, rough as a soft
velvet contrasted with a lustrous satin, yet it is, as it were, like
the skin of the ancient Greeks, which had neither been relaxed
by the constant use of warm baths,—as was the case with the
Romans after the introduction among them of effeminate
habits,—nor rubbed smooth by a scraper, but on which lay a
healthy moisture, resembling the first appearance of down
upon the chin. [1]

From **Book X Chapter 1**
Art in the Reign of Alexander the Great

Laocoön is a statue representing a man in extreme suffering
who is striving to collect the conscious strength of his soul to
bear it. While the muscles are swelling and the nerves are
straining with torture, the determined spirit is visible in the
turgid forehead, the chest is distended by the obstructed
breath and the suppressed outburst of feeling, in order that he
may retain and keep within himself the pain which tortures
him. The indrawn anxious sigh and the inhaled breath exhaust
the belly, and make the sides hollow to such a degree that we
are almost able to see the movements of the entrails. But his
own suffering seems to distress him less than that of his
children, who turn their faces to their father and shriek for
aid; the father's feelings are visible in the sorrowful eyes, and
his pity seems to float on them in a dim vapour. The

expression of the face is complaining, but not screaming; the eyes are turned for help to a higher power. The mouth is full of sorrow, and the sunken under lip is heavy with the same feeling; but in the upper lip, which is drawn upwards, this expression is mingled with one of pain, which, with an emotion of indignation at unmerited, unworthy suffering, rises to the nose, swells it, and manifests itself in the dilated and upward-drawn nostrils. The struggle between the pain and the suppression of the feelings is rendered with great knowledge as concentrated in one point below the forehead; for whilst the pain elevates the eyebrows, resistance to it presses the fleshy parts above the eyes downward and towards the upper eyelid, so that it is almost entirely covered by the overhanging skin. As the artist could not make nature more beautiful, he has sought to exhibit it more developed, more strained, more powerful; in the parts where the greatest pain is placed he shows us the greatest beauty. The left side, into which the serpent with furious bite discharges its poison, appears to suffer the most violently from its greater sensibility in consequence of its vicinity to the heart; and this part of the body may be termed a miracle of art. It seems as though he wishes to raise his legs, that he may flee from his distress; no part is in repose; even the touches of the chisel are so managed as to suggest a benumbed skin.

16 From
ROBERT WOOD
Essay on the Original Genius of Homer
(1767; third edition 1775)

For the details of Wood's life and other works, see No. 11. On his expedition to Palmyra with Dawkins, he visited Sigeum and the mouth of the Scamander; here they 'spent a fortnight with great pleasure, in writing a map of the Scamandrian plain, with Homer in our hands'. Eventually this led to *A Comparative View of the antient and present state of the Troade* to which he prefixed the essay on Homer. This was privately printed but another version of the essay on Homer appeared in 1769 and a fuller account in 1775 which had been revised by Jacob Bryant after Wood's death. This book made a major contribution to the understanding of Homer and was widely read, especially in Germany where it helped to arouse interest in poetry which was original, popular and naive.[1] Wood's study also firmly established the idea that Homer was not literate (a point slightly blunted by Bryant when he introduced the words *and Writings* into the title of Wood's book). The *ingeniosa audacia* of Wood's exposition (in the phrase of F. A. Wolf) did much to inspire that German scholar to produce his own epoch-making *Prolegomena* in 1795. Like Thomas Blackwell before him (and like Mary Wortley Montagu) Wood insisted that Homer could be best understood in terms of the environment which had produced him. Unlike Blackwell, Wood had travelled widely in and around the Homeric sites; he was even in a position to check Homer's accuracy in nautical affairs from his own experience of local conditions, both of wind and of sea. Indeed, his recurrent concern with the Homeric winds and the direct relation between his own adventures as a traveller and his interpretation of Homer give to his book a freshness and immediacy which is certainly part of its appeal. One of his first readers was so struck by this unscholarly vivacity that he told the printer: 'It is like an Oriental Novel, wild and entertaining.' [2]

Wood's approach to Homer is an empirical one: he believed that behind the Homeric epics (and he is much more concerned with the *Iliad* than with the *Odyssey*) there is a bedrock of fact the existence of which can be detected and verified by the modern enquirer. The *Iliad* is an objective work which lacks a palpable moral design; it is 'an exact transcript'. Homer's accounts of the Troade and of the siege of Troy conform to the facts: the poem 'contains in general a consistent narrative of military events, connected, and supported, by that due coincidence of the circumstances of time, and place, which History requires.' Likewise, in his accounts of navigation 'Homer ... had only the great book of Nature to peruse, and was original from necessity, as well as by genius': the same applies to his understanding of the action of the winds, where he far surpasses

Virgil who did not share his first-hand knowledge. Again, Homer was 'a faithful Historian, because he was a correct Painter'; even his chronology should not be regarded as mere fabrication. At times Homer is even too much of a realist for eighteenth-century taste: '... it is among the faults of Homer, to be too minutely descriptive. He frequently introduces superfluous circumstances of mere precision, rather than leave his object vague and uncircumscribed; even where a general view of it would have done as well, or perhaps better.'[3]

Here, perhaps, Wood is allowing the taste of his own period to cloud his understanding of Homer; in particular, he is not fully aware of the characteristics and conventions of oral poetry. This would be no surprise were it not for the fact that part of the originality of Wood's approach was his recognition that Homer probably could not read or write. Wood argues at some length that prose writing was not known in Greece until long after Homer; the Greeks did not have an alphabet and employed verse and music to help in the recording of important facts and events. Homer belonged to an oral tradition like the Mexican poets and the Celtic Bards and Fili of the Irish. However, the oral traditions of a learned and enlightened age are not to be properly compared with those of 'a rude and unlettered state of society'. Though Homer was an accurate observer as a traveller, he had no maps or charts and was ignorant of the sciences of geography and astronomy, of architecture and medicine. Art too was fairly rudimentary in Homer's day: 'I see nothing in the Iliad or the Odyssey like the use of the pencil and colours in producing resemblance; no hint of the Clair Obscur, or the art of raising an object on a flat surface, and approaching it to the eye by the management of light and shade.' Yet we should pay tribute to Homer's 'just conception and happy expression as a Painter'; an interesting feature of Wood's book is the way in which he applies to Homer's descriptions the criteria of the connoisseur and the drawing-master. The eighteenth century characteristically regarded poetry and painting as closely related if not interchangeable (see note on Joseph Spence's *Polymetis* (No. 8)) but it is strange that Wood should attempt to find the same connection in Homer when he has so forcefully demonstrated that Homer's cultural context was dramatically different from his own. Conversely, it might be imagined that Wood's penchant for the picturesque would have informed his approach to Pope's translation, which may be lacking in geographical accuracy but which is strongly conditioned by painterly considerations.[4]

Wood has much to say on the nature of the society which produced so great a poet. Again, the approach is largely empirical: Wood found the manners of the *Iliad* still preserved in parts of the East, 'nay retaining, in a remarkable degree, that genuine cast of natural simplicity, which we admire in his works and the sacred books . . .' (for the comparison between Homer and the Bible, see Nos. 2 and 3). The main characteristics of Arab society can all be paralleled in the world of the Homeric warriors. First, there is dissimulation: 'The arts of disguise are in those countries the great arts of life; and the character of Ulysses would form a perfect model for those, who wish to make their way in it with security and respect.' Secondly, there is bloodshed, treachery, cruelty and violence: 'Some of the favourite personages of the Iliad and Odyssey had fled their country for this crime [homicide]; and most of Homer's heroes would, in the present age, be capitally convicted, in any country in Europe, on the Poet's evidence.' Thirdly, there is hospitality. Fourthly, there is an unfortunate attitude to women which is reflected in certain crudenesses and insensitivities in Homeric language. Fifthly, there is the well-recognized association between royalty and the pastoral life, which are not considered incompatible in this kind of society. Finally, there is the connection with the primitive life of a rather coarse kind of wit and humour. Most, if not all, of these features had been recognized long before; what gives them greater force in Wood's account is his ability to relate them to life as he encountered it in the Near East, though it must be said that the sense of direct experience is much less pervasive here than in the navigational and geographical investigations.

There can be no doubt that Wood finds much in Homeric society of which he disapproves; but he also believes that Homer lived in a time and place which were eminently propitious for the production of great poetry. The social and political environment was highly favourable to the development of language. There was little room for pedantry and affectation. In Homer's day the Greek language was magnificently functional. Thus, particles 'are to hexameter verse, what small stones are to a piece of masonry, ready at hand to fill up the breaks and interstices, and connect those of a larger size, so exactly as to give a smooth compactness to the whole'. As for compound epithets, 'Even at this day the expression in modern languages is enriched by a Greek compound, coined for the purpose of expressing much in a single word'. Wood concludes with a celebration of the Homeric style, which takes as its unexpressed opposite the over-sophistication of Virgil and Pope and of Wood's poetic contemporaries.

NOTES

1 For Wood's influence in Germany, see FOERSTER, pp. 93–113.
2 John Nichols, *Literary Anecdotes of the Eighteenth Century*, 1812–15, iii. 83.
3 Cf. Blackwell, p. 71, Cowper, Preface to the *Iliad*, 2nd ed., 1802, p. xxxv.
4 See David Ridgley Clark, 'Landscape Painting Effects in Pope's Homer', *Essential Articles for the study of Alexander Pope*, ed. Maynard Mack, Hamden, Conn., 1968, pp. 668–74. Pope regarded Homer's epithets as pictorial and he frequently drew specific comparisons with the genres or techniques of painting. In the Preface to his translation he remarks that Homer's 'Expression is like the colouring of some great Masters' while he characterizes Book X of the *Iliad* as 'the most natural Night-scene in the World . . .' (note to l. 667). The interchangeability of painting and poetry was the guiding concept behind *Tableaux tirés de l'Iliade, de l'Odyssée d'Homère et de l'Énéide de Virgile*, 1757, by Comte de Caylus, which provided a reservoir of images from classical epic for the use of painters. See Jean Hagstrum, *The Sister Arts*, Chicago, Ill., 1958, especially pp. 229–33.

From **Homer's Country**

I shall begin with that beautiful comparison of the wavering and irresolute perplexity of the Greeks, to an agitated sea; and take this passage into consideration the more willingly, as it has given occasion to some severe strictures on the Poet's Geography.

As from its cloudy dungeon issuing forth
A double tempest of the west and north
Swells o'er the sea, from Thracia's frozen shore,
Heaps waves on waves, and bids the Ægean roar;
This way and that, the boiling deeps are tost;
Such various passions urg'd the troubled host.

POPE.[1]

Here we not only find a happy allusion, but, if I am not
mistaken, a beautiful sea piece: and in order to do justice to
its perspective, we should place ourselves on the spot, or in
the point of view, where the Painter made his drawing; which
will only answer to some part of the Asiatic coast, or its
islands.

It would be a false and affected refinement to suppose, that
the simile acquires any additional beauty by the discovery of
a real landscape in those lines. The Poet's purpose, which was
to paint the struggle of wavering indecision in the people,
distracted between a sense of honour and of danger, and
alternately resolving to fly or to stay, is, no doubt, completely
satisfied in the general image, which he makes use of. But
though his meaning went no farther, I am not less of opinion,
that, upon this occasion, his imagination suggested to him a
storm, which he had seen: and having myself had more than
once an opportunity of observing from the coast of Ionia the
truth of this picture in every circumstance; I cannot help
giving it as an instance of the Poet's constant original manner
of composition, which faithfully (though perhaps in this case
inadvertently) recalls the images, that a particular striking
appearance of Nature had strongly impressed upon his
youthful fancy, retaining the same local associations, which
accompanied his first warm conception of them.

But lest my testimony, as an eye-witness of the exact
correspondence of this copy to the original, from which I

suppose it taken, should not be satisfactory; I would propose a test of this matter, upon which every Reader will be enabled to form his own judgement. Suppose a painter to undertake this subject from Homer, he will find each object, not only clearly expressed, though within the compass of four hexameters; but its particular place on the canvas distinctly marked; and the disposition, as well as perspective, of the whole ascertained, with a precision of out-line, from which it is impossible to depart. The Thracian mountains must form the back ground, thence the tempest is to burst on the Ægean sea, which has its proper stormy colouring; while the Ionian shore covered with sea-wreck, by a succession of waves breaking on its beach, will make the fore-ground, where the Poet views, admires, and describes the whole.

A curious and attentive observer of Nature is perhaps most liable to retain those marks of locality, which it has been my object to trace in the Poet. An elegant conception of external forms cannot easily divest itself of the precise order and arrangement of objects, with which it has at any time connected the idea of beauty; and this may account for that Ionian point of view, to which Homer's scenery is so much adapted, sometimes even in violation of those rules, which critics have since laid down in regard to unity of place.

We shall find this negligence more excusable, if we credit that probable tradition of the wandering Bard's chanting his compositions to his countrymen, in the manner practised at this day in the East: a tradition which is favoured by the dramatic cast of the Iliad and Odyssey. I have often admired the spirited theatrical action of Italian and Eastern poets, when they recite in the open air, pointing out each object of description in an imaginary scenery of their own extemporaneous creation, but availing themselves at the same time of every real appearance of Nature within view of their Audience, that is applicable to their subject, and connects it, in some degree, with the spot, where the recital is made.

After what has been said on this passage, I should think it

needless to mention the censure Eratosthenes passed upon it, had it not been so frequently produced to the Poet's disadvantage, and urged as a proof of his ignorance in geography. The error laid to his charge is, that of making the West wind blow from Thrace. I rest his defence against this accusation upon the obvious answer of Strabo to so strange a piece of criticism; which is, in substance, that Eratosthenes mistakes the Poet, when he concludes from this passage, that he asserts, as a general proposition, that the West wind blows from Thrace; the wind here mentioned blows from the Thracian mountains upon the Ægean sea, and must of course be a West wind in respect to Ionia.[2]

For though this may not be exactly true, if we are to talk with the precision of a modern seaman; yet we should remember, that in Homer's time there were but four points to the compass. I must observe, that there are but two passages in the Iliad, where winds are described as blowing from the Thracian mountains across the Ægean upon the Asiatic coast; and in both cases Boreas and Zephyrus are employed together.[3]

But to proceed to other instances of the same kind; when the formidable march of Ajax with his corps is compared to a threatening storm coming from the sea, I must observe (as an illustration, not of the obvious beauties of the simile, but of the Poet's country) that this can be no other than an Ionian, or, at least, an Asiatic storm; for it is raised by a West wind, which in those seas, can blow on that coast alone.[4]

When, again, the irresistible rage of Hector is compared to the violence of Zephyrus buffeting the waves, we are not immediately reconciled to this wind's appearance in that rough character, so little known to western climates, and so unlike the playful Zephyr of modern Poetry.[5] But, before we condemn Homer as negligent of nature, we should see, whether he is not uniform in this representation, and whether this is not the true Ionian character of Zephyrus.

The very next simile of the same book is as much to our

purpose, where the numbers, tumult, and eagerness of the Grecian army collecting to engage, are compared to a growing storm, which begins at sea, and proceeds to vent its rage upon the shore. [6]The West wind is again employed in this Ionian picture; and we shall be less surprised to see the same allusion so soon repeated, when we find, that of all the appearances of nature, of a kind so generally subject to variation, there is none so constant upon this coast. For at Smyrna the West wind blows into the gulph for several hours, almost every day during the summer season, generally beginning, in a gentle breeze, before twelve o'clock, but freshening considerably towards the heat of the day, and dying away in the evening. During a stay of some days in this city, at three different times, I had an opportunity of observing the various degrees of this progress, from the first dark curl on the surface of the water, to its greatest agitation, which was sometimes violent. Though these appearances admit of variation, both as to the degree of strength, and the precise time of their commencement, yet they seldom fail entirely. This wind, upon which the health and pleasure of the inhabitants so much depend, is, by them, called the Inbat. The Frank merchants have long galleries running from their houses, supported by pillars, and terminating in a chiosque, or open summer-house, to catch this cooling breeze, which, when moderate, adds greatly to the Oriental luxury of their coffee and pipe.

We have seen how happily the Poet has made use of the growing violence of this wind, when he paints the increasing tumult and agitation of troops rushing to battle; but, in a still silent picture, the allusion is confined to the first dubious symptoms of its approach, which are perceived rather by the colour, than by any sound or motion of the water, as in the following instance:

When Hector challenges the most valiant of the Greeks to a single combat, both armies are ordered to sit down to hear his proposal. The plain, thus extensively covered with shields, helmets, and spears, is, in the moment of this solemn pause, compared to the sea, when a rising western breeze has spread a dark shade over its surface. [7]

From **Homer's Geography and Pope's Translation**

That Homer should escape so entire, out of the hands of Lawyers and Grammarians, is a piece of good fortune to letters, upon which his friends have great reason to congratulate themselves. For, considering how cruelly both his compositions and the countries they describe have been tortured by barbarous treatment of various kinds, and the changes they have undergone in so great a length of time, his descriptions correspond more with present appearances, than could be reasonably expected.

Not only the permanent and durable objects of his description, such as his rock, hill, dale, promontory, &c. continue in many instances to bear unquestionable testimony of his correctness, and shew, by a strict propriety of his epithets, how faithfully they were copied; but even his more fading and changeable landscape, his shady grove, verdant lawn, and flowery mead, his pasture and tillage, with all his varieties of corn, wine, and oil, agree surprisingly with the present face of those countries.

So remarkable a resemblance between periods so distant from each other would induce us to believe, what is not otherwise improbable, that agriculture is pretty much in the same neglected state, in that part of the world, at present, as it was in the time of the Poet. I doubt much, whether his descriptions of this kind could have so well stood the test of our examination, two thousand years ago, in those days of elegance and refinement, when nature was probably decked out in a studied dress, unlike the elegant dishabille in which Homer and we found her.

But, I must own that great part of the amusement, which we enjoyed in Homer and Strabo's company, on the spot, arose as much from the investigation, as the discovery of the correspondence and resemblance ... Now, though it must be acknowledged, that Mr Pope is the only translator, who has, in a certain degree, kept alive that divine spirit of the Poet, which has almost expired in other hands; yet I cannot help thinking, that those, who wish to be thoroughly acquainted, either with the manners and characters of Homer's age, or the landscape and geography of his country, will be disappointed, if they expect to find them in this translation. Had Mr Pope preserved the first; viz. the manners and characters, Homer would have continued to speak Greek to most of his English readers. For, though the disguise of several passages in a modern dress may sometimes proceed from his not being very conversant with ancient life and manners; yet he often purposely accommodates his author to the ideas of those, for whom he translates; substituting beauties of his own (as similar as he can bring them to the original) in the room of those which he despaired of making intelligible.

But as a truly poetical translation could not be effected, even by Mr Pope, without his "venturing to open the prospect a little, by the addition of a few epithets, or short hints of description;" so "the most valuable piece of geography left us, concerning the state of Greece in that early period," has of course suffered by such liberties; and, when every descriptive epithet in Homer should have been religiously preserved, Mr Pope's alterations have produced a new map of his own, and deprived us of that merit of the original which he called upon us to admire. Thus the Græa and spacious Mycalessus of Homer become by translation,

> Græa near the main,
> And Mycalessia's ample piny plain.[8]

Had it been proper to describe the narrow streight of the Euripus, by the name of the main, yet it is not at all distinguished, by such a situation, from several other places mentioned on this shore; and as to the ample piny plain, we searched for it to no purpose. It is, therefore, matter of doubt, whether it existed in the time of Homer, though mentioned by Statius about a thousand years after. Indeed it would be difficult to assign any reason for the addition in the English, except that the rhyme requires that Græa should be near the main in the first line, and that Mycalessia (for so the translator was obliged to write it in order to make out the line) owes both to rhyme and measure her piny plain in the second . . .

In short, those concise, but descriptive, and therefore interesting, sketches of antient arts, customs, and manners, with which Homer has enlivened his map of Greece, cannot be translated faithfully, and at the same time poetically. Mr Pope has succeeded surprisingly in the latter; but then his study of a flowing and musical versification frequently betrays him into a florid profusion of unmeaning ornament, in which the object is greatly disguised, if not totally lost . . .

From **Homer's Religion and Mythology**

If we form to ourselves a just idea of the respective situation, distance, and perspective, of Olympus, Ida, the Grecian camp, &c. we shall find Homer's celestial geography (if I may so call it) so happily connected with his Map of Troy, that the scene is shifted from one to the other naturally, and with a certain mixture of circumstantial truths, which operates unobserved, and throws at least an air of possibility into the wildest excursions of fancy. I shall explain myself by example.

Jupiter, seated on Mount Gargara, the summit of Ida, not suspecting, that any of the gods would violate the neutrality he had so strictly enjoined, turns his eyes from the slaughter upon the Scamandrian plain to the peaceful scenes of Thrace and Mysia. But Neptune, anxious for the distressed Greeks, had placed himself on the top of Samothrace, which commands a prospect of Ida, Troy, and the fleet. Having from hence observed Jupiter turn his back upon the scene of action, he resolves to seize that opportunity of annoying the Trojans. With this view he goes home to Aegos for his armour, and proceeds thence to the field of battle, putting up his chariot and horses between Imbros and Tenedos. At the same time Juno, not less interested in the Grecian cause, discovers from Olympus, what is passing at the ships. And watching the motions of Jupiter and Neptune, she forms her plan accordingly for rendering the operations of the latter effectual, by keeping Jupiter's attention diverted another way. Having with this view procured the cestus or girdle of Venus, she proceeds, first to Lemnos, to sollicit the aid of the god of Sleep, and thence to Jupiter on Gargara.[9]

I doubt much, whether any Reader has ever suspected, that this fanciful piece of machinery is so strictly geographical, that we cannot enter into the boldness and true spirit of the Poet's conceptions upon this occasion, without a map. But if he examines it in that light, he will be pleased to find, that a view of the land and water here described, under a certain perspective, clears up the action, and converts, what may otherwise appear crowded and confused, into distinct and pleasing variety. He will then see, that the mere change of Jupiter's position, while it introduces a most beautiful contrast between scenes of innocence and tranquillity, and those of devastation and bloodshed, is essential to the episode of Neptune and Juno. He will attend those Divinities with new pleasure, through every step of their progress. The mighty strides of the first, and the enchanting description of his voyage, long admired as one of the happiest efforts of a truly poetical imagination, will improve upon a survey of the original scenery, when its correspondence with the fable is discovered. Juno's stages are still more distinctly marked: she goes from Olympus by Pieria and Æmathia, to Athos; from Athos, by sea, to Lemnos, where, having engaged the god of

Sleep in her interests, she continues her course to Imbros; and from Imbros to Lectum, the most considerable promontory of Ida; here leaving the sea, she proceeds to Gargara, the summit of that mountain.

When I attempted to follow the steps of these poetical journies, in my eye, from Mount Ida, and other elevated situations on the Æolian and Ionian side of the Ægean sea; I could not take in so many of them as to form a tolerable picture of the whole. But I could not make this experiment with the same success from any station in European Greece. This induces me to suppose the composition to be Asiatic, and that the original idea of Neptune and Juno's journey was most probably conceived in the neighbourhood of Troy.

I must own, that in this sort of inquiry we are apt to indulge our fancy; and it is not without some apprehensions of falling into this error, that, by way of farther explanation, I risk the following conjecture. When I was in these classical countries, I could not help tracing one of the most ancient pieces of heathen Mythology up to its source, I mean the war of the Titans with the gods. For though the scene of this story lies in old Greece, yet some of its embellishments look very like the production of an Ionian imagination. I have already taken notice of the beauties of a western evening prospect from this coast. When the sun goes down behind the cloud-capped mountains of Macedonia and Thessaly, there is a picturesque wildness in the appearance, under certain points of view, which naturally calls to mind the old fable of the rebel giants bidding defiance to Jupiter, and scaling the heavens, as the fanciful suggestion of this rugged perspective. And we find this striking face of nature adapted to so bold a fiction with the fitness and propriety, which its extravagance would forbid us to expect; for it was by no means a matter of indifference, which mountains were to be employed, or in what order they were to be piled, to effect this daring escalade. If we compare Homer and Virgil's account of this matter with the present state of the country, we shall find a variation in their descriptions, which, while it sufficiently distinguishes the Roman copy from the Greek original, will best explain my meaning.

There was an old tradition in Greece, which is preserved there to this day, that Ossa and Olympus were originally different parts of the same mountain, of which the first formed the summit, and the latter the base, till they were separated by an earthquake. It is not improbable that their size and shape, as they appear under an eastern point of view, should have given rise to this tradition, and perhaps suggested to the inventor of the fable, or, if you please, to the Poet, who first adapted it to this Grecian scenery, the order of piling them one upon another. But Virgil, who never saw, or never attended to, this prospect, has deviated both from Homer, and Nature, in placing those mountains so as to form an inverted pyramid. [10]

17 *From*
SIR WILLIAM CHAMBERS
Notes on the Revival of Greek Architecture
(1768–71)

The much-travelled Sir William Chambers (1723–1796) was architectural tutor to the future George III, Architect of the Royal Works, Comptroller and finally Surveyor-General of the Office of Works. He was also the first treasurer of the Royal Academy. Chambers was one of the most powerful and outspoken opponents of the Greek Revival, which offended his Palladian sense of the architectural proprieties. When the first volume of *Ionian Antiquities* was published in 1769 he complained to Charlemont:

The dilettanti book is published, and a cursed book it is, between friends, being composed of some of the worst architecture I ever saw; there is a degree of madness in sending people abroad to fetch home such stuff.[1]

His highly critical notes, unedited and unpolished extracts from which are printed here, were probably intended for the second edition of his *Treatise on Civil Architecture* (1st ed. 1759); in the event, they appeared in slightly modified form in the third edition of 1791.

Like many of those who admired the Greek achievement, Chambers attributed it to social and geographical factors; unlike them, he saw it as a beginning rather than the attainment of an unrivalled artistic perfection. Greek society was fragmented, geographically and politically; economically, it was underdeveloped. These factors, to which Thomas Blackwell had traced the particular excellences of Homer, were seen by Chambers as obstacles to the full flowering of art and architecture: in his view Greek architecture was less mature than that of the Romans because Greek society was at an earlier stage of development. Chambers was not alone in holding this view[2] but he was swimming against the tide; the very primitivism which he criticized was what attracted many of his contemporaries to Homer and to the Doric temples at Paestum.

Chambers was answered directly in the preface to the third volume of the *Antiquities of Athens*; his antagonist was Willey Reveley, who had once trained as an architect under his tutelage but had later spent five years with Sir Richard Worsley as architect and draughtsman on a tour of Italy, Greece and Egypt. Reveley argued that Chambers knew little of his subject at first-hand. He had produced too little in the way of specific detail and he was far too strong in his assertions. Reveley claimed that he was also faulty in his measurements, since he appeared to believe that the Lantern of Demosthenes and the Parthenon were similar in size and that the Parthenon was smaller than St Martin in the Fields:

Artists who ever saw an antique temple or ever read Vitruvius, know, that Saint Martin's church, though one of the best in London, is no more than a very inferior imitation of the Greek Prostyle temple, and will not enter into the slightest degree of comparison with the chaste grandeur, the dignified simplicity, and sublime effect, of the Parthenon. Sir William seems to insinuate in his opinion upon the subject, that the Parthenon would gain considerably with respect to beauty by the addition of a steeple. A judicious observer of the fine arts would scarcely be more surprized were he to propose to effect this improvement by adding to it a Chinese pagoda.

Reveley also defended the 'masculine boldness and dignity' of the

Grecian Doric, the effect of which 'can scarcely be understood by those who have never seen it'. He had no doubt that Greek architecture could throw open 'a grand field for the display of genius'.

NOTES

1   *Manuscripts and Correspondence of Charlemont*, 1891–4, i. 298.
2   Writing in 1823 James Elmes remembered how most architects had hated 'the new-fangled "Doric" without a base, as much as they did a shirt without ruffles, or a wig without two good portly curls over each ear, and half a yard of tail behind; scorning its simpler flutes without fillets, which they compared to ribbed stockings' (CROOK (*The Greek Revival*, 1968), p. 15).

How distant the Grecians were from Perfection in Proportions in the Art of Profiling & I may venture to say in the whole Detail of the Decorative Part of Architeckture will appear at first Sight to every one whether Ignorant or informed who unprejudiced compares the Columns, Capitals, Bases Pedestals, Entablatures & Ornaments in the Works of Messrs le Roy, Revet & Stewart[1] and other ingenious travelers with the Antiquities of Rome which those who have not had or are not likely to have an Opportunity of seeing in the Originals may find in Palladio, Serlio, Desgodets, Sandrart, Piranesi & many other Books in which they are delineated with sufficient accuracy [2] But should any Man be diffident of his own Judgement, or trusting to the Encomiums of a few Ingenious but too partial Travellers, discredit the Testimony of his own Eyes, he cannot have a more corroborating Proof of the Imperfection of the Grecian Architecture than that it is diametrically opposite in almost every Particular to that of the Romans, whose Works have been admired, copied & imitated by all the great Architects from the fourteenth Century when the antient Stile of Architecture began to revive, till this Day, although these great Architects were by no means unacquainted with the Grecian Manner of Building Calabrea, Sicily & even Rome furnished Examples, which had they deserved the Preference would no doubt have been copied or had they deserved Notice would at least have been mentioned in their Work besides Greece & its Antiquities are not a discovery of Yesterday. Accounts of them were published in the last Century & when Desgodets was employed to measure the Antiquities of Rome other Artists were sent for the same purpose to Greece, had what they collected there merited a Publication it would probably have made its Appearance in the World a hundred Years ago.

But supposing for Argument Sake that the Grecian Architecture was intrinsically more perfect than the Roman yet the Fashion or habit of Admiring the latter is of so long a standing our Prepossessions are so strong in its favor & its Reputation is established upon such indisputable Authority that it would be almost impossible to remove them, a general Outcry of Artists & Connoisseurs would perhaps bring even the Gothic Architecture into Vogue again, & might cheat us into a Reverence for Attic Deformity but the Opinions of two or three or half a dozen can have but little Weight in a matter of this Nature, they might with equal success oppose a Hottentot & a Baboon to the Apollo & the Gladiator as set up the Grecian Architecture against the Roman the *Ton* in anything is not easily given and it would be absurd to suppose that Monsieur or Mr such a one should turn the torrent of Prejudice in any particular Branch of Art as it would be to imagine that a Peasant could set the Fashion of a dress. Things that do not admit of absolute Demonstration are measured by the number and Reputation of those that adopt them & either esteemed or despised in Proportions as they are well or ill protected.

It hath afforded Occasion of Laughter to every intelligent Architect to see with what Pomp the Grecian Antiquities have lately been ushered into the World & what Encomiums have been lavished upon things that in Reality deserve little or no Notice, it is however to be lamented that these Encomiums ill grounded as they are, have made strong Impressions on many ingenious Men chiefly Men of Learning who accustomed to admire and to taste the Beauties of Grecian Literature have easily been persuaded into a belief of Grecian Superiority in an Art of which they were themselves no Judges, A few Remarks upon some of these celebrated Trifles may here be permitted they are not made with any invidious Design but merely to set them in a proper light, & with an Intent to undeceive such as have been led astray by fine words & elegant Publications.

The celebrated Lantern of Demosthenes or Choragic Monument of Lysicrates or the Temple of Hercules with all its other Names is in Reality not quite so large as one of the Centry Boxes in Portman Square its Form and Proportions resemble those of a silver Tankard excepting that the Handle is wanting. Messrs. Steward & Ryvet have given twenty six Plates of this Edifice well drawn & well engraved in which all its Parts are represented with the utmost Accuracy & from an Inscription upon the Architrave it appears that this Monument was erected in the Days of Alexander the Great when the Grecian Arts were at the highest Pitch of Excellence so that we may look upon this Building as a Cryterion of the Grecian Taste in Architecture when its utmost Perfection which as the learned Architect will perceive bore a very exact Resemblance to the Taste of Boromini[3] universally & Justly esteemed the most licentious & Extravagant of all the modern Italians.

The celebrated Temple of the Winds or Tower of Andronicus Cyrrhestes to vulgar Eyes resembles exactly one of the Dove houses usually erected on Gentlemens Estates in the Country of England, excepting that the Roof is somewhat flatter & there is no Turret for the Pigeons to creep in & fly out at, but we are assured that a more nice observer will be greatly pleased with its Elegance & extraordinary Beauty . . .

At first Sight it appears extraordinary that a People so renowned for Poetry, Rhetoric, & every sort of Polite Literature and who carried Sculpture farther than any of the antient nations should be so deficient in Architecture yet upon Reflection many Reasons will suggest themselves to us why it naturally should be so.

Greece a Country small in itself was divided into a Great Number of little States none of them extremely powerful populous nor Rich so that they could attempt no very considerable Works in Architecture neither having the Space nor the Hands nor the Treasures necessary for that Purpose it must be owned Says Monsieur d'Ablancourt[4] that Grece eaven in the Zenith of its greatness had more ambition than Power we find Athens flattering herself with the Conquest of the Universe though unable to Deffend her own territories against the Incursions of her neighbors and we find despairing reduced to sue for peace upon the loss of four hundred men. The Lake of Moeris would have drowned Peloponessus and beggard Greece, Babylon only one of the many famous cities, with which the Assyrian Empire abounded would have covered Attica, & more Men were employed to build it than there were inhabitants in all the Grecian States the Egyptian Labyrinth was an hundred times larger than that built in Imitation of it by Dedalus in Crete & there is more stone in the great Pyramid than there was in all the Public Buildings of Athens, if we recollect at the same time that whilst divided into many Governments Greece was constantly harressed with domestic Wars and from the time of its union under Phillip always in an unsettled State that an uncommon Simplicity of Manner prevailed amongst the Grecian Nations & that the Strickest Maxims of Equality were jealously adhered to in most of their States it will be easy to account for the little Progress the Grecians made in Architecture Demosthenes observes that the Houses of Aristides, Miltiades or any other of the great Men at that Time were no finer than those of their Neighbors such was their Moderation & so steadily did they adhere to the antient Manners of their Country one of the Laws of Lycurgus ordained that the Ceilings of Houses should only be wrought by an Ax.

What little Magnificence the Grecians then displayed in their Structures was confined to public Buildings which were chiefly Temples in which there appears to have been nothing very surprizing either for Dimensions or ingenuity of contrivance. Greece almost constantly the Theatre of War abounded not like Italy in magnificent Villas where the richest Productions of the Pencil & Chizel were displayed, their Roads were not adorned with Mausoleums to commemorate their Heroes, nor their Towns with Arches to celebrate their Triumphs, the Grecian Theatres were trifling compared with those of Italy the Numachia[5] and Amphitheatres unknown amongst them as were also the Thermini in which the Romans displayed so much splendor . . .

It will perhaps be alledged that as the Greeks brought the Arts of Painting & Sculpture to Perfection they must necessarily have done so with Architecture likewise it being closely connected with them, but that is by no means a consequence for both Sculpture & Painting are much more easily cultivated than Architecture & being in a great Degree Arts of Imitation & having in a great measure their Cryterion in Nature they would of course make quicker strides towards Perfection than Architecture which has no such guides.

Architecture is a creative Art & that of a very complicated kind the hints which it collects from Nature are rude & imperfect a tree is the model of a Column a basket & a Dock Leaf those of a Capital & a hut is the Original of a Temple, the precise form, the exact Proportion, & degree of Strength, with a thousand other Particulars are left to the Determination of the Art & can only be attained by a number of Experiments & a long Series of Observations not easily made but in times of profound Peace in Countries where Wealth abounds & where Splendor prevails.

Since therefore it appears that the Grecian Structures are neither the most considerable nor the most varied in the World & since it has been proved as clearly as the Nature of the Subject will admit that they are not the most perfect it naturally follows that our knowledge ought not to be collected from thence but from some purer & more abundant Source and this in whatever relates to the Ornamental branch of the Art can be no other than the Roman Antiquities still existing in Italy, France & many other Countries remains of Buildings erected in the politest Ages & by the Richest most Splendid & most Powerful People in the World who after having transported to Rome from Carthage, Sicily & Greece the rarest Productions of the Art of Design as also the ablest Artists of the Times were constantly employed during many Centuries in the Construction of all kinds of Buildings that either Use, Convenience or Pomp requires, & must therefore have improved upon the Grecian Architecture & carried the Art to a very high degree if not to the highest degree of perfection ...

... Nature is the Supreme & Ultimate Model of the imitative Arts upon which every great Artist must finish his Idea of the Profession in which he means to excell The Antique is to the Architect what Nature is to the painter or Sculptor the Source from whence his chief Knowledge must be collected and the model upon which his Taste must be formed.

But as in Nature few Objects are faultless so neither must it be imagined that every antient Production in Architecture eaven amongst the Romans was perfect or a fit Model for Imitation as some Blind Adorers of Antiquity would insinuate, on the Contrary their Remains are so extremely unequal that it will require the greatest Circumspection and Effort of Judgement to make a proper Choice, the Roman Arts like those of other Nations had their Rise their Era of Perfection and their decline at Rome as in London or Paris there were few great Architects & many very indifferent ones and they had their Connoisseurs as we have ours who sometimes would dictate to the Artist and cramp the happy Sallies of their Genius, or Force upon the world their own insipid Productions, promote ignorant Sycophants and discourage and even oppress honest Merit . . .

In the Constructive Part of Architecture the Antients were no great Proficients. I believe many of the Deformities which we observe in the Grecian Buildings must be ascribed to their Ignorance in this Particular such as their Gouty Columns their narrow Intervals their disproportionate Architraves their Ipetral Temples which they knew not how to cover and their Temples with a Range of Columns running in the Center to support the Roof contrary to every Rule both of Beauty and Conveniency.

18   *From*
NORTON NICHOLLS
Reminiscences of Gray
(1805)

Thomas Gray (1716–1771) was not only a poet and one of the great letter writers of the eighteenth century but Regius Professor of Modern History at Cambridge. He was a man of great learning, very widely read and in advance of his age in many of his literary tastes. The passage from Norton Nicholls, which should be compared with Gray's highly detailed notes on his reading of Plato, is of interest because it shows that, although Plato was generally ignored or neglected in the eighteenth century, he did have intelligent and sympathetic readers. Perhaps the greatest problem was the lack of translations: there was no complete version in English until Thomas Taylor brought to a conclusion in 1804 what Floyer Sydenham had begun in 1759. Before this the reader without Greek was the victim of a vicious circle in which the lack of translations seemed to justify and deepen the prejudice which had discouraged the translators in the first place; before Sydenham and Taylor the reader had to rely mainly on selections translated from

Dacier's French version which was first published in England in 1701. The fact that in order to understand Plato you had to read him in the original ensured that he remained an unfashionable taste.

This tendency was further encouraged by the confusion of Plato with neo-Platonism and esoteric and mystical pursuits (as exemplified by Taylor himself). Gray's approach is sympathetic but very much of its time. The strengths and limitations of this approach are precisely analyzed by Coleridge in No. 34, where he points out that Gray's major deficiency is his lack of interest in Plato's philosophy. In one particular at least, Coleridge appears to be understating the case against Gray's version of Plato: in spite of Coleridge's claim to the contrary, Gray is not truly responsive to Plato the poet. This enthusiasm (not for Plato's epigrams but for the poetic qualities of his prose) belongs more properly to the Romantic period, where it was given expression by Coleridge himself in *Biographia Literaria* and by Shelley in his essays and translations, not least in the *Defence of Poetry* where he claims: 'Plato was essentially a poet—the truth and splendour of his imagery, and the melody of his language, is the most intense that it is possible to conceive'.[1]

NOTES

1   *Shelley's Prose*, ed. D. L. Clarke, Albuquerque, N. Mex., 1966, p. 280. A much earlier example can be found in Sidney's *The Defence of Poesie*: 'of all *Philosophers* he is the most *Poeticall* '.

It is not pedantry but truth to say that the minds of those are best cultivated who have cultivated them by Greek literature; more vigorous writers have written in that language than in any other and the language itself is the best vehicle that has yet existed for the highest and noblest ideas of which the mind of man is capable. Mr. Gray thought so; and had read and studied every Greek author, I believe, of note or importance:—Plato perhaps more than any other person. He lost all patience when he talked of the neglect of his favourite author at the University.——He was astonished that its members should in general read and admire Cicero, and yet not think it worth while to pay any attention to him whom Cicero called 'Divinus ille Plato.'[1] What he admired in Plato was not his mystic doctrines, which he did not pretend to understand, nor his sophistry, but his excellent sense, sublime morality, elegant style, and the perfect dramatic propriety of his dialogues.——I was reading Plato to him one evening, and stopped at a passage which I did not understand, he said, 'Go on, for if you stop as often as you do not understand Plato, you will stop very often.' He then added, that, finding what he did understand so admirable, he was inclined to think that there might be a meaning in the rest which at this distance of time, and for want of proper *data*, we might not be able to reach.

19   From
RICHARD CHANDLER
Travels in Asia Minor (1775)
Travels in Greece (1776)

Richard Chandler (1738–1810), classical antiquary and traveller, first became known as the author of *Marmora Oxoniensia* (1763). In 1764 the Society of Dilettanti invited him to lead an 'Ionian Mission' with the help of Nicholas Revett and William Pars (for details of this expedition, see No. 28). The party travelled widely in Asia Minor and Greece between 9 June 1764 and 2 November 1766. The first volume of *Ionian Antiquities* was published in 1769 to great acclaim and the second in 1797. Chandler's two volumes of travels were based on the journals which he had kept during the expedition. While the value of *Ionian Antiquities* is that it provides a strictly technical account of the architectural remains, the value of the *Travels* is that they provide a human setting for the great cities and the architectural sites so meticulously delineated in the plates and the accompanying descriptions.

Not everyone has admired the *Travels*. Summing up his

reactions to the second volume, Horace Walpole accused Chandler of pedantic quibbling and pronounced that he was more of an antiquarian than a writer.[1] The high-spirited J. B. S. Morritt (see No. 27) regarded him as scholarly to a fault.[2] In contrast, Chandler's travelling companion Revett questioned the accuracy of his observation; his copy of the *Travels* in the British Library is quite heavily annotated with criticisms and corrections, many of which were included in the 1825 edition. Revett, who was certainly embittered by the unequal share of the credit for the *Antiquities of Athens* which was generally accorded to 'Athenian' Stuart, may also have felt some resentment of Chandler. He comments brusquely, 'A Mistake', 'Unintelligible', 'It did occur, therefore your conclusion is erroneous', while Chandler's 'colour as resembling chalk' is directly rebutted ('The colour has no resemblance to chalk') and 'whitish shining' is corrected to 'dark greyish'. Chandler's accuracy, it would seem, was not above suspicion, as Colonel Leake the topographer was later to confirm;[3] on the other hand, his status as a writer was seriously underestimated by Horace Walpole, as Gibbon would have agreed when he praised the description of the solitariness and desolation of Laodicea.[4] A fair proportion of the two books is devoted to detailed historical or archaeological description and, while the solidity of the account depends on this very accumulation of detail, it must be confessed that much of it does not make very interesting reading for anyone but the specialist; on the other hand, though Chandler rarely enjoys the adventures of travel or the beauty of landscape as keenly as Morritt or Byron, there are many passages where his imagination is fired by the strangeness of his surroundings, the Turkishness of the Turks and the picturesqueness of Eastern customs. His very detachment gives to his observations a special clarity of focus.

This detachment also manifests itself in a somewhat critical aloofness both from Turks and from Greeks. The Turks who are his travelling companions are referred to, patronisingly, as 'our savages' while he is openly contemptuous of the churches of the Greeks, whose interiors 'are covered with representations of the exploits of their saints ... extravagant, ridiculous, and absurd beyond imagination'. One is reminded of Sir George Wheler's hostility to the Greek Orthodox Church and in particular of his gleeful interpretation of the ruins of Laodicea as a sign of the wrath of God. This is precisely where Chandler comes into his own for, though he had little sympathy with the religion of the Greeks, he felt keenly the desolation of great cities such as Laodicea and responded to their ruins with a poetic power which was laconic but evocative. The strength of Chandler's book depends very much on his sense of the gap between the present and the past: this involves not only his meditations among the ruins but his informed attention to local detail (see Introduction, pp. 4–5).

NOTES

1   *The Letters of Horace Walpole*, ed. Peter Cunningham, Edinburgh, 1906, vi. 322.
2   MORRITT, p. 191.
3   (Quoted in *Dictionary of National Biography*).
4   Note to Chapter 2 of *The Decline and Fall of the Roman Empire*.

Travels in Asia Minor
From   **Chapter VIII**

About a quarter after three we landed near the antient port of Troas.

We immediately began a cursory survey of this deserted place; ascending to the principal ruin, which is at some distance from the shore. The whole site was overspread with stones and rubbish intermingled with stubble, plantations of cotton and of Turkey wheat, plats of long dry grass, thickets and trees, chiefly a species of low oak which produces valanea or large acorns for exportation, to be used in tanning. A solemn silence prevailed, and we saw nothing alive, but a fox and some partridges. In the mean time, the Turks, who were left in the wherry, removed about three miles lower down, towards Lectos, where the beach afforded a station less exposed to the wind and more secure.

The evening coming on, we were advised to retire to our boat. By the way, we saw a drove of camels feeding. We came to a shed, formed with boughs round a tree, to shelter the flocks and herds from the sun at noon; and under it was a peasant, who had an ass laden, besides other articles, with a goatskin containing four curds, called *Caimac*. On these and some brown bread our Turks made their evening meal. A goatskin, with the hair on, served likewise for a bucket. It was distended by a piece of wood, to which a rope was fastened. He drew for us water from a well not far off, and promised to bring us milk and a kid the next day. We found our cook, a Jew, busy by the sea-side preparing supper; his tin-kettle boiling over a fire, in the open air.

The beauty of the evening in this country surpasses all description. The sky glowed with the rich tints of the setting sun, which now, skirting the western horizon, raised as it were up to our view the distant summits of the European mountains. We saw Mount Athos distinctly, bearing from us 55m. west of north, of a conical form, and so lofty, that on the top, as the antients relate, the sun-rising was beheld four hours sooner than by the inhabitants of the coast; and at the solstice, its shade reached into the Agora or *Market-place* of Myrina a town in Lemnos, which island was distant eighty-seven miles eastward. [1] The shore was strewed with pumice-stones, once perhaps floating from Ætna or Vesuvius, unless ejected by some nearer Volcano. [2] The pikes of Athos and of Tenedos suggest the idea, that their mountains have burned; and it is possible, that these, with many of the islands in this sea, may have been the produce of eruptions, which happened at a period too early to be recorded in history.

We had here no choice, but were forced to pass the night on the beach, which was sandy. The Turks constructed a half-tent for us near our boat, with the oars and sail. We now discovered that we had neglected to procure wine and candles at Tenedos. We did not, however, remain in the dark. An extemporary lamp supplied one omission. It was a cotton-wick swimming in oil, on a bit of cork, in a drinking-glass suspended by a string. By this light the Turks, sitting before us on the ground, cross-legged, endeavoured to amuse us, by teaching us the numbers in their language, or by learning them in English. Some desired us to distinguish each by his name, *Mahmet*, *Selim*, *Mustapha* and the like. They were liberal of their tobacco, filling their pipes from their bags, lighting and presenting them to us, as often as they saw us unprovided. Our janizary, who was called Baructer Aga, played on a Turkish instrument like a guittar. Some accompanied him with their voices, singing loud. Their favourite ballad contained the praises of Stamboul or Constantinople. Two, and sometimes three or four, danced together, keeping time to a lively tune, until they were almost breathless. These extraordinary exertions were followed with a demand of bac-shish, *a reward or present*, which term from its frequent use, was already become very familiar to us. We were fatigued by our rough hot walk among the ruins, and growing weary of our savages, gladly lay down to rest under the half-tent. The Turks slept by us upon the ground, with their arms ready in case of an alarm, except two, who had charge of the boat. The janizary, who watched, sate smoking, cross-legged, by the fire. The stars shone in a clear blue sky, shedding a calm serene light; the jackalls howled in vast packs, approaching near us, or on Mount Ida; and the waves beat gently on the shore in regular succession.

We rose with the dawn, ready dressed, hoping to get to the ruins in the cool of the morning. It was necessary to take water with us, as none could be procured there. A well, by which the peasant had agreed to leave his bucket for our use, with his ass, was known only to the janizary, and we resolved to accompany him to the place rather than wait for his return. Some of the Turks carried an umbrella for us, an earthen jar, and instruments for measuring or drawing. After going about half a mile by the sea toward Lectos, we turned to the left, and crossing the plain, and two water-courses, one of which was not quite dry, came to a root of Mount Ida, and a vineyard. We entered and saw nobody, but gathered as many grapes as we chose, and loading the ass with our luggage, repassed the plain to the great ruin at Troas, distant about an hour. Some peasants were employed in a field of Turkey wheat on the way, and their dogs worried us exceedingly.

From **Chapter XXXVI**

The Ephesians are now a few Greek peasants, living in extreme wretchedness, dependance, and insensibility; the representatives of an illustrious people, and inhabiting the wreck of their greatness; some, the substructions of the glorious edifices which they raised; some beneath the vaults of the stadium, once the crouded scene of their diversions; and some, by the abrupt precipice, in the sepulchres which received their ashes. We employed a couple of them to pile stones, to serve instead of a ladder, at the arch of the stadium, and to clear a pedestal of the portico by the theatre from rubbish. We had occasion for another to dig at the Corinthian temple; and sending to the stadium, the whole tribe, ten or twelve, followed; one playing all the way before them on a rude lyre, and at times striking the sounding-board with the fingers of his left-hand in concert with the strings. One of them had on a pair of sandals of goat-skin laced with thongs. After gratifying their curiosity, they returned back as they came, with their musician in front.

Such are the present citizens of Ephesus, and such is the condition to which that renowned city has been gradually reduced. It was a ruinous place, when the emperor Justinian filled Constantinople with its statues, and raised his church of St. Sophia on its columns. Since then it has been almost quite exhausted. Its streets are obscured, and overgrown. A herd of goats was driven to it for shelter from the sun at noon; and a noisy flight of crows from the quarries seemed to insult its silence. We heard the partridge call in the area of the theatre and of the stadium. The glorious pomp of its heathen worship is no longer remembered; and christianity, which was there nursed by apostles, and fostered by general councils, until it increased to fullness of stature, barely lingers on in an existence hardly visible.

Travels in Greece
From **Chapter VIII**

The acropolis, asty, or citadel, was the city of Cecrops [Athens]. It is now a fortress, with a thick irregular wall, standing on the brink of precipices, and inclosing a large area, about twice as long as broad. Some portions of the antient wall may be discovered on the outside, particularly at the two extreme angles; and in many places it is patched with pieces of columns, and with marbles taken from the ruins. A considerable sum had been recently expended on the side next Hymettus, [3] which was finished before we arrived. The scaffolding had been removed to the end toward Pentele,[4] but money was wanting, and the workmen were withdrawn. The garrison consists of a few Turks, who reside there with their families, and are called by the Greeks *Castriani* or the soldiers of the castle. These hollow nightly from their station above the town, to approve their vigilance. Their houses overlook the city, plain, and gulf, but the situation is as airy as pleasant, and attended with so many inconveniences, that those who are able and have the option prefer living below, when not on duty. The rock is lofty, abrupt, and inaccessible, except the front, which is toward the Piraeus; and on that quarter is a mountainous ridge,[5] within cannon-shot. It is destitute of water fit for drinking, and supplies are daily carried up in earthen jars, on horses and asses, from one of the conduits in the town.

The acropolis furnished a very ample field to the antient virtuosi. It was filled with monuments of Athenian glory, and exhibited an amazing display of beauty, of opulence, and of art; each contending, as it were, for the superiority. It appeared as one entire offering to the deity, surpassing in excellence, and astonishing in richness. Heliodorus, named Periegetes, *the guide*, had employed on it fifteen books. The curiosities of various kinds, with the pictures, statues, and pieces of sculpture, were so many and so remarkable, as to supply Polemo Periegetes with matter for four volumes; and Strabo affirms, that as many would be required in treating of other portions of Athens and of Attica. In particular, the number of statues was prodigious. Tiberius Nero, who was fond of images, plundered the acropolis, as well as Delphi and Olympia; yet Athens, and each of these places, had not fewer than three thousand remaining in the time of Pliny. Even Pausanias seems here to be distressed by the multiplicity of his subject. [6] But this banquet, as it were, of the senses has long been withdrawn; and is now become like the tale of a vision. The spectator views with concern the marble ruins intermixed with mean flat-roofed cottages, and extant amid rubbish; the sad memorials of a nobler people; which, however, as visible from the sea, should have introduced modern Athens to more early notice. They who reported it was only a small village, must, it has been surmised, have beheld the acropolis through the wrong end of their telescopes. [7]

From **Chapter XI**

The marbles, which recorded these riches of the Athenians, have not all perished. We discovered some, which I carefully copied, among the rubbish at the farther end of the parthenon; and purchased one of a Turkish woman living in the acropolis. Another had been conveyed down to the French convent, and, after we left it, was placed as a step in the staircase of a kitchen erected by the friar. All these inscriptions, which are very antient, commemorate jewels,

Victories, and crowns of gold, rings, and a variety of curiosities consecrated by eminent persons; giving some, though an inadequate, idea of the nature and quality of the treasure. Another marble, which has been engraved at the expense of the society of DILETTANTI, was discovered at a house not far from the temple of Minerva Polias, placed, with the inscribed face exposed, in the stairs. The owner, who was branded for some unfair dealing with the appellative *Jefut* or *the Jew*, prefixed to his name, seeing me bestow so much labour in taking a copy, became fearful of parting with the original under its value. When the bargain was at length concluded, we obtained the connivance of the Disdar,[8] his brother, under an injunction of privacy, as otherwise the removal of the stone might endanger his head, it being the property of the Grand Signior. Mustapha delivered a ring, which he commonly wore, to be shown to a female black slave who was left in the house alone, as a token; and our Swiss, with assistants and two horses, one reputed the strongest in Athens, arrived at the hour appointed, and brought down the two marbles, for which he was sent, unobserved; the Turks being at their devotions in the mosque, except the guard at the gate, who was in the secret. The large slab was afterwards rendered more portable by a mason. We saw many other inscribed marbles, besides these: some fixed in the walls or in the pavement of the portico of the mosque; some in the floors and stairs of the houses; or lying in the courts and among rubbish; all which we were permitted to copy; the Turks even prying into corners, and discovering several, which they had often passed before without notice.

From **Chapter XV**

On the left hand, returning from the aquæduct, is the bed of the Ilissus; and higher up, the junction of it and of the Eridanus. The water of this river was so bad that the cattle would scarcely drink of it. The Ilissus is now, as it ever was, an occasional torrent. In Summer it is quite dry. During our residence at Athens, I several times visited the bed, after snow had fallen on the mountains, or heavy rain, hoping to see it filled to the margin, and rushing along with majestic violence; but never found even the surface covered; the water lodging in the rocky cavities, and trickling from one to another.

And here it may be remarked, that the poets who celebrate the Ilissus as a stream laving the fields, cool, lucid, and the like, have both conceived and conveyed a false idea of this renowned water-course. They may bestow a willow fringe on its naked banks, amber waves on the muddy Maeander, and hanging woods on the bare steep of Delphi, if they please;[9] but the foundation in nature will be wanting; nor indeed is it easy for a descriptive writer, when he exceeds the sphere of his own observation, to avoid falling into local absurdities and untruths.

Going on by the bed of the Ilissus, as before, toward the town, you come to a ruinous bridge of three arches, the stones massive, and without cement. A piece of ordinary wall, standing on it, is part of a monastery, which was abandoned after the Turks took Athens. The ingenious Frenchman,[10] who, in a view of this spot, has exhibited the bridge standing in a full stream, may justly plead, that the same liberties have been indulged to the painter as to the poet.

From   **Chapter XVI**

In one of the dialogues of Plato, Socrates is represented as meeting Phaedrus, who was going from a house by the temple of Jupiter Olympius toward the Lycéum, which was without the city. [11]Perceiving, as they walked, that he had a book in his left hand, under his garment, Socrates proposed turning out of the road, and sitting down by the Ilissus. Phædrus consents, pointing to a lofty plane-tree as a proper place; and observing, that as both had their feet naked, it would not be disagreeable to wet them, especially at that time of the year and day. The conversation changes to a local story, that Boreas had carried off Orithyia, daughter of Erectheus, as she was sporting by the Ilissus, not by the fountain, but two or three stadia lower down, where was the crossing over to go to the temple of Diana Agræa, and where was the altar of Boreas. On their arrival at the chosen spot, Socrates admires it, like a stranger or one rarely stirring out of the city into the hilly country round about. He praises the large and tall tree; the thicket of Agnus Castus, high and shady, then in full flower and fragrant; the cool delicious fountain running near, with the girls by it, and the images, which made it seem a temple of the Nymphs and Achelous; the grateful and sweet air; the shrill summer-chorus of locusts; and the elegance of verdure, prepared as it were to meet the reclining head.

The vicinity of Enneacrunus has ceased to deserve encomiums like those bestowed on it by Socrates, since it has been deprived of the waste water of the fountain, which chiefly nourished the herbage and the plane-tree. The marble-facing and the images are removed; and the place is now dry, except a pool at the foot of the rock, down which the Ilissus commonly trickles. The water, which overflows after rain, is used by a currier, and is often offensive. The church in this dell occupies, it is probable, the site of the altar of the Muses, to whom, among other deities, the Ilissus was sacred. One lower down stands perhaps where Boreas had an altar. This God was believed to have assisted the Athenians in the Persian war, and was on that account honoured with a temple. By the Ilissus Codrus was slain. [12]

The tower of the winds is now a *Teckeh* or place of worship belonging to a college of Dervishes. I was present, with my companions, at a religious function, which concluded with their wonderful dance. The company was seated on goat-skins on the floor cross-legged; forming a large circle. The chief Dervish, a comely man, with a gray beard and of a fine presence, began the prayers, in which the rest bore a part, all prostrating themselves, as usual, and several times touching the ground with their foreheads. Of a sudden, they leaped up, threw off their outer garments, and joining hands, moved round slowly, to music, shouting *Alla*, the name of God. The instruments sounding quicker, they kept time, calling out *Alla. La illa ill Alla. God. There is no other God, but God.* Other sentences were added to these as their motion increased; and the chief Dervish, bursting from the ring into the middle, as in a fit of enthusiasm, and letting down his hair behind, began turning about, his body poised on one of his great toes as on a pivot, without changing place. He was followed by another, who spun a different way, and then by more, four or five in number. The rapidity with which they whisked round was gradually augmented, and became amazing; their long hair not touching their shoulders but flying off; and the circle still surrounding them, shouting, and throwing their heads backwards and forwards; the dome re-echoing the wild and loud music and the noise, as it were of frantic Bacchanals. At length, some quitting the ring and fainting, at which time it is believed they are favoured with extatic visions, the spectacle ended. We were soon after introduced into a room furnished with skins for sofas, and entertained with pipes and coffee by the chief Dervish, whom we found, with several of his performers, as cool and placid as if he had been only a looker-on. [13]

20 From
GEORGE FORSTER
A Voyage Round the World
(1777)

George (Johann Georg Adam) Forster (1754–1794) was the son of the scholar and naturalist John Reinhold Forster whom, it is said, he helped to translate Bougainville's *Voyage* into English in 1772. When his father was appointed naturalist on Captain Cook's second expedition, he took George as his assistant; George's highly readable account of the voyage was published in English in 1777 and in German in 1779.

Though he was open-minded and objective, George Forster interpreted certain features of life in the South Seas in terms of classical antiquity. In this he was following the example of explorers and naturalists such as Bougainville and his father's predecessor on Cook's first voyage, Sir Joseph Banks. Banks, the President of the Royal Society, was also a member of the Society of Dilettanti, whose fine collection of marbles was kept in his house at Soho Square; he had responded to the beauty of the Tahitians by exclaiming that they 'might even defy the imitation of the chizzel of a Phidias or the Pencil of an Apelles'.[1] Forster develops this connection between Greece and Tahiti when he writes of the islanders: 'This climate, and its salubrious productions, contribute to the strength and elegance of their form. They are all well-proportioned, and some would have been selected by Phidias or Praxiteles, as models of masculine beauty. Their features are sweet, and unruffled by violent passions'.

Clearly, Forster's response has been conditioned by Winckelmann, both in his account of the relation between classical beauty and generous climate and in the association of the highest form of beauty with serenity. He was not guilty of the romanticizing or the simple-minded adulation of the natives which marks the *Voyage* of Hawkesworth, the translator of Fénelon, who had compiled his book in the seclusion of his study (see No. 1). Obviously, he was aware of the typical vices of soft primitivism and the danger for the South Sea islanders that 'the corruption of manners which unhappily characterizes civilized regions, may reach that innocent race of men, who live here fortunate in their ignorance and simplicity'.[2] On the other hand, he greatly admired the heroic qualities of the chieftains of Tahiti whom he compares to Homeric warriors in the extract printed below.

In discovering these analogies and connections, Forster was in line with many of his contemporaries. The increasing interest in so-called primitive societies was broad enough to include both Greece and the South Pacific. Homer had been identified as the product of such a society by Thomas Blackwell, Robert Wood and others and the primitivist movement had acquired even greater momentum with the appearance of Macpherson's *Ossian*; in such circumstances, it was as natural for Sir Joseph Banks to remark that the natives of the South Seas 'sang many songs, generally in praise of us, for these gentlemen, like Homer of old, must be poets as well as musicians'[3] as it was for Forster to be reminded of Homer by the giant stature and the heroic appetites of the chieftains of Tahiti. In 1775 the Society of Dilettanti invited Thomas Jones, the artist, to accompany Cook on his next voyage (Jones refused). Richard Payne Knight, who was one of the principal figures in the Society of Dilettanti, himself proposed a comparison between the Greeks of the golden age and the Tahitians in his *Analytical Enquiry into the Principles of Taste* (1801).[4] Cook's own death as depicted by Zoffany (painted *c.* 1789–97) was largely modelled on classical statues. Cook appears in the pose of the *Dying Gaul*, while other figures are based on the *Discobolos* in the Townley Collection, a dying gladiator and the statue of a faun.[5]

NOTES

1 *Thoughts on the Manners of Otaheite*, cited in B. SMITH, p. 26. Cf. Flaxman: 'The Greeks had a sort of nude original art among themselves—like the people of Otaheite' (Sketchbook, 832/11, Fitzwilliam Museum, Cambridge, cited in THE AGE OF NEO-CLASSICISM, p. 183).
2 *A Voyage Round the World*, i. 303.
3 *Journal*, ed. J. D. Hooker, (1896), p. 99. Entry for 12 June 1769.
4 The relevant passage is cited in B. SMITH, p. 26.
5 For further details and discussion, see THE AGE OF NEO-CLASSICISM, p. 183; B. SMITH, p. 84; HONOUR, p. 116, plate 56.

Some of the canoes likewise performed part of their manoeuvre. They came singly one after another through the narrow entrance of the reef; but as soon as they were within, they formed in a line, and joined close together. On the middlemost canoe there was a man placed behind the fighting stage, who gave signals with a green branch to the rowers, either to paddle to the right or left. The movement in consequence of his command was in perfect tune, and so very regular, that it seemed as if all the paddles were parts of the same machine which moved some hundred arms at once. This man might be compared to the Κελευστής [1] in the ships of the ancient Greeks: indeed, the view of the Taheitian fleet frequently brought to our mind an idea of the naval force which that nation employed in the first ages of its existence, and induced us to compare them together. The Greeks were doubtless better armed, having the use of metals; but it seemed plain, from the writings of Homer, in spight of poetical embellishment, that their mode of fighting was irregular, and their arms simple, like those of Taheitee. The united efforts of Greece against Troy, in remote antiquity, could not be much more considerable than the armament of O-Too against the isle of Eimeo; and the boasted *mille carinae*, [2] were probably not more formidable than a fleet of large canoes, which require from fifty to an hundred and twenty men to paddle them. The navigation of the Greeks in those days was not more extensive than that which is practised by the Taheitians at present, being confined to short passages from island to island; and as the stars at night directed the mariners through the Archipelago at that time, so they still continue to guide others in the Pacific ocean. The Greeks were brave; but the numerous wounds of the Taheitian chiefs, are all proofs of their spirit and prowess. It seems to be certain, that in their battles they rouze themselves into a kind of phrenzy, and that their bravery is a violent fit of passion. From Homer's battles it is evident, that the heroism which produced the wonders he records, was exactly of the same nature. Let us for a moment be allowed to carry this comparison still farther. The heroes of Homer are represented to us as men of supernatural size and force. The Taheitian chiefs, compared to the common people, are so much superior in stature and elegance of form, that they look like a different race. [3] It requires a more than ordinary quantity of food to satisfy stomachs of unusual dimensions. Accordingly we find, that the mighty men at the siege of Troy, and the chiefs of Taheitee, are both famous for eating; and it appears that pork was a diet no less admired by the Greeks, than it is by the Taheitians at this day. Simplicity of manners is observable in both nations; and their domestic character alike is hospitable, affectionate, and humane. There is even a similarity in their political constitution. The chiefs of districts at Taheitee are powerful princes, who have not more respect for O-Too, than the Greek heroes had for the "King of men;" [4] and the common people are so little noticed in the Iliad, that they appear to have had no greater consequence, than the towtows in the South Sea. In short, I believe the similitude might be traced in many other instances; but it was my intention only to hint at it, and not to abuse the patience of my readers. What I have here said is sufficient to prove, that men in a similar state of civilization resemble each other more than we are aware of, even in the most opposite extremes of the world.

WILLIAM COWPER
Critical Remarks on Pope's Homer (1785)

William Cowper (1731–1800) was embarking on his own translation of Homer at about the time when this essay was published in the *Gentleman's Magazine*; the *Iliad* and the *Odyssey* eventually appeared in 1791. According to his own account, the inadequacy of Pope's version was one of the driving forces behind his decision to make a translation: 'There is', he wrote, 'hardly the thing in the world of which Pope is so entirely destitute as a taste for Homer'.[1] Cowper's review-article was published under the pseudonym *Alethes* (= Truthful), which crystallizes his own position: not only is he setting out to tell the truth about Pope but he is also committed to a notion of faithful translation which involves the directness he attributes to Homer himself, 'speaking the thing as it was'. Cowper's dissatisfaction with Pope primarily derives from his failure to achieve an appropriate simplicity, a point which is made in a telling image in a letter of 1791: 'I have two French prints in my study, both on *Iliad* subjects; and I have an English one in the parlour, on a subject from the same poem. In one of the former, Agamemnon addresses Achilles exactly in the attitude of a dancing master turning miss in a minuet; in the latter the figures are plain, and the attitudes plain also. This is, in some considerable measure, I believe, the difference between my translation and Pope's ...'[2] The dismissal of the French print is symptomatic of the age: the urbanities and artifices of Pope were usually associated with the French view of Homer, to which Pope was much indebted, particularly in the persons of Fénelon, Le Bossu and Anne Dacier. For all its intelligence, or so Cowper and his contemporaries would have claimed, this tradition was more concerned with gentlemen than with heroes.

One of Cowper's examples is the famous simile of the moon and stars at the end of the Eighth Book of the *Iliad*. Here again his basic criticism is that Pope is too elaborate and his diction too obviously elegant to capture or imitate successfully the 'almost divine simplicity' of Homer. This passage in the translation was to become something of a *cause célèbre*, incurring the wrath of Wordsworth, Coleridge and Southey, all of whom acknowledged the general merits of Pope's version but took exception to the 'glare and glitter' of his poetic diction. Cowper also criticizes Pope for his failure to respond to the more savage elements in Homer; these elements had long been recognized, particularly by those who were interested in comparative studies of primitive societies, but it was only in the later part of the century that Pope's reluctance to present this brutality in all its nakedness began to be regarded as a serious flaw. Eventually, Chapman's ability to reproduce what Cowper characterizes as 'smartness and acrimony' where Pope substituted 'good christian meekness' was one of the factors which led to his popularity with the Romantics and the corresponding decline in the fortunes of Pope (see Introduction, pp. 15–16). This shift of taste also involved the supposedly coarse and the indelicate—for example, Phoenix' memory of how the young Achilles had, as Cowper's prose puts it, 'wetted all my raiment'. The Augustan sense of the decorum which was appropriate to epic prevented Pope from emulating the bluntness of Hobbes, who translated 'And often on my breast you puked my wine'. It is an interesting indication of the strength of this convention that Cowper, who criticized Pope's weakness in omitting this detail altogether, resorted in his own version to the most pompously periphrastic diction: 'and many a time, in fits / Of infant frowardness, the purple juice / Rejecting thou hast deluged all my vest, / And fill'd my bosom'.

The fact that Cowper was impelled to undertake another translation of Homer to make up for the inadequacies of Pope is perhaps more important than Cowper's translation itself. His criticism of Pope is acute and catches very well the growing spirit of dissatisfaction not only with Pope's Homer but with Augustan poetry in general. On the other hand, as Cowper soon discovered, the difficulties which Pope encountered were no less intractable when he came to grapple with them in his own person. Cowper was essentially a master of the miniature, whether a poem or a letter, a fact that was harshly recognized by the artist Henry Fuseli, who had helped with the translation: 'I heartily wish that Cowper had trusted to his own legs instead of a pair of stilts to lift him to fame . . .'[3] For Pope as translator, see No. 2 and pp. 141–3.

1 *The Correspondence of William Cowper*, ed. T. Wright, 1904, iii. 233.
2 Letter to Joseph Hill, 10 March 1791.
3 IRWIN, p. 46. Fuseli himself did some finely spirited illustrations of the *Iliad*.

Pope was a most excellent rhymist; that is to say, he had the happiest talent of accommodating his sense to his rhyming occasions. Formerly, to discover homotonous words in a language abounding with them like ours, is a task that would puzzle no man competently acquainted with it. But for such accommodation as I have mentioned, when an author is to be translated, there is little room. The sense is already determined. Rhyme, therefore, must, in many cases, occasion, even to the most expert in the art, an almost unavoidable necessity to depart from the meaning of the original. For Butler's remark is as true as it is ludicrous, that

> —Rhyme the rudder is of verses,
> With which, like ships, they steer their courses."[1]

Accordingly, in numberless instances, we may observe in Pope a violation of Homer's sense, of which he certainly had never been guilty, had not the chains with which he had bound himself constrained him. It is, perhaps, hardly worth while to mention the aukward effect that the barbarous abridgement of proper names produces in his work; an effect for which he was entirely indebted to his rhyme: for blank verse, being of loftier construction, would have afforded sufficient room for *Idomeneus* and *Meriones*, with several others, to have stood upright, while the two heroes whom I have specified, being shortened by the foot, and appearing under the appellations of *Idomen* and *Merion*, lose much of their dignity, and are hardly to be known for the same persons. But rhyme has another unhappy effect upon a poem of such length. It admits not of a sufficient variety in the pause and cadence. The ear is fatigued with the sameness of the numbers, and satiated with a tune, musical indeed, but for ever repeated.—Here, therefore, appears to have been an error in the outset, which could never afterward be corrected. It is to be lamented, but not to be wondered at. For who can wonder, since all men are naturally fond of that in which they excell, that Pope, who managed the bells of rhyme with more dexterity than any man, should have tied them about Homer's neck? Yet Pope, when he composed an epic poem himself, under the title of *Alfred*, wrote it in blank verse, aware, no doubt, of its greater suitableness, both in point of dignity and variety, to the grandeur of such a work. And though Atterbury advised him to burn it, and it was burnt accordingly, I will venture to say, that it did not incur that doom by the want of rhyme. It is hardly necessary for me to add, after what I have said on this part of the subject, that Homer must have suffered infinitely in the English representation that we have of him; sometimes his sense is suppressed, sometimes other sense is obtruded upon him; rhyme gives the word, and a miserable transformation ensues; instead of Homer in the graceful habit of his age and nation, we have Homer in a straight waistcoat.

The spirit and the manner of an author are terms that may, I think, be used conversely. The spirit gives birth to the manner, and the manner is an indication of the spirit. Homer's spirit was manly, bold, sublime. Superior to the practice of those little arts by which a genius like Ovid's seeks to amuse his reader, he contented himself with speaking the thing as it was, deriving a dignity from his plainness, to which writers more studious of ornament can never attain. If you meet with a metaphorical expression in Homer, you meet with a rarity indeed. I do not say that he has none, but I assert that he has very few. Scriptural poetry excepted, I believe that there is not to be found in the world poetry so simple as his. Is it thus with his translator? I answer, No, but exactly the reverse. Pope is no where more figurative in his own pieces, than in his translation of Homer. I do not deny that his flowers are beautiful, at least they are often such; but they are modern discoveries, and of English growth. The Iliad and the Odyssey, in his hands, have no more of the air of antiquity than if he had himself invented them. Their simplicity is overwhelmed with a profusion of fine things, which, however they may strike the eye at first sight, make no amends for the greater beauties which they conceal. The venerable Grecian is as much the worse for his new acquisitions of this kind, as a statue by Phidias, or Praxiteles would be for the painter's brush. [2]The man might give to it the fashionable colour of the day, the colour of the Emperor's eye, or of the hair of the Queen of France, but he would fill up those fine strokes of the artist which he designed should be the admiration of all future ages. Do you ask an instance in point? I will give you one. At the assault made by the Trojans on the Grecian wall, in the twelfth book of the Iliad, Ajax kills Epicles, the friend of Sarpedon, with a great stone, which he casts down upon him from the top of the fortification. Homer says, simply, that he raised it on high, and that he cast it down. What says Pope?

> He pois'd and swung it round; then, toss'd on high,
> It flew with force, and *labour'd up the sky*.
> Full on the Lycian's helmet *thund'ring* down
> The pond'rous ruin crush'd his batter'd crown.[3]

Had the stone been discharged from a mortar, with a design that it should fall on the roof of some distant citadel besieged by the Duke of Marlborough, there would have been great beauty in the expression *labour'd up the sky*; but in the present case it is doubtless a most gross absurdity; and yet, absurd as it is, for the sake of its poetical figure, it found admittance.

As he inserts beauties of his own, so, not unfrequently, he rejects the beauties of his author, merely because they were of a kind not easily susceptible of that polish on which he insists upon all occasions. Thus, when Idomeneus, planted in the

Grecian van, is said to occupy his station with the sturdiness of a boar, the comparison is sunk.[4] Again, when Phoenix, who had been a kind of foster-father to Achilles, in order to work upon his affections, and to prevail with him, by doing so, to engage in the battle, reminds him of the passages of his infancy, he tells the hero, that in his childish fondness for his old tutor he would drink from no cup but his; 'and often,' says he, 'when thou hast filled thy mouth with wine, sitting upon my knee, thou hast returned it into my bosom, and hast wetted all my raiment.'[5] The delicacy of Pope seems to have been shocked at this idea, for he has utterly passed it over; an omission by which it is not easy to say whether he has more dishonoured Homer or himself. A more exquisite stroke of nature is hardly to be found, I believe, in any poet.

The style of Homer is terse and close in the highest possible degree; insomuch that his introductory lines excepted, in which the same adjuncts or ascriptions of wisdom, strength, or swiftness, constantly recur, as Ulysses, Diomede, or Achilles, happen to be mentioned, it were not easy to find, in many lines, perhaps in any, a single word that could be spared without detriment to the passage. He has no expletives except such as he uses avowedly for that purpose. I cannot pay the same compliment to his translator. He is so often diffuse, that he is indeed seldom otherwise, and seems, for the most part, rather to write a paraphrase than to translate. The effect of which management is a weakness and flimsiness to which Homer is completely a stranger. The famous simile at the end of the 8th book, in which the fires kindled in the Trojan camp are compared to the moon and stars in a clear night, may serve as a specimen of what I blame. In Homer it consists of five lines; in Pope, of twelve. I may be told, perhaps, that the translation is nevertheless beautiful, and I do not deny it; but I must beg leave to think that it would have been more beautiful, had it been more compressed. At least I am sure that Homer's close is most to be commended. He says, simply, The shepherd's heart is glad;—a plain assertion, which in Pope is rendered thus:

> The conscious swains, rejoicing in the sight,
> Eye the blue vault, and bless the useful light.[6]

Whence the word *conscious* seems to be joined with *swain*, merely by right of ancient prescription, and where the blessing is perfectly gratuitous, Homer having mentioned no such matter. But Pope, charmed with the scene that Homer drew, was tempted to a trial to excel his master, and the consequence was, that the simile, which in the original is like a pure drop, of simple lustre, in the copy is like that drop dilated into a bubble, that reflects all the colours of the bow. Alas! to little advantage; for the simplicity, the almost divine simplicity, of Homer is worth more than all the glare and glitter that can be contrived.

I fear, Sir, that I have already trespassed upon your paper, and, lest I should trespass upon your patience also, will hasten, as fast as possible, to a conclusion, observing only, as I go, that the false delicacy, of which I have a proof in the instance of Phoenix, has, in other particulars also, occasioned a flatness in the English Homer that never occurs in the Greek. Homer's heroes respected their gods just as much as the Papists respect their idols. While their own cause prospered they were a very good sort of gods, but a reverse of fortune taking place, they treated them with a familiarity nothing short of blasphemy. These outrages Pope has diluted with such a proportion of good christian meekness, that all the spirit of the old bard is quenched entirely. In like manner the invective of his heroes is often soothed and tamed away so effectually, that, instead of the smartness and acrimony of the original, we find nothing but the milkiness of the best good manners. In nice discriminations of character Homer is excelled by none; but his translator makes the persons of his poems speak all one language; they are all alike, stately, pompous, and stiff. In Homer we find accuracy without littleness, ease without negligence, grandeur without ostentation, sublimity without labour. I do not find them in Pope. He is often turgid, often tame, often careless, and, to what cause it was owing I will not even surmise, upon many occasions has given an interpretation of whole passages utterly beside their meaning.

If my fair countrywomen will give a stranger credit for so much intelligence novel at least to them, they will know hereafter whom they have to thank for the weariness with which many of them have toiled through Homer; they may rest assured that the learned, the judicious, the polite scholars of all nations have not been, to a man, mistaken and deceived, but that Homer, whatever figure he may make in English, is in himself entitled to the highest praise that his most sanguine admirers have bestowed upon him. Pope resembles Homer just as Homer resembled himself when he was dead. His figure and his features might be found, but their animation was all departed.

22
JOHN GILLIES

Dedication to the *History of Ancient Greece*
(1786)

John Gillies (1747–1836) was a translator, historian and classical scholar. As tutor to the Hon. Henry Hope he travelled in Europe. Later he became royal historiographer for Scotland. His *History*, which was almost immediately translated into French, had reached a third edition by 1792–3. For a discussion of his politics, see Introduction, pp. 28–9; for other dedications, see p. 206.

TO THE KING
Sir,
The History of Greece exposes the dangerous turbulence of Democracy, and arraigns the despotism of Tyrants. By describing the incurable evils inherent in every form of

Republican policy, it evinces the inestimable benefits, resulting to Liberty itself, from the lawful dominion of hereditary Kings, and the steady operation of well-regulated Monarchy. With singular propriety, therefore, the present Work may be respectfully offered to Your MAJESTY, as Sovereign of the freest nation upon earth; and *that* Sovereign, through whose discerning munificence, the interest of those liberal arts, which distinguished and ennobled Greece beyond all other countries of antiquity, has been more successfully promoted in Your MAJESTY's dominions, than during any former period in the British annals. That Your MAJESTY may long reign the illustrious Guardian of public freedom, and the unrivalled Patron of useful learning, is the fervent prayer of

YOUR MAJESTY's

Most dutiful Subject and Servant,

London, Feb. 10, 1786.

JOHN GILLIES.

23   *From*
THOMAS TAYLOR
The Mystical Initiations; or
Hymns of Orpheus
(1787)

Thomas Taylor (1758–1835) was one of the most prolific and industrious translators of his time and a vigorous and influential spokesman for 'the long lost *philosophy* of *Pythagoras* and *Plato*', who was sometimes known as 'the English Pagan'. He abandoned Christianity and devoted himself to translating and expounding the works of the Greek philosophers; his Aristotle was financed by a wealthy merchant and his monumental translation of Plato, which completed the work begun by Floyer Sydenham, received the support of the Duke of Norfolk. Taylor's interests were unfashionable. Plato was either abused (see No. 5) or passed over in favour of later Greek philosophers such as Epictetus and Roman interpreters of Greek philosophy such as Cicero. Some index of taste is provided by the fact that Elizabeth Carter made £1,000 from her translation of Epictetus (1758, 1807)[1] while Floyer Sydenham who translated nine dialogues of Plato between 1759 and 1780 suffered neglect and poverty. Plato was admired by the perceptive few: these included Gray (see No. 18) and Fielding, who took a volume on his last voyage. Even his admirers took a strictly limited interest in his achievement, and he was largely ignored by the universities and by English publishers, editors and translators. The Renaissance had produced approximately thirty complete editions of Plato, yet between 1602 and the appearance of Taylor's translation in 1804 there was only one complete edition in a modern language and only one in Greek. A complete Greek edition was not published in England till 1826.

It was against this combination of ignorance and misunderstanding that Taylor launched himself both as translator and as interpreter. He rejected the pseudo-Platonism of commentators such as Ficino, Pico della Mirandola and Henry More, which was based on a desire to establish conformity between Plato and the doctrines of Christianity; instead, he insisted on the importance of Greek theology and the necessity of acknowledging its polytheistic tendencies. Plato he regarded as no more than the most important link in 'the golden chain of deity' which went back through Pythagoras to Orpheus and which was continued after his death by the Alexandrian Platonists. Plato was not the father of a philosophy but the inheritor of an unrecognized religious tradition. Taylor's interpretations of Plato were largely based on the writings of the latter Platonists of Alexandria (the term 'Neo-Platonist' was a later invention). He translated copiously from the works of these writers, who were mostly neglected or derided by his contemporaries. This extraordinary enterprise was an attempt to shift the emphasis from the customary moral or political reading of Plato to his spiritual doctrine which was (in Taylor's view) the most consummate exposition of the lost religion of ancient Greece.

Armed with this symbolical key, Taylor approached literature with an eye to exegesis. A good example of his method is his commentary on the *Hymns of Orpheus* from which the general introduction and part of the concluding note are here reprinted. A more extensive example is his translation of Porphyry's *De Antro Nympharum* (*Concerning the Cave of the Nymphs*) which first appeared as part of an essay on the latter Platonists in 1787 or 1788 and was included in the second volume of the *Commentaries of Proclus* (1789). Porphyry's essay is a detailed reading of a passage in Book XIII of the *Odyssey* which 'contains some deep arcana of the natural and symbolical theology of the ancients, together with some beautiful observations respecting the allegory of Ulysses'. Taylor adopts the method for his own purposes in an ingenious supplementary essay in which he interprets the wanderings of Ulysses in terms of the fundamental principles of symbolic thought: this reading, which is based on a detailed knowledge of Greek sources, makes an interesting contrast to the more plainly allegorical interpretations favoured by many earlier commentators and imitated by writers such as Fénelon, and to the naive investigations of scholars such as Jacob Bryant in his *A New System . . . of Ancient Mythology* (1774–6).

Taylor was much abused, sometimes for being unscholarly, sometimes for being incomprehensible, sometimes no doubt because his interests ran counter to accepted taste. Horace Walpole was irritated because 'this half-witted Taylor prefers them [the Neo-Platonists] to Bacon and Locke, who were almost the first philosophers who introduced common sense into their writings, and were as clear as Plato was unintelligible—because he did not understand himself'.[2] Clearly, Walpole was finding fault not only with Taylor but with Proclus and Plato. On the other hand, Coleridge who was so much at home in the company of Plato and the Neo-Platonists that he was himself considered a victim to their contagious obscurity, complained that Taylor had translated Proclus from 'difficult Greek into incomprehensible English'.[3]

Whatever the errors and infelicities of his translations, Taylor's achievement was a considerable one and his courage and dedication should not be forgotten. Coleridge owned and annotated the *Commentaries*, even though he did not admire Taylor's translation; Blake's interests had much in common with those of Taylor, though there is no direct evidence that they met or that Blake possessed any of Taylor's books; Shelley and Taylor shared a number of friends and were linked by contemporary gossip; Peacock numbered Taylor among his 'six especial friends' and introduced him as a character in *Melincourt* (1818) where he parodied his exegetic method in the thirty-first chapter. Taylor or his books (or both) were known to Southey, Wordsworth, Lamb, Hunt and probably Keats. Yet, the exact nature and scope of Taylor's influence are difficult to determine. It would perhaps be claiming too much to see him as the originator of the mythological narratives of the Romantic period or the creator of a new mode of perception; for all his originality, he was the product of his own age as well as one of its determining forces. Yet, at the least, there is a remarkable correspondence between Taylor's concerns and the direction which Romantic poetry was to take: this can be observed in its special concern for 'intellectual beauty', in its polytheistic tendencies and its interest in spirits and daemons, and in its richly symbolic versions of narrative.[4] See Nos. 25 and 26 and Introduction, p. 23.

NOTES

1 CLARKE, p. 115.
2 *The Letters of Horace Walpole*, ed. Peter Cunningham, Edinburgh, 1906, ix. 237 (26 November 1791).
3 Cited in TAYLOR (ed. Raine and Harper), p. 18.
4 For the possible significance of Plotinus for Romantic poetry, see M. H. Abrams, *Natural Supernaturalism*, 1971, pp. 146f.

From **Preface**

There is doubtless a revolution in the literary, correspondent to that of the natural world. The face of things is continually changing; and the perfect, and perpetual harmony of the universe, subsists by the mutability of its parts. In consequence of this fluctuation, different arts and sciences have flourished at different periods of the world: but the complete circle of human knowledge has I believe, never subsisted at once, in any nation or age. Where accurate and profound researches into the principles of things have advanced to perfection; there, by a natural consequence, men have neglected the disquisition of particulars: and where sensible particulars have been the general object of pursuit, the science of universals has languished, or sunk into oblivion and contempt.

Thus wisdom, the object of all true philosophy, considered as exploring the causes and principles of things, flourished in high perfection among the Egyptians first, and afterwards in Greece. Polite literature was the pursuit of the Romans; and experimental enquiries, increased without end, and accumulated without order, are the employment of modern philosophy. Hence we may justly conclude, that the age of true philosophy is no more. In consequence of very extended natural discoveries, trade and commerce have increased, while abstract investigations have necessarily declined: so that modern enquiries, never rise above sense; and every thing is despised, which does not in some respect or other, contribute to the accumulation of wealth; the gratification of childish admiration; or the refinements of corporeal delight. The author of the following translation, therefore, cannot reasonably expect, that his labours will meet with the approbation of the many: since these Hymns are too ancient, and too full of the Greek philosophy, to please the ignorant, and the sordid. However, he hopes they will be acceptable to the few, who have drawn wisdom from its source; and who consider the science of universals, as first in the nature of things, though last in the progressions of human understanding.

The translator has adopted rhyme, not because most agreeable to general taste, but because he believes it necessary to the poetry of the English language; which requires something as a substitute for the energetic cadence, of the Greek and Latin Hexameters. Could this be obtained by any other means, he would immediately relinquish his partiality for rhyme, which is certainly when well executed, far more difficult than blank verse, as the following Hymns must evince, in an eminent degree.

And, here it is necessary to observe, with respect to translation, that nothing is more generally mistaken in its nature, or more faulty in its execution. The author of the Letters on Mythology, [1] gives it as his opinion, that it is impossible to translate an ancient author so as to do justice to his meaning. If he had confined this sentiment, to the beauties of the composition, it would doubtless have been just; but to extend it, to the meaning of an author, is to make truth and opinion, partial and incommunicable. Every person, indeed, acquainted with the learned languages, must be conscious how much the beauty of an ancient author generally suffers by translation, though undertaken by men, who have devoted the greatest part of their lives to the study of words alone. This failure, which has more than any thing contributed to bring the ancients into contempt with the unlearned, can only be ascribed to the want of genius in the translators: for the sentiment of Pythagoras is peculiarly applicable to such as these; that many carry the Thyrsus, [2] but few are inspired with the spirit of the God. But this observation is remarkably verified, in the translators of the ancient philosophy, whose performances are for the most part without animation; and consequently retain nothing of the fire and spirit of the original. Perhaps, there is but one exception to this remark, and that is Mr Sydenham: [3] whose success in such an arduous undertaking can only be ascribed to his possessing the philosophical genius, and to his occasionally paraphrasing passages, which would otherwise be senseless and inanimate.

Indeed, where languages differ so much as the ancient and modern, the most perfect method, perhaps, of transferring the philosophy from the one language to the other, is by a faithful and animated paraphrase: faithful, with regard to retaining the sense of the author; and animated, with respect to preserving the fire of the original; calling it forth when latent, and expanding it when condensed. Such a one, will every where endeavour to improve the light, and fathom the depth of his author; to elucidate what is obscure, and to amplify, what in modern language would be unintelligibly concise.

Thus most of the compound epithets of which the following Hymns chiefly consist, though very beautiful in the Greek language; yet when literally translated into ours, lose all their propriety and force. In their native tongue, as in a prolific soil, they diffuse their sweets with full-blown elegance; but shrink like the sensitive plant at the touch of the verbal critic, or the close translator. He who would preserve their philosophical beauties, and exhibit them to others in a different language, must expand their elegance, by the supervening and enlivening rays of the philosophic fire; and, by the powerful breath of genius, scatter abroad their latent but copious sweets.

If some sparks of this celestial fire shall appear to have animated the bosom of the translator, he will consider himself as well rewarded, for his laborious undertaking. The ancient philosophy, has been for many years, the only study of his retired leisure; in which he has found an inexhaustible treasure of intellectual wealth, and a perpetual fountain of wisdom and delight. Presuming that such a pursuit must greatly advantage the present undertaking, and feeling the most sovereign contempt for the sordid drudgery of hired composition, he desires no other reward, if he has succeeded, than the praise of the liberal; and no other defence if he has failed, than the decision of the candid, and discerning few.

From **Note to Hymn LXXXVI**

And thus much for a Commentary on the Hymns or Initiations of Orpheus. But before I conclude the present work, I beg leave to address a few words to the liberal and philosophical part of my readers. You then, as the votaries of truth, will, I doubt not, unite with me in most earnest wishes, that every valuable work on the Platonic philosophy was well translated into our native tongue; that we might no longer be subject to the toil of learning the ancient languages. The mischief, indeed, resulting from the study of words is almost too apparent to need any illustration; as the understanding is generally contracted, its vigour exhausted; and the genius fettered to verbal criticism, and grammatical trifles. Hence an opinion is gradually formed, that the Greek philosophy can alone be understood in the Greek tongue: and thus the books containing the wisdom of antiquity, are for the most part deposited in the hands of men, incapable of comprehending their contents. While an opinion so sordid prevails, amidst all our refinements in arts, and increasing mass of experiments, we must remain with respect to philosophy in a state of barbarous ignorance. We may flourish, indeed, as a commercial people; and stretch the rod of empire over nations as yet unknown. The waters of Thames, heavy laden with the wealth of merchandize, and sonorous with the din of trade, may devolve abundance in a golden tide; but we must remember that the Daemon of commerce is at the same time advancing with giant strides, to trample on the most liberal pursuits, and is preparing with his extended savage arm, to crush the votaries of truth, and depopulate the divine retreats of philosophy. Rise then ye liberal few, and vindicate the dignity of ancient wisdom. Bring truth from her silent and sacred concealments, and vigorously repel the growing empire of barbaric taste; which bids fair to extinguish the celestial fire of philosophy in the frigid embraces of philology, and to bury the divine light of mind, in the sordid gloom of sense. But if your labours should prove abortive; if the period is yet at a distance, when truth shall once more establish her kingdom; when another stream like that of Ilissus, shall become tuneful with the music of philosophy; and other cities like those of Athens and Alexandria, be filled with the sacred haunts of philosophers: there yet remains an inheritance for the lovers of wisdom in the regions of intellect, those fortunate islands of truth, where all is tranquil and serene, beyond the power of chance, and the reach of change. Let us then fly from hence my friends, to those delightful realms: for there, while connected with body, we may find a retreat from the storms and tempests of a corporeal life. Let us build for ourselves the raft of virtue, and departing from this region of sense, like Ulysses from the charms of Calypso, direct our course by the light of ideas, those bright intellectual stars, through the dark ocean of a material nature, until we arrive at our father's land. For there having divested ourselves of the torn garments of mortality, as much as our union with body will permit, we may resume our natural appearance; and may each of us at length recover the ruined empire of his soul.

24   From
JEAN-JACQUES BARTHÉLEMY
Les Voyages du jeune Anacharsis en Grèce
(1788; tr. W. Beaumont ?1791; second edition 1794)

Barthélemy (1716-1795) spent two years in Italy observing art and monuments at first hand and meeting scholars and archaeologists. It was at this time that he conceived the *Travels of Anacharsis* which he began in 1757 but did not complete for over thirty years. The book has a slight narrative thread but it is essentially an account not only of Greece in the fourth century B.C., during which period it is set, but of the whole of Greek history in all its branches, as it was understood by contemporary scholars. The book is encyclopaedic and its meticulous detail is corroborated by references to classical authorities. On this foundation of scholarship Barthélemy builds an account of the travels in Greece of a young Scythian who has the good fortune to meet most of the leading figures of the time, including Aristotle, Plato and Euclid. Particular attention is paid to Athens and its history which is finally overshadowed by the emerging power of Philip of Macedon.

Anacharsis was a great success. By 1799 it was already in a sixth edition. One of the main reasons for its popularity was the coincidence of its completion with the beginning of the French Revolution; its glorification of the democratic political theory of the Greeks and its idealization of the ancient at the expense of the modern were in keeping with the spirit of the times. Yet, for all its popularity, *Anacharsis* had its weaknesses. Barthélemy's limitations were shrewdly recognized by A. W. Schlegel and by Shelley, who commented that he 'never forgets that he is a Christian and a Frenchman'.[1]

Two excerpts are included here: the first is from the Author's Preface, while the second describes a visit to Sunium and involves a lecture from Plato which is stitched together from a number of passages in his works; Plato's views seem to lean towards Christianity and a belief in a single god. This recreation of the past to serve the purposes of the present combined with the evocation of sunset in the setting of the temple (restored to its prelapsarian wholeness in the engraving by Barbié du Bocage) is characteristic both of Barthélemy and of Romantic Hellenism in general.

NOTE

1 *Lectures on Dramatic Art and Literature*, tr. J. Black, 1815, p. 47; *Shelley's Prose*, ed. D. L. Clark, 1966, p. 219.

From **Advertisement by the Author**

I imagine a Scythian, named Anacharsis, to arrive in Greece, some years before the birth of Alexander; and that from Athens, the usual place of his residence, he makes several excursions into the neighbouring provinces; every where observing the manners and customs of the inhabitants, being present at their festivals, and studying the nature of their governments; sometimes dedicating his leisure to enquiries relative to the progress of the human mind, and sometimes conversing with the great men who flourished at that time; with Epaminondas, Phocion, Xenophon, Plato, Aristotle, Demosthenes, &c. As soon as he has seen Greece enslaved by

Philip, the father of Alexander, he returns into Scythia, where he puts in order an account of his travels; and, to prevent any interruption in his narrative, relates in an introduction the memorable events which had passed in Greece before he left Scythia.

The æra I have chosen, which is one of the most interesting that the history of nations presents, may be considered in two points of view. With respect to literature and the arts, it connects the age of Pericles with that of Alexander. My Scythian has conversed with a number of Athenians, who had been intimately acquainted with Sophocles, Euripides, Aristophanes, Thucydides, Socrates, Zeuxis, and Parrhasius. I have mentioned some of the celebrated writers who were known to him. He has seen the masterly productions of Praxiteles, Euphranor, and Pamphilus, make their appearance, as also the first essays of Apelles and Protogenes; and in one of the latter years of his stay in Greece Epicurus and Menander were born.

Under the second point of view, this epocha is not less remarkable. Anacharsis was a witness to the revolution which changed the face of Greece, and which, some time after, destroyed the empire of the Persians. On his arrival, he found the youth Philip with Epaminondas: he afterwards beheld him ascend the throne of Macedon; display, in his contests with the Greeks, during two-and-twenty years, all the resources of his genius; and, at length, compel those haughty republicans to submit to his power.

I have chosen to write a narrative of travels rather than a history, because in such a narrative all is scenery and action; and because circumstantial details may be entered into which are not permitted to the historian. These details, when they have relation to manners and customs, are often only indicated by ancient authors, and have often given occasion to different opinions among modern critics. I have examined and discussed them all before I have made use of them; I have even, on a revisal, suppressed a great part of them, and ought perhaps to have suppressed still more.

I began this work in the year 1757, and, since that time, have never intermitted my labours to complete it. I should not have undertaken it if, less captivated by the beauty of the subject, I had consulted my abilities more than my courage . . .

From **Chapter LIX**

We had not informed Plato of our journey to the mines. He wished to accompany us to Cape Sunium, distant from Athens about three hundred and thirty stadia. On it stands a superb temple consecrated to Minerva, of white marble, and of the Doric order, surrounded by a peristyle, and having, like that of Theseus, which it resembles in its general disposition, six columns in front, and thirteen on the sides.

From the summit of the promontory is seen, at the foot of the mountain, the harbour and town of Sunium, which is one of the fortresses of Attica. But a grander scene excited our admiration. Sometimes we permitted our eyes to wander over the vast plains of the sea, and at length to repose on the prospects presented by the neighbouring islands. Sometimes pleasing recollections seemed to bring nearer to us the isles which escaped our sight. We said: On that side of the horizon is Tenos, in which we find such fertile valleys; and Delos, where such delightful festivals are celebrated. Alexis said to me, in a whisper: There is Ceos, where I saw Glycera for the first time. Philoxenus shewed me, with a sigh, the island which bears the name of Helen; in which, ten years before, he had with his own hands erected, amid myrtles and cypresses, a monument to the affectionate Coronis, and whither for ten years he had resorted, on certain days, to sprinkle with his tears her cold ashes, still dear to his heart. Plato, on whom great and sublime objects had always made a strong impression, seemed to have fixed his whole attention on the gulfs which nature has excavated to receive the waters of the ocean.

In the mean time the horizon began to be overclouded at a distance with hot and gloomy vapours; the sun grew dim, and the smooth and motionless surface of the waters assumed a melancholy hue, the tints of which incessantly varied. Already the heavens, shut in on every side, only presented to our view a dark vault, from which issued streams of flame. All nature appeared to be in silent and fearful expectation, and in a state of inquietude, which communicated itself to the inmost recesses of our souls. We sought an asylum in the vestibule of the temple, and quickly the thunder, with redoubled peals, broke the barrier of darkness and fire suspended over our heads, thick clouds rolled their heavy masses through the air, and descended in torrents on the earth, while the winds, unchained, rushed impetuously on the sea, and upturned its enormous billows. The united roarings of the thunder, the winds, the waves, and the re-echoing caverns and mountains, produced a dreadful sound, which seemed to proclaim the approaching dissolution of the universe. At length, the north wind having redoubled its efforts, the storm departed, to carry its rage into the burning climates of Africa. We followed it with our eyes, and heard it howl at a distance, while with us the sky again shone with a purer splendour, and that sea, which had so lately dashed its foaming surges to the clouds, now scarcely impelled its languid waves to the shore.

At the sight of so many unexpected and rapid changes, we remained for some time motionless and mute; but they quickly reminded us of those doubts and questions which have exercised the curiosity of mankind for such a number of ages. Why these seeming errors and revolutions in nature? Are they to be attributed to chance? But whence then is it that the close-connected chain of beings, though a thousand times on the very verge of being broken, is yet perpetually preserved? Are tempests excited and appeased by an intelligent cause? But what end does that cause propose in them, and whence is it that he darts his lightnings on the desert, while he spares the nations whose guilt loudly calls for his vengeance? From these enquiries we proceeded to the existence of the gods, the reduction of chaos to form and order, and the origin of the universe. Wandering and lost in the mazes of these ideas, we conjured Plato to guide us to the truth. He was absorbed in profound meditation; it seemed as if the terrible and majestic voice of nature still resounded in his ears. At length, overcome by our entreaties, and the truths which he revolved in his labouring mind, he seated himself on a rustic seat, and having placed us by his side, began his discourse as follows:

Feeble mortals that we are! is it for us to penetrate the secrets of the Divinity; for us, the wisest of whom is to the Supreme Being only what an ape is to us? Prostrate at his feet, I entreat him to inspire me with such ideas and such language as shall be pleasing to him, and shall appear to you conformable to reason.

If I were obliged to explain myself in the presence of the multitude concerning the first Author of all things, the origin of the universe, and the cause of evil, I should be compelled to speak in enigmas; but in these solitary places, where I am only heard by God and my friends, I shall have the satisfaction of rendering homage to truth.

The God which I declare unto you, is a God, single, immutable and infinite, the centre of all perfections, and the inexhaustible source of intelligence and being. Before he had created the universe, before he had externally displayed his power, he was, for he had no beginning; he was in himself, he existed in the profundity of eternity. No; my expressions do not correspond to the elevation of my ideas, nor my ideas to the sublimity of my subject.

THOMAS TAYLOR
The Cratylus, Phaedo, Parmenides and Timaeus of Plato
(1793)

See introduction to No. 23; see also Nos 5, 18, 26, 34.

From **Preface**

The Dialogues of Plato are such rare and admirable pieces of composition, that it is alike impossible to explain the beauty of their construction to such as are ignorant of the Greek tongue, or translate them into any other language without at least frequently losing something of their native elegance and grace. Plato's style indeed has been justly celebrated in the warmest terms by the literati of every age. Aristotle, from considering its animated, vehement, and luminous nature, places it as a medium between poetry and prose; and Ammianus, from regarding as we may suppose its elevation and majesty, asserts, that if Jupiter were to speak in the Attic tongue, he would use the diction of Plato. But his language principally demands our admiration, when we attend to the abstruse meaning of his sentences in conjunction with the beauty of their composition. For then we shall find that Plato possessed the happy art of uniting the blossoms of elocution with the utmost gravity of sentiment; the precision of demonstration with the marvellous of mystic fables; the venerable and simple dignity of *scientific* dialectic with the enchanting graces of poetical imagery; and in short, that he every where mingles rhetorical ornament with the most astonishing profundity of conception. Such indeed is the unparalleled excellence of Plato's composition, that notwithstanding all the artifice of the style, almost every word has a peculiar signification, and contains some latent philosophical truth; so that at the same time it both gives elegance to the structure, and becomes necessary to the full meaning of the sentence with which it is connected. He who desires to be convinced of the truth of this observation, need only consult any one of the invaluable commentaries of the latter Platonists on Plato's dialogues; and if he has a genius for such speculations, he will perceive with astonishment that Plato is as close in his reasoning, as skilful in *vulgar* dialectic, and as prolific in his conceptions, as the Stagirite[1] himself; at the same time that his language is incomparably more magnificent, and his doctrine in some particulars infinitely more sublime.

Thus much I thought it necessary to premise, as an apology for the literal exactness of the following translations. Had I indeed been anxious to gratify the false taste of the moderns with respect to composition, I should doubtless have attended less to the precise meaning of the original, have omitted almost all connective particles, have divided long periods into a number of short ones, and branched out the strong, deep, and rapid river of Plato's language, into smooth-gliding, shallow, and feeble streams. But as the present volume was composed with an eye to the commentaries of the latter Platonists, and with the hope of obtaining the approbation of more equitable posterity, and benefiting *men of elevated souls*, I have endeavoured not to lose a word of the original; and yet at the same time have attempted to give the translation as much elegance as such verbal accuracy can be supposed capable of admitting. How well I have succeeded, cannot I fear be justly determined by any writer of the present period. For as unfortunately there does not appear to be any living author besides myself who has made the acquisition of the Platonic philosophy the great business of his life, without regarding the honours of the multitude, or paying the smallest attention to the accumulation of wealth;—as this is the case, who of the present day can equitably decide the merit of the ensuing work? Surely no one can be so ignorant, as to think that a bare knowledge of the Greek tongue, such as is acquired at universities, can be a sufficient qualification for appreciating his labours who has studied the Greek philosophy, or for passing judgement on a translation from a species of Greek so different from that which is generally known. Philosophy indeed in any language must vindicate to itself a number of peculiar terms; but this is so remarkably the case with the philosophy of Plato in the original, that he who should attempt to translate any one of his dialogues without understanding his secret doctrine, would produce nothing but a heap of absurdities, would only abuse the credulity of the simple reader, and would himself in the end sink into silent contempt. Let the reader, if he has any knowledge of Platonism, compare the following version of the Phædo with that of Dacier; and then, from the difference in point of meaning between the two, let him either subscribe to the truth of my assertion, or prove that my translation is false.

I take this opportunity therefore of publicly declaring, that during the course of my translating all the remaining dialogues of Plato, which have not been attempted by Mr. Sydenham, I shall pay no attention whatever to the criticisms of any writer who has not legitimately studied the philosophy of Plato, unless it shall appear that his criticisms are not only dictated by ignorance, but are the result of malevolent design. For in this case, merely from regard to the philosophy which I am so anxious to propagate, and not from any resentment for the personal injuries which I may sustain, I shall not fail to expose the infamy of such conduct with all the ability I am capable of exerting.

But here it is necessary to observe, that by a legitimate student of the Platonic philosophy, I mean one who both from nature and education is properly qualified for such an arduous undertaking. That is one who possesses a naturally good disposition; is sagacious and acute, and is inflamed with an ardent desire for the acquisition of wisdom and truth; who from his childhood has been well instructed in the mathematical disciplines; has diligently studied the whole or at least the greater part of Aristotle's works, as a preparative for the more profound speculations of Plato; and who, after this gradual and scientific progression, has for many years with unabated ardour strenuously laboured through the works of Plato and his disciples; who, besides this, has spent whole days, and frequently the greater part of the night, in profound meditation; and, like one triumphantly sailing over a raging sea, or skilfully piercing through an army of foes, has successfully encountered an hostile multitude of doubts;—in short, who has never considered *wisdom* as a thing of trifling estimation and easy access, but as that for which every thing is to be sacrificed; which cannot be obtained without the most generous and severe endurance, and whose intrinsic worth surpasses all corporeal good, far more than the ocean the fleeting bubble which floats on its surface. To the judgement of such a character as this I cheerfully and joyfully submit my past, present, and future productions. The censure of such a one I should reverence; his approbation, should I be fortunate enough to obtain it, I shall receive with transport; and his friendship would be a felicity which language is unable to describe.

26   *From*
THOMAS TAYLOR
The Description of Greece, by Pausanias
(1794)

See introduction to No. 23; see also No. 25 and Introduction, pp. 28–9.

From   **Preface**

Some fashionable readers will, I doubt not, think that my translation abounds too much with connective particles. To such I shall only observe, that beauty in every composite consists in the apt connexion of its parts with each other, and is consequently greater where the connexion is more profound. It is on this account that the sound of the voice in singing is more pleasing than in discourse, because in the former it is more connected than in the latter; that a palace is more beautiful than a rude heap of stones; a kingdom than a democracy; and in short whatever is orderly and regular, than whatever is disordered and confused. In the present age indeed, it cannot be an object of wonder, that books are composed with scarcely any connective particles, when men of all ranks are seized with the mania of lawless freedom, bear indignantly all restraint, and are endeavouring to introduce the most dire disorder, by subverting subordination, and thus destroying the bond by which alone the parts of society can be peaceably held together. Of the truth of this observation the French at present are a remarkable example, among whom a contempt of orderly connexion has produced nothing but anarchy and uproar, licentious liberty and barbaric rage, all the darkness of atheism, and all the madness of democratic power.

27   From

J. B. S. MORRITT

*Letters . . . descriptive of Journeys in Europe
and Asia Minor in the Years 1794–1796*
(ed. G. E. Marindin 1914)

John Bacon Sawrey Morritt (1772?–1843) travelled in Greece and Asia Minor between 1794 and 1796. Although he never produced a formal account of his travels, part of his journal was published in 1817[1] and a collection of his letters appeared in 1914. The main interest of his letters, extracts from two of which are included here, is that they represent the reactions of a high-spirited and adventurous young man whose Grand Tour took in the famous sites of classical antiquity. He visited the remote temple of Apollo at Bassae, where a previous visitor had probably been murdered, and he identified strongly with the banditti of Maina, who displayed the virtues and vices of 'a half civilized nation' and who were still 'free in the midst of slavery'.

His attitude to the collecting of marbles is by no means untypical of the period: Morritt was yet another in a long line of English travellers who appropriated what they could, with little or no regard for the feelings or the claims of the Greeks.[2] At Megara Morritt found a small statue half buried in the ground: 'At least, it was not expensive; for, giving half a crown to a priest that belonged to a chapel near it, we pretended to have a firman, and carried it off from the Greeks in triumph'. While he was in Athens he visited Fauvel, who was living in the so-called Lantern of Demosthenes; Fauvel was the most famous foreigner then resident in Athens and an enterprising collector of antiquities—in 1787 alone he had sent to the Comte de Choiseul-Gouffier in France sixteen cases of marbles and forty of plaster-casts. When Morritt tried to persuade the Turkish commander of the Acropolis to knock down the best of the Parthenon metopes, it was Fauvel who frightened the *disdar* into calling off the deal (the death penalty could be invoked on Turks or Greeks who disposed of antiquities without permission from the Sultan).

Morritt also made a survey of the scene of the *Iliad*. When Jacob Bryant tried to prove that Troy had never existed, Morritt refuted him in *A Vindication of Homer* (1798), which led to a further flurry of controversy. Morritt became a member of the Society of Dilettanti and wrote the introductory essay to the Society's second volume of *Specimens of Ancient Sculpture Preserved in Great Britain* (1835). He was also one of the founders of the Travellers' Club (1819). He became friendly with Walter Scott who visited the family estate at Rokeby and was inspired by it to produce his poem of the same name.

NOTES

1   In WALPOLE.
2   See BRACKEN and p. 109 above.

The country beyond Ephesus is fine, especially when we came to the banks of the sea, with views of Samos, a high, black, mountainous island, separated from the grand, rocky range of Mycale by the narrow strait of three-quarters of a mile, so famous for the last great triumph of Grecian liberty.[1] The south side of Mycale, which we afterwards rode along, is bold, high, and craggy. Round its points we saw several eagles skimming round in circles, and sometimes sitting on its crags and screaming, which gave what Mr. Gilpin[2] would call *infinite character* to the scene. In the large plain on the left we had the Maeander; it resembles that of the Cayster, but is much larger, and, like it too, has been formed by the river. Priene, once a seaport, is now four or five miles from the shore, and Myus still further.

The ruins of the temple at Priene are a great and splendid heap of architectural fragments, all on the ground; the blocks of marble are immense, and the worked stones very elegant. The walls under it, of which part remain, and those of the city, which do not seem likely to fall, gave us the highest idea of the ancient skill in masonry. After looking at the ruins, talking over Bias and old stories, we turned across the plain to the Maeander. The sun was now setting, the sky in a glow with its rays, and the islands and mountains round us glorious. Opposite us was the woody ridges and summits of Latmos, and more to the left a high, conical mountain whose outline was everywhere broken with crags and glittering in the parting lights of the sun. The moon over it grew brighter as the sun set, and when the evening came on—in memory, I suppose, of Endymion—did the honours of Mount Latmos gloriously. [3]

We at last ferried over the Maeander to the ruins of Miletus here. There is only a Turkish hut or two, already full of their own inhabitants, not counting fleas, bugs, etc., so we made our beds under a tree and slept in open air, though now in

October. I despair of giving you an idea of this climate. Its mildness and the beauty of its mornings and evenings exceed what I could have conceived. Barthélemy in "Anacharsis"[4] makes his hero speak of himself as "assis sur les bords du Méandre, ne pouvant se rassasier ni de cet air ni de cette lumière dont la douceur égale la purité." It cannot be more spiritedly or more justly described. The theatre at Miletus still remains pretty perfect—that is to say, the shape of it in the side of the hill, one or two of the marble seats, and the entrance; the communications with the seats and the upper passages, though a good deal filled with dirt, are very tolerably perfect.

Among the ruins are several Turkish ones, and two palm trees, the only ones we have seen, which looked very oriental. We went on southward over Mount Latmos, which, being a charming hill for hunting, was chosen by Endymion for the scene of his amusements, and where he fell asleep for Diana's. In four hours we came to a poor village, with ruins of the famous temple of Apollo at Branchidae. Three columns are standing, two still support the architrave and frieze. They are about forty feet high, fluted, and of the most beautiful Ionic proportions. The area of the temple has been immense, and from two points of the rising ground it stands upon the sea opens. A setting sun, when we saw it, shone full on the temple; beyond, the sea was as smooth as a mirror, and the eye wandered over the neighbouring islands, or fancied distant ones. Samos, Icaria, Patmos, Leros, Calymna, and some smaller islands near us, were all scattered over it, and you can hardly conceive a more delicious scene. The moon at night, and the sun at daybreak the day after, showed it off still more, in new lights and equal beauty.

We attempted to sleep in a miserable mud cottage, but before midnight turned out with a legion of fleas and vermin and again took our station in open air, where we should have managed very well if we could have left all our fleas behind. Yesterday we returned in hopes of getting here time enough to sail for Samos. We had been on the point of embarking before, where the passage was longer; we thank our stars some accident made us ride forwards, because the boat could not very well get to shore, and we did not like being carried to it, I believe, and a man happened to say the wind was rather against us. We crossed the plain of the Maeander, when the wind rose to a storm you can scarce conceive. The clouds gathered over Mount Mycale, along which they swept, casting a shade like night; the promontories out at sea and the whole sky in that part were as black as ink. It was worth being wet through to see the scene. The effect of Mount Mycale's summits and promontories as the cloud advanced was inconceivably grand. At last it burst over us in such a storm of thunder and lightning as I never in my life witnessed. The sea flew on one side of us, the thunder roared like a cannonade, almost deafening us with the sound among the tops of the mountain. The lightning was forked and continual, often followed immediately by the thunder.

Suppose every effect you can, you will never imagine a sublimer scene. We were very wet, and took refuge in a Greek village; the storm lasted about five hours. Thunder in England is a perfect popgun to it. We were very glad of our lucky escape, for had we put to sea there is no doubt you would have read that disagreeable paragraph Abney talks of, as how Mr. Morritt, a most amiable and accomplished youth, had with such and such companions been most classically shipwrecked and drowned off Mount Mycale. No open boat could have stood it. This morning we rode here where the boat is lying—being detained, have cooked some fish and our dinner in the cave whilst I am writing, my draughtsman taking views of and from the cave, and the weather is cleared up, so now we have only to dine, and are within about an hour's sail of Samos, whence we shall sleep to-night. Adieu till then.

It is very pleasant to walk the streets here. Over almost every door is an antique statue or basso-rilievo, more or less good though all much broken, so that you are in a perfect gallery of marbles in these lands. Some we steal, some we buy, and our court is much adorned with them. I am grown, too, a great medallist, and my collection increases fast, as I have above two hundred, and shall soon, I hope, have as many thousands. I buy the silver ones often under the price of the silver, and the copper ones for halfpence. At this rate I have got some good ones, and mean to keep them for the alleviation of Sir Dilberry's visits, as they will be as good playthings as the furniture and pictures for half an hour before dinner. Don't you think the whole family much indebted to me; I am sure you are sensible of the obligation. The conjecturing on defaced medals is very ingenious, and I begin to grow quite a connoisseur. Thus employed, guess with what spirit our tour goes on; I really fear I shall never get out of Greece. Our house, to be sure, is not so good as Rokeby, but what signifies a house here, where I am now really writing at ten o'clock at night without a fire, with half my clothes off because they were too hot, though our windows and door are half an inch open at every chink. This is the case whenever the south wind blows, and the weather is really like May. We live here most luxuriously in other respects, and our larder contains hares, woodcocks, and wild ducks in abundance. We had two days ago eighteen woodcocks together, some of which fell by our own hands on a shooting-party. Amongst our other delicacies I must mention the famous honey of Hymettus, which is better than I can describe or you imagine easily, without I could enclose you some. We are very well with the Turks here, and particularly with the governor of the town, who has called on us, sent us game, made coursing-parties for us, offered us dogs, horses, etc., and is a very jolly, hearty fellow. We often go and smoke a pipe there, and are on the best of terms. I shall really grow a Mussulman.[5] If they are ignorant it is the fault of their government and religion, but I shall always say I never saw a better disposed or manlier people. Their air, from the highest to the lowest, is that of lords and masters, as they are, and their civility has something dignified and hearty in it, as from man to man; while I really have English blood enough in me almost to kick a Greek for the fawning servility he thinks politeness. They salute you you putting their hand to their heart; and I should not have mentioned this trifle but that, as some of them do it, it has the most graceful air in the world.

The Greeks are, you will see, in *très mauvaise odeur* with us; and I would much rather hear that the Turks were improving their government than hear that the Empress had driven them out, for I am sure, if left to the Greeks in their present state, the country would not be passable. We have just breakfasted, and are meditating a walk to the citadel, where our Greek attendant is gone to meet the workmen, and is, I hope, hammering down the Centaurs and Lapithae, like Charles's mayor and aldermen in the "School for Scandal."[6] Nothing like making hay when the sun shines, and when the commandant has felt the pleasure of having our sequins for a few days, I think we shall bargain for a good deal of the old temple . . .

I am wanted by the Centaurs and Lapithae. Goodbye for a moment. Scruples of conscience had arisen in the mind of the old scoundrel at the citadel; that is to say, he did not think we had offered him enough. We have, however, rather smoothed over his difficulties, and are to have the marble the first opportunity we can find to send it off from Athens. I, only being sensible of the extreme awkwardness of Grecian workmen, tremble lest it should be entirely broken to pieces on taking it out; if any accident happens to it I shall be quite crazy, as now there is nothing damaged but the faces and one of the hands. If I get it safe I shall be quite happy, and long to show it you at Rokeby.

In 1764 the Society of Dilettanti invited Richard Chandler (see No. 19) to lead an 'Ionian Mission' in which his colleagues were to be Nicholas Revett, the architect and draughtsman who had worked on *The Antiquities of Athens* with James Stuart (see No. 9), and William Pars, the young painter whose brother Henry was William Blake's drawing-master. The party travelled widely in Asia Minor and Greece and not without adventure, for they were interrupted by an outbreak of the plague. They returned to England in 1766. The first volume of *Ionian Antiquities* appeared in 1769 but the second was delayed till 1797; still further volumes were published in 1840, 1881 and 1915. Together with Stuart and Revett's magnificent first volume, *Ionian Antiquities* played an important role in establishing the supremacy of Greece over Rome and eventually in shaping a phase of British architecture known as the Greek Revival.[1]

The preface to the second volume, part of which is printed here, reflects a desire to recapture 'the genuine simplicity of ancient taste' which was gaining momentum at the time. Its account of Athenian politics is critical of those who make a simple-minded equation between the artistic achievements of cities like Athens and their supposedly 'democratic' forms of government. On the other hand, the preface has even less sympathy for those 'shallow retailers of the froth of history' who try to depreciate the very real achievements of Greek architecture, which are infinitely superior to the buildings erected by despotic states, whether ancient or modern. The touchiness at the thought of 'equal rights' is not perhaps surprising in the 1790s: Paine's *The Rights of Man* had appeared in 1791–2 and the French Revolution was deeply disturbing, not least to students of ancient history (see Thomas Taylor's outburst on grammar and politics in No. 26). Presumably, the idealizing historians are the Whigs and the radicals to whom Greece (and Athens in particular) sometimes suggested an incarnation of the spirit of Liberty (see Introduction, pp. 29–31). There is a strong similarity here to the attitudes of John Gillies (see No. 22), who appreciated the virtues and achievements of Athens but who was quick to point out 'the evils inherent in every form of Republican policy'. Unlike the idealizers, the anonymous author of the preface is also concerned with the importance of trade; in fact, he suggests it was the commercial spirit rather than democratic institutions which fostered the arts. Byron, for one, would not have agreed; for him, the charm of ancient Greece was partly based on its dedication to arms and arts and its neglect of the restricting concerns of commerce.[2]

Like *Antiquities of Athens*, the first volume of *Ionian Antiquities* was dedicated to the king; though George III was not himself a discriminating connoisseur, he was an important patron and collector (see William Whitehead's Birthday Ode for 1769). In 1762 he acquired a collection of gems and drawings from the British Consul at Venice. In the same year he purchased a collection of drawings and prints of classic art from Winckelmann's patron Cardinal Albani; this was 'the largest, single collection of archaeological information anywhere in Europe, a mine of material not only for archaeologists, but also for painters and sculptors'.[3]

NOTES

1 See CROOK (*The Greek Revival*, 1972). Chandler's descriptions of Ionia also had an influence on Goethe and Hölderlin (see HIGHET, p. 664).
2 *Hints from Horace*, ll. 509–12.
3 IRWIN, p. 17.

From **To the Reader**

After having, in our volume of Ionian Antiquities, presented the Public with specimens of the elegant, luxuriant, and in some instances fanciful, Architecture of the Asiatic Greeks, we now offer to their consideration a few examples of the more chaste and severe style, which prevailed in Greece itself and its European colonies; where a greater degree of rigour, both in private manners and public discipline, maintained for a longer time the genuine simplicity of ancient taste.

This style of Architecture is commonly called *Doric*, but might more properly be called *Grecian*, as being the only style employed, either in Greece, or its European colonies, prior to the Macedonian conquest; when all the distinctive characteristics of the different nations, which became incorporated in that empire, were, by the policy of the conqueror and his successors, gradually blended and lost in each other. Hence, from the combined tastes and habits of different countries, arose fanciful and capricious designs and compositions; and that restless desire of novelty, which has always been the bane of true taste.

Prior to that period, all the temples of Greece, Sicily, and Italy, appear to have been of one Order, and of one general form; though slightly varied in particular parts, as occasional convenience or local fashion might chance to require . . .

Prior to the establishment of trades, when every man made the utensils of his own household, it must have been a matter of little importance to him, whether the cup out of which he drank was of a rude or elegant form; since the only advantage or distinction which he could hope to obtain by possessing it, would be the reputation of possessing a little more skill than his neighbours, in matters of handicraft; and this is a species of reputation never very highly valued in the infancy of civil society; but when he carried any productions of his labour in this way to a foreign market, where art had not made even this little progress, or nature supplied the materials for it, the admiration of the purchaser would be raised in proportion to the beauty of the form and brilliancy of the colours; and the vanity of possession would increase with the difficulty of acquiring: hence, the industry and ingenuity of the maker would be excited by a certain prospect of reward, and the success of an accidental effort render him, thenceforward, an artist by profession . . .

In considering these facts, and reflecting on this real state of things in those ancient republics, which have been so generally admired, as models of the most free, and happy government, we cannot but smile at the presumptuous ignorance and temerity of those pretended politicians and philosophers of modern times, who are perpetually recommending their wild and impracticable theories of equal liberty, and pure democracy, by the glorious examples of Athens and Rome; and justifying their extravagant projects of anarchy with the names of Pericles, Cato, and Brutus. In superficial abridgements, indeed, of ancient history, we may find many high sounding sentences in praise of the liberty of those states, and of the patriots, who, at the expence of every private virtue, defended it; but such general sentences of indiscriminate applause are very easily made, and still more easily repeated; though, to those who inquire accurately into the detail of facts, they will appear wholly unfounded, unless taken in a very limited sense. The citizens might, indeed, have enjoyed some degree of liberty, and even of license; though without much security either of person or property. But the citizens constituted, in every state, but a very small proportion of the people; the bulk of whom were slaves, absolutely at the disposal of their owners: by them, almost all the manual labour was done; so that there was scarcely any freeman, who could not afford to give some time to public affairs; and who was not qualified, by education and habits of life, to understand something of the business, on which he was to deliberate. These admired constitutions of government were, therefore, all completely aristocratical; and as for the chiefs above mentioned, who have been quoted with such ridiculous ostentation, as patrons of the general and equal rights of man, they were all (particularly Marcus Brutus, who has been most quoted) leaders of oligarchical parties in those aristocracies, and only hostile to that monopolized power, of which they could not partake.

Other modern sophists, of a very different kind from these shallow retailers of the froth of history, have taken the contrary extreme; and because their deep researches could not discover that liberty, happiness, and security, for individuals, in ancient states, which superficial declaimers attributed to them, have questioned all the accounts of their energy, power, and population; and thus endeavoured to subvert all the authority of ancient history. The learned and elaborate essay of a late very acute and ingenious sceptic on this subject, is well known;[1] but without entering into any critical discussions concerning the corruptions of the texts, or the uncertainty of numerals in the Greek historians; or repeating any of the commonplace accusations of their disposition to exaggerate; we may, in answer to all the sceptical reasoning that human ingenuity can produce, point to the vast remains of splendour and power in the mouldered ruins of their public buildings; not only in the great ruling states, such as Athens, Corinth, and Syracuse, but in little obscure republics, such as Paestum, Segesta, and Selinus, whose names alone can be gleaned from history by the diligence of the antiquary; yet has the last and most obscure of these little states, left buildings, which surpass in size, strength, and solidity of construction, not only all that the greatest potentates of modern times have been able to accomplish, but all that was ever produced by the unlimited resources and unlimited despotism of the Roman emperors.

SAMUEL TAYLOR COLERIDGE
Letter on Chapman's Homer
(?1808)

This letter was sent to Sara Hutchinson with a copy of Chapman's translation. For the Romantic rediscovery of Chapman, see Introduction, pp. 15–16.

Chapman I have sent in order that you might read the *Odyssey*—the Iliad is fine, but less equal in the Translation, as well as less interesting in itself. What is stupidly said of Shakespeare is really true & appropriate of Chapman —'mighty faults counterpoised by mighty Beauties.' Excepting his quaint epithets which he affects to render literally from the Greek, a language above all others 'blest in the happy marriage of sweet words,' & which in our language are mere printer's compound epithets—such as quaff'd divine *Joy-in-the-heart-of-man-infusing* Wine——(the undermarked is to be one word, because one sweet mellifluous Word expresses it in Homer)—excepting this, it has no look, no air, of a translation. It is as truly an original poem as the Fairy Queen—it will give you small idea of Homer, tho' a far truer one than Pope's *Epigrams* or Cowper's cumbersome most anti-Homeric *Miltonized* [translation]—for Chapman writes & feels as a Poet—as Homer might have written had he lived in England in the reign of Queen Elizabeth—in short, it is an exquisite poem, in spite of its frequent & perverse quaintnesses & harshnesses, which are however amply repaid by almost unexampled sweetness & beauty of language, all over spirit & feeling. In the main it is an English Heroic Poem, the *tale* of which is borrowed from the Greek— ...

30   From
AUGUST WILHELM von SCHLEGEL
Vorlesungen über dramatische Kunst und Literatur
(*Lectures on Dramatic Art and Literature*)
(delivered at Vienna 1808; published 1809–11;
translated into English by J. Black 1815)

Schlegel (1767–1845), poet, critic a d scholar, translated from Shakespeare, Petrarch, Dante, Calderón and the *Bhagavadgita*. This impressive range of interests indicates both the comparative tendency and the openness of mind which characterized his criticism. Nicety of discrimination within the safe precincts of a narrow circle was never his ambition: '. . . no man can be a true critic or connoisseur who does not possess a universality of mind, who does not possess the flexibility, which, throwing aside all personal predilections and blind habits, enables him to transport himself into the peculiarities of other ages and nations, to feel them as it were from their proper central point . . .'[1]

The *Lectures* are an attempt to put this philosophy into practice. They cover a wide range of European drama with varying degrees of flexibility and sympathy; Schlegel does not succeed in feeling the drama of Racine, Corneille and Molière from its proper central point and even his enthusiastic account of Greek tragedy is distorted by certain cultural assumptions. Whatever their shortcomings, the *Lectures* mark an important phase in European criticism, not least in their formulation of the essential differences between the spirit of ancient and modern art and literature, which Schlegel identifies respectively as the classical and the romantic. This contrast is richly suggestive though the dialectical sweep of the argument involves some simplification. The Greeks are characterized as the finest products of a natural education and the inventors of 'the poetry of gladness': in this response to Greek civilization Schlegel owes much to Winckelmann, particularly to his insistence on the favourable influence of Greek climate and the ideal and untroubled beauty of Greek art and literature. Like Winckelmann, too, Schlegel stresses the importance of the Greek devotion to liberty; in his interpretation, the openness of the Greek theatre and the publicity of its transactions, which always took place out of doors, is directly related to Greek republican ideals.

Unlike Winckelmann, however, for whom the Greeks represented a pagan ideal which was much to be desired, Schlegel did not admire the Greeks unreservedly. For all their grace and beauty, Schlegel suspected that they lacked a spiritual dimension. In spite of the undeniable glory of their achievements, they were complacent and lacking in that subjectivity and that troubled introspective sense of human imperfection which characterizes the moderns and the northern peoples (who seem here to be more or less identified). Unfortunately, the Greeks were inescapably handicapped because they had lived before the advent of Christianity. This fact disturbed Wordsworth and seriously affected his response to Greek mythology, which he could never fully accept because of its pagan associations; it also troubled Coleridge, who was deeply indebted to Schlegel's ideas on this subject as on many others.[2]

Schlegel was well qualified to assess the problems of translation and to gauge the failure of the available renderings from Greek drama to capture the true spirit of the original. So he advises those who cannot read the plays in the original Greek that the surest way to feel the ancients as we ought is to study the antique, especially through the medium of sculpture. The 'best key to enter this sanctuary of beauty' is the writings of Winckelmann since, unlike Barthélemy, the great historian of art 'transformed himself completely into an ancient'. The influence of Winckelmann is evident in Schlegel's own approach, both in the detailed comparison between Greek literature and Greek art and more particularly in the analogies between sculpture and the Greek tragedians. The tragic mode is analyzed in terms of the *Niobe* and the *Laocoön*, both of which Winckelmann had famously celebrated, while Aeschylus is compared to Phidias, Sophocles to Polycleitus and Euripides to Lysippus.[3] Winckelmann's conception of the ideal nobility of Greek sculpture also lies behind Schlegel's analysis of the moral contours of Greek tragedy; like the sculpture which Winckelmann celebrated for its technical excellence as well as for its aesthetic perfection, Greek tragedy succeeded in combining the real and the ideal. For English reactions, see reviews of the French translation by Francis Hare-Naylor, *Quarterly Review*, xii (1814), 112–46 and of Black's translation by Hazlitt, *Works*, ed. Howe, 16.57–99.

1   Cf. Novalis to Schlegel: 'It requires a high degree of poetic morality, sacrifice of one's inclinations, to submit oneself to true translation. One translates because of genuine love of the beautiful and of one's country's literature. Translating is as good as writing new poetic works—only it is more difficult, depends on a rarer gift' (*Briefe und Dokumente*, ed. E. Wasmuth, Heidelberg, 1954, pp. 367–8; tr. S. S. Prawer, *Comparative Literary Studies: an introduction*, 1973, p. 86).

2   See 'Coleridge's Indebtedness to A. W. Schlegel' in Thomas McFarland, *Coleridge and the Pantheist Tradition*, Oxford, 1969, pp. 256–61.

3   Eighteenth-century writers were fond of comparing the tragedians to painters: in *A Dissertation on Ancient Tragedy* (1760) Thomas Francklin characterized Aeschylus as the Giulio Romano of Greek drama, Sophocles as the Raphael and Euripides as the Correggio, while Robert Potter the translator compared Raphael to Euripides and invoked Michelangelo, Salvator Rosa, Claude and Poussin to suggest the varied and powerful talents of Aeschylus.

From   **Lecture 1**

The formation of the Greeks was a natural education in its utmost perfection. Of a beautiful and noble race, endowed with susceptible senses and a clear understanding, placed beneath a mild heaven, they lived and bloomed in full health of existence; and, under a singular coincidence of favourable circumstances, performed all of which our circumscribed nature is capable. The whole of their art and their poetry is expressive of the consciousness of this harmony of all their faculties. They have invented the poetry of gladness.

Their religion was the deification of the powers of nature and of the earthly life: but this worship, which, among other nations, clouded the imagination with images of horror, and filled the heart with unrelenting cruelty, assumed, among the Greeks, a mild, a grand, and a dignified form. Superstition, too often the tyrant of the human faculties, seemed to have here contributed to their freest developement. It cherished the arts by which it was ornamented, and the idols became models of ideal beauty.

But however far the Greeks may have carried beauty, and even morality, we cannot allow any higher character to their formation than that of a refined and ennobled sensuality. Let it not be understood that I assert this to be true in every instance. The conjectures of a few philosophers, and the irradiations of poetical inspiration, constitute an exception. Man can never altogether turn aside his thoughts from infinity, and some obscure recollections will always remind him of his original home; but we are now speaking of the principal object towards which his endeavours are directed.

Religion is the root of human existence. Were it possible for man to renounce all religion, including that of which he is unconscious, and over which he has no control, he would become a mere surface without any internal substance. When this centre is disturbed the whole system of the mental faculties must receive another direction . . .

Among the Greeks human nature was in itself all-sufficient; they were conscious of no wants, and aspired at no higher perfection than that which they could actually attain by the exercise of their own faculties. We, however, are taught by superior wisdom that man, through a high offence, forfeited the place for which he was originally destined; and that the whole object of his earthly existence is to strive to regain that situation, which, if left to his own strength, he could never accomplish. The religion of the senses had only in view the possession of outward and perishable blessings; and immortality, insofar as it was believed, appeared in an obscure distance like a shadow, a faint dream of this bright and vivid futurity. The very reverse of all this is the case with the Christian: every thing finite and mortal is lost in the contemplation of infinity; life has become shadow and darkness, and the first dawning of our real existence opens in the world beyond the grave. Such a religion must waken the foreboding, which slumbers in every feeling heart, to the most thorough consciousness, that the happiness after which we strive we can never here attain; that no external object can ever entirely fill our souls; and that every mortal enjoyment is but a fleeting and momentary deception. When the soul, resting as it were under the willows of exile, breathes out its longing for its distant home, the prevailing character of its songs must be melancholy. Hence the poetry of the ancients was the poetry of enjoyment, and ours is that of desire: the former has its foundation in the scene which is present, while the latter hovers betwixt recollection and hope. Let me not be understood to affirm that every thing flows in one strain of wailing and complaint, and that the voice of melancholy must always be loudly heard. As the austerity of tragedy was not incompatible with the joyous views of the Greeks, so the romantic poetry can assume every tone, even that of the most lively gladness; but still it will always, in some shape or other, bear traces of the source from which it originated. The feeling of the moderns is, upon the whole, more intense, their fancy more incorporeal, and their thoughts more contemplative. In nature, it is true, the boundaries of objects run more into one another, and things are not so distinctly separated as we must exhibit them for the sake of producing a distinct impression.

The Grecian idea of humanity consisted in a perfect concord and proportion between all the powers,—a natural harmony. The moderns again have arrived at the consciousness of the internal discord which renders such an idea impossible; and hence the endeavour of their poetry is to reconcile these two worlds between which we find ourselves divided, and to melt them indissolubly into one another. The impressions of the senses are consecrated, as it were, from their mysterious connexion with higher feelings; and the soul, on the other hand, embodies its forebodings, or nameless visions of infinity, in the phenomena of the senses.

In the Grecian art and poetry we find an original and unconscious unity of form and subject; in the modern, so far as it has remained true to its own spirit, we observe a keen struggle to unite the two, as being naturally in opposition to each other. The Grecian executed what it proposed in the utmost perfection; but the modern can only do justice to its endeavours after what is infinite by approximation; and, from a certain appearance of imperfection, is in greater danger of not being duly appreciated.

From **Lecture 3**

The theatres of the Greeks were quite open above, and their dramas were always acted in open day, and beneath the canopy of heaven. The Romans, at an after period, endeavoured by a covering to shelter the audience from the rays of the sun; but this degree of luxury was hardly ever enjoyed by the Greeks. Such a state of things appears very inconvenient to us; but the Greeks had nothing of effeminacy about them, and we must not forget, too, the beauty of their climate. When they were overtaken by a storm or a shower, the play was of course interrupted; and they would much rather expose themselves to an accidental inconvenience, than, by shutting themselves up in a close and crowded house, entirely destroy the serenity of a religious solemnity, which their plays certainly were. To have covered in the scene itself, and imprisoned gods and heroes in dark and gloomy apartments with difficulty lighted up, would have appeared still more ridiculous to them. An action which so nobly served to establish the belief of the relation with heaven could only be exhibited under an unobstructed heaven, and under the very eyes of the gods as it were, for whom, according to Seneca, the sight of a brave man struggling with adversity is a becoming spectacle.[1] With respect to the supposed inconvenience, which, according to the assertion of many modern critics, was felt by the poets from the necessity of always laying the scene of their pieces before houses, a circumstance that often forced them to violate probability,

216

this inconvenience was very little felt by tragedy and the older comedy. The Greeks, like many southern nations of the present day, lived much more in the open air than we do, and transacted many things in public places which usually take place with us in houses. For the theatre did not represent the street, but a place before the house belonging to it, where the altar stood on which sacrifices to the household gods were offered up. Here the women, who lived in so retired a manner among the Greeks, even those who were unmarried, might appear without any impropriety. Neither was it impossible for them to give a view of the interior of the houses; and this was effected, as we shall immediately see by means of the encyclema.

But the principal reason for this observance was that publicity, according to the republican notion of the Greeks was essential to a grave and important transaction. This is clearly proved by the presence of the chorus, whose remaining on many occasions when secret transactions were going on has been judged of according to rules of propriety inapplicable to that country, and most undeservedly censured . . .

We come now to the essence of the Greek tragedy itself. In stating that the conception was ideal, we are not to understand that the different characters were all morally perfect. In this case what room could there be for such an opposition or conflict, as the plot of a drama requires?—Weaknesses, errors, and even crimes, were pourtrayed in them but the manners were always elevated above reality, and every person was invested with such a portion of dignity and grandeur as was compatible with the share which he possessed in the action. The ideality of the representation chiefly consisted in the elevation to a higher sphere. The tragical poetry wished wholly to separate the image of humanity which it exhibited to us, from the ground of nature to which man is in reality chained down, like a feudal slave. How was this to be accomplished? By exhibiting to us an image hovering in the air? But this would have been incompatible with the law of gravitation and with the earthly materials of which our bodies are framed. Frequently, what we praise in art as ideal is really nothing more. But the production of airy floating shadows can make no durable impression on the mind. The Greeks, however, succeeded in combining in the most perfect manner in their art ideality with reality, or, dropping school terms, an elevation more than human with all the truth of life, and all the energy of bodily qualities. They did not allow their figures to flutter without consistency in empty space, but they fixed the statue of humanity on the eternal and immoveable basis of moral liberty; and that it might stand there unshaken, being formed of stone or brass, or some more solid mass than the living human bodies, it made an impression by its own weight, and from its very elevation and magnificence it was only the more decidedly subjected to the law of gravity.

Inward liberty and external necessity are the two poles of the tragic world. Each of these ideas can only appear in the most perfect manner by the contrast of the other. As the feeling of internal dignity elevates the man above the unlimited dominion of impulse and native instinct, and in a word absolves him from the guardianship of nature, so the necessity which he must also recognize ought to be no mere natural necessity, but to lie beyond the world of sense in the abyss of infinitude; and it must consequently be represented as the invincible power of fate. Hence it extends also to the world of the gods: for the Grecian gods are mere powers of nature; and although immeasurably higher than any mortal man, yet, compared with infinitude, they are on an equal footing with himself. In Homer and the tragedians, the gods are introduced in a manner altogether different. In the former their appearance is arbitrary and accidental, and can communicate no higher interest to the epic poem than the charm of the wonderful. But in tragedy the gods either enter in obedience to fate, and to carry its decrees into execution; or they endeavour in a godlike manner to assert their liberty of action, and appear involved in the same struggles with destiny which man has to encounter.

31   *From*
BENJAMIN ROBERT HAYDON
Autobiography
(ed. Tom Taylor 1853)

Haydon (1786–1846) was a historical painter whose ambition to produce paintings of epic proportions and heroic conception was never attuned to the needs of his age or the limitations of his own talent. He was one of the most eloquent champions of the artistic value of the Elgin Marbles which the British Government finally purchased from Lord Elgin in 1816. One of the leading opponents of this acquisition was Richard Payne Knight (1750–1824), an influential figure described by the *Quarterly Review* as the 'arbiter of fashionable virtu'. When in 1803 the Society of Dilettanti had been asked to provide Elgin with financial assistance and perhaps to consider electing him as a member, it was Payne Knight who vetoed the suggestion. When Elgin arrived in France in 1806, Payne Knight told him: 'You have lost your labour, my Lord Elgin. Your marbles are over-rated: they are not Greek: they are Roman of the time of Hadrian'.[1] He had not even seen the marbles. In 1809 he continued the attack in *Specimens of Antient Sculpture*, which was published by the Society of Dilettanti and contained engravings of sixty-three works of art belonging to its members (twenty-three were the property of Payne Knight himself). Here he shifted the basis of his attack to the supposedly inferior quality of the Elgin Marbles, claiming that some of those who had worked on the metopes 'would not have been entitled to the rank of artists in a much less cultivated and fastidious age'. In his view, the Elgin Marbles were not in keeping with those standards of Ideal Beauty which characterized Roman and Graeco-Roman sculptures such as the *Apollo Belvedere*; they were grand but naturalistic rather than softly graceful. In fact, they challenged the artistic premises on which many of the Dilettanti (not least Payne Knight) had assembled their own collections of sculpture. So there is a particular significance in the title of Haydon's important defence of the Elgins which appeared in 1816—*The Judgement of Connoisseurs upon Works of Art compared with that of Professional Men*. The implication is that the Dilettanti are dilettanti, that they do not understand the true basis of art.

The passages extracted here are not from this significant though technical account but from Haydon's *Autobiography*, which is his one undoubted masterpiece. The first and second extracts refer to the period when the first collection of marbles was on display at Elgin's home in Park Lane; the third extract refers to the period beginning in 1811 when the marbles were moved to a windowless half-timbered outhouse in the yard of Burlington House, where they were joined in 1812 by the second collection, some of which had to be left in the open air.[2] Haydon's delight in these sculptures is based on a detailed appreciation of their anatomical realism, a realism which was not deflected by the demands of the fashionable or the superficially graceful. His friendship with David Wilkie puts this into convenient perspective. Wilkie's paintings at this time were mostly in the style of Ostade and Teniers and his planned picture of boys playing in a greenhouse shows that his realism was essentially grotesque or sentimental; the realism that Haydon recognized in the Elgin Marbles was grand, heroic, and uncompromising. Here, nature and idea coincided; or, as Keats's Grecian urn was to claim, 'Beauty is truth, truth beauty . . .'.[3]

The significance of Haydon's response, analytical but also highly emotional, extended beyond the world of painters and sculptors; his informed enthusiasm for Greek art had a profound influence on his young friend John Keats, both directly and through the *Annals of the Fine Arts* (1817–20), which was dedicated to principles very similar to his own and to which he frequently contributed. ('Ode to a Nightingale' and 'Ode on a Grecian Urn' were also first published in its pages.) Haydon took Keats to see the Marbles in March 1817: two sonnets resulted immediately but a more lasting consequence was the enriching of Keats's iconography and the confirmation of his natural tendency to interweave the images of life and of art.[4] For other reactions to the Elgin Marbles, see p. 115.

1 Haydon, *Autobiography and Memoirs*, ed. Tom Taylor, London, 1926, i. 207.
2 See Plates VII–VIIIb in ST CLAIR.
3 A different appreciation of the accuracy of the sculptures was demonstrated by the riding-master who took his pupils to admire the horsemanship on the Frieze (J. T. Smith, *Nollekens and his Times* [1828], 1929, p. 198).
4 For Haydon's influence on Keats, see Ian Jack, *Keats and the Mirror of Art*, Oxford, 1967.

1808

To Park Lane then we went, and after passing through the hall and thence into an open yard, entered a damp, dirty penthouse where lay the marbles ranged within sight and reach. The first thing I fixed my eyes on was the wrist of a figure in one of the female groups, in which were visible, though in a feminine form, the radius and ulna. I was astonished, for I had never seen them hinted at in any female wrist in the antique. I darted my eye to the elbow, and saw the outer condyle [1] visibly affecting the shape as in nature. I saw that the arm was in repose and the soft parts in relaxation. That combination of nature and idea which I had felt was so much wanting for high art was here displayed to midday conviction. My heart beat! If I had seen nothing else I had beheld sufficient to keep me to nature for the rest of my life. But when I turned to the Theseus and saw that every form was altered by action or repose,—when I saw that the two sides of his back varied, one side stretched from the shoulder-blade being pulled forward, and the other side compressed from the shoulder-blade being pushed close to the spine as he rested on his elbow, with the belly flat because the bowels fell into the pelvis as he sat,—and when, turning to the Ilissus, I saw the belly protruded, from the figure lying on its side,—and again, when in the figure of the fighting metope I saw the muscle shown under the one arm-pit in that instantaneous action of darting out, and left out in the other arm-pits because not wanted—when I saw, in fact, the most heroic style of art combined with all the essential detail of actual life, the thing was done at once and for ever.

Here were principles which the common sense of the English people would understand; here were principles which I had struggled for in my first picture with timidity and apprehension; here were the principles which the great Greeks in their finest time established, and here was I, the most prominent historical student, perfectly qualified to appreciate all this by my own determined mode of study under the influence of my old friend the watchmaker[2]—perfectly comprehending the hint at the skin by knowing well what was underneath it!

Oh, how I inwardly thanked God that I was prepared to understand all this! Now I was rewarded for all the petty harassings I had suffered. Now was I mad for buying Albinus [3] without a penny to pay for it? Now was I mad for lying on the floor hours together, copying its figures? I felt the future, I foretold that they would prove themselves the finest things on earth, that they would overturn the false beau-ideal, where nature was nothing, and would establish the true beau-ideal, of which nature alone is the basis.

I shall never forget the horses' heads—the feet in the metopes! I felt as if a divine truth had blazed inwardly upon my mind and I knew that they would at last rouse the art of Europe from its slumber in the darkness.

I do not say this *now*, when all the world acknowledges it, but I said it then, *when no one would believe me*. I went home in perfect excitement, Wilkie [4] trying to moderate my enthusiasm with his national caution.

Utterly disgusted at my wretched attempt at the heroic in the form and action of my Dentatus, I dashed out the abominable mass and breathed as if relieved of a nuisance. I passed the evening in a mixture of torture and hope; all night I dozed and dreamed of the marbles. I rose at five in a fever of excitement, tried to sketch the Theseus from memory, did so, and saw that I comprehended it. I worked that day and another and another, fearing that I was deluded. At last I got an order for myself; I rushed away to Park Lane; the impression was more vivid than before. I drove off to Fuseli,[5] and fired him to such a degree that he ran upstairs, put on his coat and away we sallied. I remember that first a coal-cart with eight horses stopped us as it struggled up one of the lanes of the Strand; then a flock of sheep blocked us up; Fuseli, in a fury of haste and rage, burst into the middle of them, and they got between his little legs and jostled him so much that I screamed with laughter in spite of my excitement. He swore all along the Strand like a little fury. At last we came to Park Lane. Never shall I forget his uncompromising enthusiasm. He strode about saying, "De Greeks were godes! de Greeks were godes!" We went back to his house, where I dined with him, and we passed the evening in looking over Quintilian and Pliny.[6] Immortal period of my sanguine life! To look back on those hours has been my solace in the bitterest afflictions. . . .

I saw that the essential was selected in them [the marbles] and the superfluous rejected; that first, all the causes of action were known and then all of those causes wanted for any particular action were selected; that then skin covered the whole and the effect of the action, relaxation, purpose or gravitation was shown on the skin. This appeared, as far as I could see *then*, to be the principle. For Dentatus I selected all the muscles requisite for human action, no more nor less, and then the members wanted for *his* action, and no more nor less.

I put a figure in the corner of a lower character, that is, more complicated in its forms, having parts not essential, and this showed the difference between the form of a hero and common man. The wiseacres of the time quizzed me, of course, for placing a naked soldier in a Roman Army, a thing never done by any artist. Raffaele did so in Constantine's battle, but they had nothing to do with Raffaele and perhaps never heard of Raffaele's battle. [7]

I drew at the marbles ten, fourteen, and fifteen hours at a time; staying often till twelve at night, holding a candle and my board in one hand and drawing with the other; and so I should have stayed till morning had not the sleepy porter come yawning in to tell me it was twelve o'clock, and then often have I gone home, cold, benumbed and damp, my clothes steaming up as I dried them; and so, spreading my drawings on the floor and putting a candle on the ground, I have drank my tea at one in the morning with ecstacy as its warmth trickled through my frame, and looked at my picture and dwelt on my drawings, and pondered on the change of empires and thought that I had been contemplating what Socrates looked at and Plato saw,—and then, lifted up with my own high urgings of soul, I have prayed God to enlighten my mind to discover the principles of those divine things,—and then I have had inward assurances of future glory, and almost fancying divine influence in my room have lingered to my mattress bed and soon dozed into a rich, balmy slumber. Oh, those were days of luxury and rapture and uncontaminated purity of mind! No sickness, no debility, no fatal, fatal weakness of sight. I arose with the sun and opened my eyes to its light only to be conscious of my high pursuit; I sprang from my bed, dressed as if possessed, and passed the day, the noon, and the night in the same dream of abstracted enthusiasm; secluded from the world, regardless of its feelings, unimpregnable to disease, insensible to contempt, a being of elevated passions, a spirit that

> Fretted the pigmy body to decay,
> And o'erinformed its tenement of clay. [8]

1811

I now returned to Macbeth with my principles of form quite settled. I finished the king, whom everybody liked, and was soon buried in application. I used to go down in the evenings with a little portfolio and bribe the porter at Burlington House, to which the Elgin Marbles were now removed,[9] to lend me a lantern, and then locking myself in, take the candle out and make different sketches, till the cold damp would almost put the candle out. As the light streamed across the room and died away into obscurity, there was something solemn and awful in the grand forms and heads and trunks and fragments of mighty temples and columns that lay scattered about in sublime insensibility—the remains, the only actual remains, of a mighty people. The grand back of the Theseus would come towering close to my eye and his broad shadow spread over the place a depth of mystery and awe. Why were such beautiful productions ever suffered to be destroyed? Why did not the Great Spirit of the world protect the work of minds that honour His creation? Why in a succession of ages has the world again to begin? Why is knowledge ever suffered to ebb? and why not allowed to proceed from where it left off to an endless perfection? All these beautiful forms were executed before Christianity had opened the eyes of mankind to moral principles. Why must we admire the works of those whose idolatry and vice degraded them? Genius had displayed as much vigour before Christ as after. These questionings would occur to me in the intervals of drawing and perplex my mind to an endless musing, and yet take Wilkie there at any time and he would care little about them. I remember a most remarkable example of the nature of his genius. I think it was the second time we were ever there, when I and everybody else had been excessively excited by these ruins of Athens. Wilkie, when we came out into Piccadilly, said in great glee to me: "I have been thinking of a capital subject." "Well done," said I; "while there?" "Yes, to be sure," said he; "it is some boys playing with a garden engine; some throwing the water over others; some inside a greenhouse laughing heartily at their poor unfortunate companions outside, and some squeezing their noses and mouths flat aginst panes of glass, and laughing through. This would be a capital bit of fun, and I shall make a sketch when I get home." In the midst of the ruins of beautiful Athens, where every stone and fragment and pillar set the soul musing for hours, in the midst of the most beautiful productions the world ever saw, such was the peculiarity of Wilkie's faculty that there it operated in spite of gods and goddesses totally uninterrupted by the association of the grand things round about it.

32   *From*
THOMAS CAMPBELL
Life and Letters
(ed. William Beattie 1849)

Thomas Campbell (1777-1844), Scottish poet and man of letters, was in Paris in 1814, where he met Mme de Staël, Cuvier, Schlegel, Humboldt and the great English actress Sarah Siddons. In the company of Mrs Siddons he visited the Louvre and was overwhelmed by the presence of the celebrated statues which Napoleon had removed from Italy and put on display: these included the *Apollo Belvedere*, the *Venus de Medici*, the *Laocoön*, the *Torso Belvedere* and the *Horses* of Lysippus. Campbell's reaction was extravagant but not uncharacteristic of the Romantic age. Napoleon himself had shown signs of strong emotion when discussing the *Venus de Medici*, shortly after the French had taken possession of her: 'Bonaparte ... turned round to those about him, and said, with his eyes lit up, "She's coming!" as if he had been talking of a living person'.[1] It must be remembered, too, that the statues which he then saw for the first time had been celebrated throughout the eighteenth century by a wide range of poets and most fervently of all by Wincklemann. The interest of Campbell's reaction is partly in observing his own observation of Mrs Siddons (who was then fifty-nine) among the ancient marbles. Here again Campbell was influenced by the spirit of the age. Lord Elgin had once invited the artists West and Lawrence to meet Mrs Siddons among his own collection. Lawrence could not come but observed: 'Mrs Siddons can nowhere be seen with so just accompaniments as the works of Phidias, nor can they receive nobler homage than from her praise. She is of his age, a kindred genius, though living in our times'.[2] Faced with the marbles, Mrs Siddons reacted in appropriately dramatic fashion. The statues of the Fates 'so rivetted and agitated the feelings of Mrs Siddons, the pride of theatrical representation, as actually to draw tears from her eyes'.[3] The actress was not alone in her glory: the prize-fighter Gregson posed naked among the marbles while, on another occasion, three boxing matches were staged in the same setting.[4]

After the overthrow of Napoleon in 1815 the Louvre collection was returned to Italy—an event celebrated by Felicia Hemans in a poem entitled 'The Restoration of the Works of Art to Italy' (1816).

NOTES

1 *The Autobiography of Leigh Hunt,* ed. J. E. Morpurgo, London, 1949, p. 87. See p. 115.
2 A. H. Smith, 'Lord Elgin and his Collection', *Journal of Hellenic Studies,* xxxvi (1916), 306.
3 *Memorandum on the Subject of the Earl of Elgin's Pursuits in Greece,* 1811, p. 42.
4 ST. CLAIR (*Lord Elgin and the Marbles*), pp. 168–9.

1814

I write this after returning from the Louvre ... You may imagine with what feelings I caught the first sight of Paris, and passed under Montmartre, the scene of the last battle between the French and Allies. ... It was evening when we entered Paris. Next morning I met Mrs. Siddons; walked about with her, and then visited the Louvre together... Oh, how that immortal youth—Apollo! in all his splendour —majesty—divinity—flashed upon us from the end of the gallery! What a torrent of ideas—classically associated with this godlike form—rushed upon me at this moment! My heart palpitated—my eyes filled with tears—I was dumb with emotion.

Here are a hundred other splendid statues—the Venus—the Menander—the Pericles—Cato and Portia—the father and daughter in an attitude of melting tenderness ... I wrote on the table where I stood with Mrs. Siddons, the *first* part of this letter in pencil—a record of the strange moments in which I felt myself suddenly transported, as it were, into a new world, and while standing between the Apollo and the Venus ...

Coming home I conclude a transcript of the day:—The effect of the statue gallery was quite overwhelming—it was even distracting; for the secondary statues are things on which you might dote for a whole day; and while you are admiring one, you seem to grudge the time, because it is not spent in admiring something else. Mrs. Siddons is a judge of statuary; but I thought I could boast of a triumph over them—in point of taste—when she and some others of our party preferred another Venus to '*the* statue that enchants the world.' I bade them recollect the waist of the true Venus—the chest and the shoulders. We returned, and they gave in to my opinion, that these parts were beyond all expression. It was really a day of tremulous ecstacy. The young and glorious Apollo is happily still white in colour. He seems as if he had just leapt from the sun! All pedantic knowledge of statuary falls away, when the most ignorant in the arts finds a divine presence in this great created form. Mrs. Siddons justly observed, that it gives one an idea of God himself having given power to catch, in such imitation, a ray of celestial beauty.

The Apollo is not perfect; some parts are modern, and he is not quite placed on his perpendicular by his French transporters; but his head, his breast, and one entire thigh and leg are indubitable. The whole is so perfect, that, at the full distance of the hall, it seems to blaze with proportion. The muscle that supports the head thrown back—the mouth, the brow, the soul that is in the marble, are not to be expressed.

After such a subject, what a falling off it is to tell you I dined with human beings! yea, verily, at a hotel . . .

I was one of the many English who availed themselves of the first short peace to get a sight of the Continent. The Louvre was at that time in possession of its fullest wealth. In the Statuary-hall of that place I had the honour of giving Mrs. Siddons my arm the first time she walked through it, and the first in both our lives that we saw the Apollo Belvidere. From the farthest end of that spacious room, the god seemed to look down like a president on the chosen assembly of sculptured forms; and his glowing marble, unstained by time, appeared to my imagination as if he had stepped freshly from the sun. I had seen casts of the glorious statue with scarcely any admiration; and I must undoubtedly impute that circumstance, in part, to my inexperience in art, and to my taste having till then lain torpid. But still I prize the recollected impressions of that day too dearly to call them fanciful. They seemed to give my mind a new sense of the harmony of Art—a new visual power of enjoying beauty. Nor is it mere fancy that makes the difference between the Apollo himself and his plaster casts. The dead whiteness of the *stucco* copies is glaringly monotonous; whilst the diaphanous surface of the *original* seems to soften the light which it reflects. [1]

Every particular of that hour is written indelibly on my memory. I remember entering the Louvre with a latent suspicion on my mind, that a good deal of the rapture expressed at the sight of superlative sculptures was exaggerated or affected; but as we passed through the vestibule of the hall, there was a Greek figure, I think that of Pericles, with a chlamys [2] and helmet, which John Kemble desired me to notice; and it instantly struck me with wonder at the gentleman-like grace which Art could give to a human form, with so simple a vesture. It was not, however, until we reached the grand saloon, that the first sight of the god overawed my incredulity. Every step of approach to his presence added to my sensations; and all recollections of his name in classic poetry swarmed on my mind as spontaneously as the associations that are conjured up by the sweetest music. . . .

Engrossed as I was with the Apollo, I could not forget the honour of being before him in the company of so august a worshipper, and it certainly increased my enjoyment to see the first interview between the paragon of Art and that of Nature. Mrs. Siddons was evidently much struck, and remained a long time before the statue; but, like a true admirer, she was not loquacious. I remember, she said—'What a great idea it gives us of God to think that he has made a human being capable of fashioning so divine a form!' When we walked round to other sculptures, I observed that almost every eye in the Hall was fixed upon her and followed her: yet I could perceive that she was not known, as I heard the spectators say—'Who is she? Is she not an English woman?' At this time, though in her fifty-ninth year, her looks were so noble, that she made you proud of English beauty—even in the presence of Grecian sculpture.

33   *From*
PERCY BYSSHE SHELLEY
Letter of 23–4 January 1819

Shelley (1792–1822) lived in Italy from the spring of 1818 till his death. Soon after his arrival he began to compose for his friend Peacock a series of detailed letters describing his experiences and recording his impressions as a traveller. Among the places which Shelley visited were Paestum with its 'sublime monuments' and

Pompeii. The significance of the extract included here is that it shows Shelley reacting to Pompeii as to a Greek city; for Shelley, as for Winckelmann, Goethe and many others who were profoundly excited by the Greek example, Greece itself always remained just out of reach, partly for practical reasons but partly perhaps because it retained greater potency as a landscape of the imagination. Because of its history and its geography, Southern Italy was powerfully suggestive of the Greek tradition while it remained at a salutary distance from the realities of the unhappy modern country.

At Pompeii Shelley records with approval the intimate connection between the ruins and the landscape: the connection is incarnated in the word 'upaithric', which means 'open to the air, having no roof' and had recently been introduced to English by Peacock (who employed the more correct form 'hupaithric'). Shelley's account concludes with a characteristic mixture of lament and invective; he was not unaware of the shortcomings of 'the most admirable community ever formed' but he believed that the Greeks had attained a higher plane of civilization than any society before or since and that the advent of Christianity had gradually led to the withdrawal of the harmonizing possibilities of life.[1]

The grand object was to recover the latent possibilities of human greatness so tangibly available to the Greeks, to interpret the ruins not as a warning against hubristic aspirations as in the case of 'Ozymandias' but as an indication of what might yet be achieved if we could properly read the lesson of the past. It is not an accident that one of Shelley's sentences seems to look forward to 'Ode to the West Wind', which was written in October of the same year and which concerns itself with death and resurrection. The presence of Vesuvius also suggests *Prometheus Unbound* which Shelley was writing at this time; the investigation of our relation to history and the possibilities of regeneration is crucial to a play which is itself an attempt to transmit and reinterpret the legacy of classical literature.

Shelley's reflections among the ruins can be usefully compared with the melancholy musings of John Dyer at Rome (see No. 7) and with the reactions of Horace Walpole at Herculaneum (letter of 14 June 1740), of Robert Wood at Palmyra (see No. 11), of Goethe at Pompeii and Paestum (*Italian Journey*, 11, 13, 18 March 1787) and of Chateaubriand at Pompeii; Shelley's letter provides a detailed and carefully technical account of the architecture (mostly omitted in this extract) but its impetus and characteristic flavour are derived from a sympathetic identification with Greek culture. Pompeii was a source of imaginative stimulus to poets and novelists—Madame de Staël in *Corinne, ou l'Italie* (1807), Lamartine in *Graziella* (1849) and, most notably perhaps, Leopardi in *La Ginestra* (1836); it made little impact on art before the end of the eighteenth century, not least because the artistic remains were considered by many to be aesthetically deficient and morally offensive.[2]

NOTES

1 *Letters*, ed. F. L. Jones, Oxford, ii. 156.
2 See HONOUR, pp. 43–50; Hugh Honour, *Romanticism*, 1979, pp. 205–12.

At the upper end, supported on an elevated platform stands the temple of Jupiter. Under the colonnade of its portico we sate & pulled out our oranges & figs & bread & [?soil] apples (sorry fare you will say) & rested to eat. There was a magnificent spectacle. Above & between the multitudinous shafts of the [?sunshiny] columns, was seen the blue sea reflecting the purple heaven of noon above it, & supporting as it were on its line the dark lofty mountains of Sorrento, of a blue inexpressibly deep, & tinged towards their summits with streaks of new-fallen snow. Between was one small green island. To the right was Capua, Inarime, Prochyta and Miseno. Behind was the single summit of Vesuvius rolling forth volumes of thick white smoke whose foamlike column was sometimes darted into the clear dark sky & fell in little streaks along the wind. Between Vesuvius & the nearer mountains, as thro a chasm was seen the main line of the loftiest Apennines to the east. The day was radiant & warm. Every now & then we heard the subterranean thunder of Vesuvius; its distant deep peals seemed to shake the very air

& light of day which interpenetrated our frames with the sullen & tremendous sound. This scene was what the Greeks beheld. (Pompeii you know was a Greek city.) They lived in harmony with nature, & the interstices of their incomparable columns, were portals as it were to admit the spirit of beauty which animates this glorious universe to visit those whom it inspired. If such is Pompeii, what was Athens? what scene was exhibited from its Acropolis? The Parthenon and the temples of Hercules & Theseus & the Winds ? The islands of the Ægean Sea, the mountains of Argolis & the peaks of Pindus & Olympus, & the darkness of the Beotian forests interspersed? From the forum we went to another public place a triangular portico half inclosing the ruins of an enormous temple. It is built on the edge of the hill overlooking the sea. Λ That black point is the temple. In the apex of the triangle stands an altar & a fountain; & before the altar once stood the statue of the builder of the portico.—Returning hence & following the consular road we came to the eastern gate of the city. The walls are of enormous strength, & inclose a space of three miles. On each side of the road beyond the gate are built the tombs. How unlike ours! They seem not so much hiding places for that which must decay as voluptuous chamber[s] for immortal spirits. They are of marble radiantly white, & two especially beautiful are loaded with exquisite bas reliefs. On the stucco wall which incloses them are little emblematic figures of a relief exceedingly low, of dead or dying animals & little winged genii, & female forms bending in groupes in some funeral office. The higher reliefs, represent one a nautical subject & the other a bacchanalian one. Within the cell, stand the cinerary urns, sometimes one, sometimes more. It is said that paintings were found within, which are now—as has been every thing moveable in Pompeii—been removed & scattered about in Royal Museums. These tombs were the most impressive things of all. The wild woods surround them on either side and along the broad stones of the paved road which divides them, you hear the late leaves of autumn shiver & rustle in the stream of the inconstant wind as it were like the step of ghosts. The radiance & magnificence of these dwellings of the dead, the white freshness of the scarcely finished marble, the impassioned or imaginative life of the figures which adorn them contrast strangely with the simplicity of the houses of those who were living when Vesuvius overwhelmed their city. I have forgotten the Amphitheatre, which is of great magnitude, tho' much inferior to the Coliseum.—I now understand why the Greeks were such great Poets, & above all I can account, it seems to me, for the harmony the unity the perfection the uniform excellence of all their works of art. They lived in a perpetual commerce with external nature and nourished themselves upon the spirit of its forms. Their theatres were all open to the mountains & the sky. Their columns that ideal type of a sacred forest with its roof of interwoven tracery admitted the light & wind, the odour & the freshness of the country penetrated the cities. Their temples were mostly upaithric; & the flying clouds the stars or the deep sky were seen above. O, but for that series of wretched wars which terminated in the Roman conquest of the world, but for the Christian religion which put a finishing stroke to the antient system; but for those changes which conducted Athens to its ruin, to what an eminence might not humanity have arrived!

SAMUEL TAYLOR COLERIDGE
Note on Gray's *Platonica*
(1819)

For Gray's views on Plato, see No. 18; for other views, see Nos. 5, 23 and 25.

Whatever might be expected from a scholar, a gentleman, a man of exquisite taste, as the quintessence of sane and sound good sense, Mr Gray appears to me to have performed. The poet Plato, the orator Plato, Plato the exquisite dramatist of conversation, the seer and the painter of character, Plato the high-bred, highly-educated, aristocratic republican, the man and the gentleman of quality stands full before us from behind the curtain as Gray has drawn it back. Even so does Socrates, the social wise old man, the *practical* moralist. But Plato the philosopher, but the divine Plato, was not to be comprehended within the field of vision, or be commanded by the fixed immoveable telescope of Mr. Locke's human understanding. The whole sweep of the best philosophic reflections of French or English fabric in the age of our scholarly bard, was not commensurate with the mighty orb . . .

Appendix

The Society of Dilettanti

The Society of Dilettanti (lovers of the fine arts) was founded in 1732 by a group of noblemen; originally, membership was confined to those who had been to Italy, later it was extended by special dispensation ('it is the opinion of the Society that Avignon is in Italy'), while by 1764 it was revised to include those who had been 'upon some other Classic Ground'. At first, the Society was little more than a dining club: Horace Walpole tartly observed that 'the nominal qualification' for membership was 'having been to Italy, and the real one being drunk'.[1] By 1736 there were forty-six members. From these rather unpromising beginnings the Society developed until it became a significant force in the history of English taste in the eighteenth and early nineteenth centuries. Many of the early members were bound together by hostility to Robert Walpole as well as by noble birth; gradually, the social range of the membership was widened although the Society always retained strong connections with politics, diplomacy and public life. Members included not only politicians and diplomats but painters, travellers, collectors and historians: among the more notable were the Marquesses of Rockingham and of Hartington (both of whom became Prime Minister), Doddington, Charles James Fox, Admiral Rodney, Sir William Hamilton, the Earl of Sandwich, Sir Joseph Banks, Sir George and Sir James Gray, Sir Joshua Reynolds, Sir Thomas Lawrence, Benjamin West, David Garrick, Richard Payne Knight, Charles Townley, William Mitford, Thomas Hope, Dr Burney, John Hookham Frere, Joseph Spence, James Dawkins, James Stuart, Nicholas Revett, Robert Wood, Samuel Rogers and Sir William Gell.

Apart from the influence of individual members, the Society made its presence felt in two ways. First, it sponsored a small number of books which exercised a disproportionately significant influence both on taste and on the development of archaeology and topography: *The Antiquities of Athens* (1762, 1789, 1794, 1814, 1830; indirectly sponsored); *Ionian Antiquities* (1769, 1797, two other volumes to 1881); Richard Chandler's *Inscriptiones Antiquae* (1774), *Travels in Asia Minor* (1775) and *Travels in Greece* (1776); Richard Payne Knight's *An Account of the worship of Priapus* (1786); *Select Specimens of Antient Sculpture* (1809, 1835); and *The Unedited Antiquities of Attica* (1817). Secondly, its wealthy and often discriminating members initiated a series of collections which played an important role in the new assimilation of antiquity:

The Bessborough gems, the Ainslie coins, the Townley marbles, the Greville engravings, the Lansdowne marbles, the Sutherland paintings, the Weddell marbles, the Hamilton vases, the Worsley marbles, the Englefield vases, the Farnborough paintings, the Hope vases, the Hamilton manuscripts, the libraries of Heber, Bunbury, Windham, Storer and Cracherode—these were just a few of the rich and valuable collections built up by leading members.[2]

See also Nos. 8, 9, 11, 19 and 28.

NOTES

1 *Horace Walpole's Correspondence*, ed. W. S. Lewis, New Haven, Conn., 1937–   , xviii.211 (14 April 1743).
2 CROOK (*The Greek Revival* 1972), pp. 8–9.

Notes

2
ALEXANDER POPE

1 For an earlier version of this response, see letter cited on p. 46, n. 1.
2 ii.780. Pope's translation enhances the effect he is describing: the verbs he renders as *pour along* and *sweeps* can be translated more literally as *went* and *is consumed*.
3 Lucretius, *De Rerum Natura*, i.72.
4 Lucan (39–65), author of *Bellum Civile* (or *Pharsalia*), Statius (*c.* 45 – *c.* 96), author of *The Thebaid*.
5 *Poetics*, vi.19.
6 See No. 1.
7 *Traité du poëme épique*, Paris, 1675.

3
MARY WORTLEY MONTAGU
Letter to Pope

1 Shepherd's pipe, pipe of pan.
2 *Remarks on Several Parts of Italy* (1705), *Miscellaneous Works*, ed. A. C. Guthkelch, 1914, ii. 147.
3 The second volume of Pope's translation of the *Iliad* appeared in March 1716.
4 *Iliad*, vi.490–2, 323–4.
5 *Iliad*, iv.132–3; Pope, iv.163–4.
6 *Iliad*, iii.419. For a later account, perhaps influenced by M. W. Montagu, see P.–A. Guys, *Voyage littéraire de la Grèce*, 1771, Letters, VI, VII.
7 *Odyssey*, vi. 102 ff; *Aeneid*, i.498. Cf. Guys, *Voyage littéraire*, Letter XIII (see also XXXIII).

4
MARY WORTLEY MONTAGU
Letter to Conti

1 *Iliad*, iii.340–82.
2 For the exactness of Homer's geography, see the extracts from Robert Wood in No. 16. Don Quixote experiences his delightful

visions in the Cave of Montesinos (ii.22).

3 Actually the ruins of Alexandria Troas. See pp. 158–61 below.
4 Now known to be the temple of Poseidon.
5 The Parthenon was badly damaged by a bomb when under siege from the Venetians in 1687.

5

CHARLES CRAWFORD

1 Plato is referred to as *divinum* by Cicero (*Tusc. Disp.*, I.xxxii.79) and described as speaking *divinitus* (*De Oratore*, I.xi.49); the Florentine Neo-Platonist Marsilio Ficino refers to the divine Plato in the title of his translation of the complete works, 1482.
2 André Dacier (1651–1722), whose translation of ten Platonic dialogues appeared in an English version as *The Works of Plato Abridg'd* (1701).
3 Crawford refers to the *Life of Plato* in Diogenes Laertius and cites the epigram addressed to Stella (or Aster).

6

THOMAS BLACKWELL

1 The secondary titles of respectively *The Indian Emperour* by Dryden (1665) and *The Tempest* by Dryden and Davenant (1667).
2 A——, Earl of ——, to whom this anonymous work is addressed.
3 Herodotus.
4 'With faction, craft, crime, lust and wrath, within and without the walls of Troy all goes wrong', Horace, *Epistles*, I.ii.15–16, tr. H. Fairclough, Loeb, London and Cambridge, Mass., 1929.
5 Horace, *Epistles*, II.i.28.
6 Bard.
7 Herald.
8 Rhymers, writers of runes, traditional poets.
9 Blackwell's note cites Juvenal, *Satires*, vii.
10 Caius Gracchus (Plutarch, *Life of Tiberius Gracchus*, ii.5); Seneca, *Controversiae*, iv. Preface, 8.
11 Blackwell's note cites *Aeneid*, ii.713ff. with the comment: 'Says Aeneas to his Servants, who must have known those Places as well, or better than himself'.
12 Horace, *Ars Poetica*, l.121.
13 *Iliad*, i.106ff.
14 Aeneas' romantic interlude with Dido during the thunderstorm in *Aeneid* iv.

8

JOSEPH SPENCE

1   A religious system according to which the world is ruled equally by the power of good and by the power of evil.

2   Promontory on the Bay of Naples; note the eighteenth-century interest in grottoes.

3   Suetonius, *Life of Augustus*, xxxi.

4   Bernard de Montfaucon, *L'Antiquité expliquée et représentée en figures* (1719, 1724; Eng. tr. 1721–5).

5   According to Spence's note, the Egyptians usually represented Canopus in the shape of an earthen pot.

6   *Aeneid*, iii. 19; Tibullus, II.ii.11.

7   Spence quotes Tibullus, III.iv.23–4.

8   Spence cites Statius, Catullus and Ovid and goes on to describe how Augustus aspired to imitate the appearance of Apollo.

9   The hunter.

10 A short mantle or cloak.

11 Maximus Tyrius (*c.* 125–85), sophist and lecturer, in *Dissertations*, 72.

9
STUART AND REVETT

1   Antoine Desgodets (1653–1728) published *Les Édifices antiques de Rome* in 1682 and initiated a new method for architectural archaeology by directly consulting the monuments rather than published sources; Andrea Palladio (1508–80) was an architect and author of *I Quattro Libri dell' Architettura*; Sebastiano Serlio (1475–1564) was also an architect and author; Pietro Santo Bartoli (*c.* 1635–1700) was an engraver and antiquarian whose illustrations of Roman ruins influenced Piranesi. See p. 148.

2   Marcus Vitruvius Pollio (first century B.C.), was the author of *De Architectura*, a comprehensive guide to Hellenistic and Roman practice which provided a basis for Renaissance and Neo-classical architects.

3   Strabo (64/3 B.C. – 21 A.D.), author of *Geography* in seventeen books;Pausanias of Lydia (flourished *c.* 150), author of *Description of Greece*.

10
JOSEPH WARTON
I

1   Epistles, I.ii.17.

2   William Broome translated eight books of the *Odyssey* and compiled all the notes under strict supervision from Pope.

3 A reference to Harmodius and Aristogeiton, two Athenian youths who killed Hipparchus, tyrant of Athens, in 514 B.C.; the lyrics can be found in *Poetae Melici Graeci*, ed. Denys Page, Oxford, 1962, Nos. 893–6.

4 *Iliad*, xvi.384–6; *Odyssey*, iv.566–8. Both these translations elaborate on the original and both include details which fall outside the Greek passages quoted by Warton; in Homer the second passage, which is half the length of Pope's version, has only one adverb and no adjectives (Pope has eleven). The Greek has been omitted in the present edition.

5 v.153, 84.

6 'So slow and thankless flow for me the hours' (Horace, *Epistles*, I.i.23, tr. Fairclough).

7 'For indeed he desired to return home' (xiii.30).

8 xiii.34.

9 vii.259; a slight mistranslation since in the Greek it is the clothes rather than Calypso which are described as immortal.

10 'That there is nothing sweeter than his fatherland or his parents' (ix.34).

11 *Paradise Lost*, iv.756.

12 xi.170ff.

13 Pope's version, xxiv.375.

14 xvi.186ff.

15 xiv.56ff.

16 *Discourses*, III.ii.

17 *Lettre sur les occupations de l'Académie française*, v, 'Projet de la poétique'. See introduction to No. 1.

18 *Republic*, III.

JOSEPH WARTON
II

1 A romance by Marie Madeleine, Comtesse de Lafayette.

2 Horace, *Ars Poetica*, l.144.

3 For a detailed and appreciative analysis, see *An Essay on Homer's Battels* at the end of the Fourth Book of Pope's translation of the *Iliad*.

4 Horace, *Ars Poetica*, l. 145.

5 Milton, *Comus*, l.479.

6 vii. 72–7, 112ff.

7 vi.108.

8 vi.162ff.

9 *Iliad*, vi.466ff.; xxi.234ff.; xxii.395ff.

10 *Iliad*, xiii.17ff. (Longinus, ix.8); *Odyssey*, xvii.290ff.

11 *Iliad*, xvii.645–7 (Longinus, ix.10).
12 *Odyssey*, xviii.125–42.
13 iii.3; Aristotle himself considered this a far-fetched metaphor.

11
ROBERT WOOD

1 Leonidas, the Spartan King, resisted the Persian invasion with his three hundred soldiers at Thermopylae in 480 B.C.; Miltiades defeated the Persians at Marathon in 490 B.C.

12
WINCKELMANN
Imitation

1 *Timaeus*, 23D–24A.
2 *Aeneid*, i.498; *Odyssey*, vi.102ff.
3 One of the major sculptors of the second half of the fifth century B.C.
4 Commentary on Plato's *Timaeus*, ii.122B.
5 Euphranor, sculptor and painter of the fourth century B.C., described the *Theseus* of Parrhasius as 'rose-fed' and his own version as 'beef-fed' (Pliny, *Natural History*, XXV.xl.129).
6 Pindar's *Odes* celebrate victors in the Greek games; Diagoras of Rhodes, winner of the boxing match, is honoured in *Olympians* vii.
7 The Homeric epithet for Achilles is 'swift-footed'.
8 Magistrates.
9 For the attractiveness of Alcibiades and its effect on Socrates, see Plato's *Symposium*.
10 Claude Quillet, *Callipaedia* (1655); tr. as *Callipaedia; or, the Art of getting pretty children,* 1710; English verse, 1710; French, 1749.
11 *Politics*, V.
12 Nervous diseases, notably the spleen which had a vogue in the eighteenth century.
13 This story is told by Athenaeus (*Deipnosophistae*, i.20).
14 Athenian courtesan, supposedly the model for Aphrodite Anadyomene by Apelles and for the statue of the Cnidian Aphrodite by Praxiteles.
15 Sculptor of the first century A.D. Winckelmann's note here refers to Pliny, *Natural History*, XXXIV. xix.85.
16 V. Golzio, *Raffaello nei documenti, nelle testimonianze dei contemporanei, e nella letteratura del suo secolo*, Vatican City, 1936, p. 31.
17 Jacopo Sadoleto (1477–1547) in his poem on the *Laocoon*; tr. in BIEBER.
18 Metrodorus of Lampsacus (*c.* 330–277 B.C.), Epicurean philosopher.

19 False sentiment or affectation of style. Defined by Longinus (iii.5) as follows: 'It consists of untimely or meaningless emotion where none is in place, or immoderate emotion where moderate is in place. Some people often get carried away, like drunkards, into emotions unconnected with the subject, which are simply their own pedantic invention' (tr. D. A. Russell, *Ancient Literary Criticism*, Oxford, 1972).

20 Frankness, openness, sincerity, freedom, candour.

21 Capaneus: one of the Seven at Thebes, who climbed on the city walls boasting that not even Zeus could stand in his way; destroyed by a thunderbolt.

22 Epigrammatic philosopher (c. 500 B.C.); here linked with Aeschylus as too primitive for the taste of Winckelmann.

23 '[I shall make up my poem of known elements,] so that anyone may hope to do the same, but he'll sweat and labour to no purpose when he ventures', Horace, *Ars Poetica*, ll. 240–2, tr. D. A. Russell, *Ancient Literary Criticism*.

24 Raymond Lafage (1656–90), engraver, flouted the beauty of composition in Winckelmann's view by depicting 'wild and angry spirits'.

13
WINCKELMANN
Torso

1 'Offspring of aegis-bearing Zeus' (*Iliad*, v.635). Current scholarly opinion identifies the Torso as probably that of Philoctetes rather than of Hercules.

2 References to the labours of Hercules.

3 Combatant in contest which combines wrestling and boxing.

4 Cupid visited Psyche every night, on condition that she did not see him; when the condition was broken, he abandoned her. See *The Golden Ass* by Apuleius.

14
WINCKELMANN
Apollo Belvedere

1 *Homeric Hymn to Delian Apollo*, ll. 133–5 (tr. H. G. Evelyn-White); quoted in Greek by Fuseli.

2 A serpent who guarded the cave at Delphi and delivered oracles; when he killed this chthonic deity, Apollo took over its functions.

3 Variously mother of Phaethon, handmaiden of Helen, daughter of King of Crete, ocean nymph.

4 Delos and Lycia were both associated with Apollo; Dodona was the seat of an oracle.

5 'They will draw out living looks from the marble' (*Aeneid*, vi.848).

6 See No. 8.
7 Baron Philip von Stosch, author of *Gemmae Antiquae*.

15
WINCKELMANN
History of Art

1 Cf. 'Marble is an extraordinary material. Because of it, the Apollo Belvedere gives such unbounded pleasure. The bloom of eternal youth which the original statue promises is lost in even the best plaster cast'. (Goethe, *Italian Journey* [1786–1788], tr. Auden and Mayer, Penguin Books, Harmondsworth, 1970, p. 152).

16
ROBERT WOOD
Essay on Homer

1 *Iliad*, ix.4–8.
2 Refuting Eratosthenes, Strabo refers to 'Homer's care with respect to geographical matters' (I.ii.20). Eratosthenes of Cyrene (*c.* 275–194 B.C.) was the first compiler of a systematic geography; his *Geographica* helped to provide a basis for the authoritative work of Strabo, for whom see No. 9, n. 3.
3 *Iliad*, ix.4–8; xxiii.195ff.
4 *Iliad*, iv.275ff.
5 *Iliad*, xi.305–9.
6 *Iliad*, iv.422ff.
7 *Iliad*, vii.61ff.
8 Pope, ii.592–3.
9 *Iliad*, xiii.1–38, xiv.153–293.
10 *Odyssey*, xi.315–16; *Georgics*, i.281–2.

17
SIR WILLIAM CHAMBERS

1 For details, see Chronology.
2 Artists, architects, writers on art and architecture. For Palladio, Serlio and Desgodets, see p. 240. Joachim von Sandrart (1606–88) was a German artist and writer; Giovanni Battista Piranesi (1720–78) was an architect who recorded the ruins of antiquity in his *Vedute*, etchings of Rome which captured its poignant blend of ancient and modern.
3 Francesco Borromini (1599–1667), leading exponent of Roman High Baroque architecture.
4 Nicolas D'Ablancourt (1606–64).
5 *Numachia* (*sic*): a *naumachia* was an arena where sea-battles were staged. *Thermini*: it seems likely that this is another mistake and

refers to *Thermae* (public baths) such as the Baths of Caracalla and Diocletian, though it could refer to *Termini* (boundary stones).

18
NORTON NICHOLLS

1   See end note 1 to Crawford (No. 5).

19
RICHARD CHANDLER

1   Strabo, *Fragments*,vi.33; Pliny, *Natural History*, IV.xii.73.
2   'A mistake' (Revett's note).
3   Revett substitutes 'S. side'.
4   'Hymettus' (Revett).
5   ridge: 'the Museum and Sycabittus' (Revett).
6   Author of *Description of Greece*.
7   A reference to Sir George Wheler who commented in *A Journey into Greece* (1682) that most travellers 'perhaps have seen it [Athens] only from Sea, through the wrong end of the Perspective-Glass' (p. 347).
8   Turkish officer in charge of the fortress of the Acropolis.
9   E.g. 'Woods, that wave o'er Delphi's steep, / Isles, that crown th'Egaean deep, / Fields that cool Ilissus laves, / Or where Maeander's amber waves / In lingering Lab'rinths creep . . .' (Gray, *The Progress of Poesy*, ll. 66–70). See also Milton, *Paradise Regained*, IV.
10 Julien Davide Le Roy, author of *Les Ruines des plus beaux monuments de la Grèce* (1758).
11 *Phaedrus.*
12 Supposedly king of Athens in the eleventh century B.C.
13 Cf. the description by Edward Dodwell, which illuminates the nature of Chandler's vision by the crude robustness of its response to the alien: '. . . the spectator will find it as difficult to remain serious as it would be dangerous to appear otherwise. . . . The dance . . . is one of the most ridiculous ceremonies of Islamism. . . . After the Derwisches have continued turning and screaming for a considerable time, they at length sink into the arms of the by-standers, and are for a few minutes apparently deprived of their senses, and filled with divine enthusiasm' (text accompanying pictures entitled 'Entrance to the Tower of the Winds', 'Dance of the Derwisches', *Views of Greece* (1821)). This provides a compressed version of the more elaborate account in *A Classical and Topographical Tour through Greece* (1819), i.374–7.

20

GEORGE FORSTER

1 Boatswain.
2 *Aeneid*, ii.198, ix.148 referring to the 'thousand ships' of the Trojan expedition. According to Homer there were in fact 1186 ships.
3 Forster's note records that 'M. de Bougainville has been led by this difference of appearance to assert, that they were really two different races'.
4 Agamemnon.

WILLIAM COWPER

1 Samuel Butler, *Hudibras*, I.i.463–4.
2 An interesting example of idealization: many Greek statues were, in fact, painted.
3 xii.457–60; *Iliad*, xii.383–5.
4 *Iliad*, iv.253; Pope, iv.286–9.
5 *Iliad*, ix.488–91; Pope, ix.608–11.
6 *Iliad*, viii.553–65; Pope, viii.685–704.

THOMAS TAYLOR

1 Thomas Blackwell; see No. 6.
2 Staff carried by followers of Bacchus.
3 Floyer Sydenham (1710–1787), whose nine translations of Plato were included with Taylor's own versions of the other works in the complete edition of 1804.

THOMAS TAYLOR

1 Aristotle.

J. B. S. MORRITT

1 The Persians were defeated at Mycale in 479 B.C.
2 Gilpin: William Gilpin (1724–1804) was the author of a series of illustrated picturesque tours.
3 Associated with Endymion, with whom the moon goddess Diana fell in love.
4 See No. 24.
5 Mohammedan.
6 In Sheridan's play (first performed in 1777) Charles Surface auctions the portraits of his ancestors. The reference is to IV.i.83.

IONIAN ANTIQUITIES

1 A footnote here refers the reader to Hume's essay, 'Of the Populousness of Ancient Nations'.

A. W. VON SCHLEGEL

1 *De Providentia.*

BENJAMIN ROBERT HAYDON

1 A rounded process at the end of a bone serving to form an articulation with another bone.
2 Reynolds of Plymouth.
3 Anatomical text-book with whose help 'in the course of a fortnight, I got by heart all the muscles of the body'.
4 Sir David Wilkie (1785–1841), who was painting mostly in the style of Ostade and Teniers at this time.
5 Henry Fuseli (1741–1825), visionary artist, translator of Winckelmann and Keeper of the Royal Academy.
6 Pliny the Elder is perhaps the most important ancient source on the history of Greek and Roman art. Quintilian was the author of a treatise on oratory.
7 The *Battle of Constantine* in the Vatican Stanze is now known to be largely the work of Giulio Romano and others.
8 Dryden, *Absalom and Achitophel*, I.156–7.
9 In 1811 the marbles were moved from Lord Elgin's house in Park Lane to the back of Burlington House, where some of the larger pieces had to be left out in the open air, for lack of space. See plates in ST CLAIR.

32

THOMAS CAMPBELL

1 See end note to No. 15.
2 *Chlamys*: short mantle or cloak.

Select bibliography

The Arts Council of Great Britain, *The Age of Neo-Classicism*, London, 1972.

Badolle, Maurice, *L'Abbé Jean-Jacques Barthélemy ... et l'héllénisme en France dans la seconde moitié du XVIIIe siècle,* Paris, 1926.

Bate, W. Jackson, *The Burden of the Past and the English Poet*, Chatto & Windus, London, 1971.

Bate, W. Jackson, *From Classic to Romantic*: *Premises of Taste in Eighteenth Century England*, Harvard University Press, Cambridge, Mass., 1946.

Bentley, G. E., 'Blake's Engravings and his Friendship with Flaxman', *Studies in Bibliography*, 12 (1959), 161–88.

Bieber, Margarete, *Laocoön: the Influence of the Group since its Rediscovery*, revised ed., Wayne State University Press, Detroit, Mich., 1967.

Bindman, David, ed., *John Flaxman, R. A.,* Thames and Hudson (for the Royal Academy), London, 1979.

Bolgar, R. R., ed., *Classical Influences on Western Thought A.D. 1650–1870*, Cambridge University Press, Cambridge, 1979.

Bracken, C. P., *Antiquities Acquired: the Spoliation of Greece*, David and Charles, Newton Abbot, 1975.

Bredvold, Louis I., 'The Tendency towards Platonism in Neo-classical Esthetics', *English Literary History*, i (1934), 91–119.

Brower, Reuben, *Alexander Pope: the Poetry of Allusion*, Clarendon Press, Oxford, 1959.

Brown, W. C., 'Byron and English Interest in the Near East', *Studies in Philology*, xxxiv (1937), 55–64.

—, 'The Popularity of English Travel Books about the Near East, 1775–1825', *Philological Quarterly*, xv (1936), 70–80.

Bush, Douglas, *Mythology and the Romantic Tradition in English Poetry*, [1937], Norton, New York, 1963.

—, *Pagan Myth and Christian Tradition in English Poetry*, American Philosophical Society, Philadelphia, Pa., 1968.

Butler, E. M., *The Tyranny of Greece over Germany: a study of the influence exercised by Greek art and poetry over the great German writers of the eighteenth, nineteenth and twentieth centuries*, [1935],

Beacon Press, Boston, Mass., 1958.

Buxton, John, *The Grecian Taste: Literature in the Age of Neo-Classicism 1740–1820*, Macmillan, London, 1978.

Chandler, Richard, *Travels in Asia Minor 1764–1765*, ed. and abridged Edith Clay, British Museum, London, 1971.

Clarke, M. L., *Greek Studies in England 1700–1830*, Cambridge University Press, Cambridge, 1945.

Clogg, Richard, *The Movement for Greek Independence 1770–1821*, Macmillan, London, 1976.

Crook, J. Mordaunt, *The Greek Revival: Neo-Classical Attitudes in British Architecture 1760–1870*, John Murray, London, 1972.

—, *The Greek Revival*, Country Life Books, Feltham, Middlesex, 1968.

Cust, Lionel, *History of the Society of Dilettanti*, ed. Sidney Colvin, revised ed., Macmillan, London, 1914.

Eitner, Lorenz, *Neoclassicism and Romanticism 1750–1850*, 2 vols., Prentice-Hall, London, 1971.

Eliot, C., 'Athens in the Time of Lord Byron', *Hesperia*, xxxvii (1968), 134–58.

Evans, F. B., 'Platonic Scholarship in Eighteenth Century England', *Modern Philology*, xli (1943), 103–10.

—, 'The Background of the Romantic Revival of Platonism' (unpublished dissertation, Princeton, N.J., 1938).

—, 'Thomas Taylor, Platonist of the Romantic Period', *Publications of the Modern Language Association*, lv (1940), 1060–79.

Feldman, Burton and Richardson, Robert D., *The Rise of Modern Mythology 1680–1860*, Indiana University Press, Bloomington, Ind., and London, 1972.

Florisoone, Michael, 'The Romantic and Neo-Classical Conflict', *The Romantic Movement Exhibition Catalogue*, London, 1959, pp. 21–6.

Foerster, Donald M., *Homer in English Criticism: the Historical Approach in the Eighteenth Century*, Yale University Press, New Haven, Conn., 1957.

—, *The Fortunes of Epic Poetry: a Study in English and American Criticism 1750–1950*, Catholic University of America Press, 1962.

Foster, F. M. K., *English Translations from the Greek: a Bibliographical Survey*, Columbia University Studies in English and Comparative Literature, New York, 1918.

Fothergill, Brian, *Sir William Hamilton, Envoy Extraordinary*, Faber & Faber, London, 1973.

Frantz, R. W., *The English Traveller and the Movement of Ideas, 1660–1732*, University Studies of the University of Nebraska, Lincoln, Nebr., 1934.

Fussell, Paul, Jr., 'Patrick Brydone: the Eighteenth Century Traveler as Representative Man', *Bulletin of the New York Public Library*, 66 (1962), 349–63.

Goldberg, M. A., 'John Keats and the Elgin Marbles', *Apollo*, 82 (1965), 370–7.

Harper, George Mills, *The Neoplatonism of William Blake*, University of North Carolina Press and Oxford University Press, Chapel Hill, N.C., and London, 1961.

Hatfield, H. C., *Aesthetic Paganism in German Literature: From Winckelmann to the Death of Goethe*, Harvard University Press, Cambridge, Mass., 1964.

——, *Winckelmann and his German Critics 1755–1781: a Prelude to the Classical Age*, King's Crown Press, New York, 1943.

Highet, Gilbert, *The Classical Tradition: Greek and Roman Influences on Western Literature* [1949], Oxford University Press, London, corrected reprint, 1967.

Hipple, Walter John, *The Beautiful, the Sublime and the Picturesque in Eighteenth Century British Aesthetic Theory*, Carbondale, Ill., 1957.

Honour, Hugh, *Neo-classicism*, Penguin Books, Harmondsworth, 1968.

Hungerford, Edward B., *Shores of Darkness* [1941], World Publishing Company, Cleveland, Ohio and New York, 1963.

Hutton, C. A., 'The Travels of "Palmyra" Wood in 1750–51', *Journal of Hellenic Studies*, xlvii (1927), 102–28.

Irwin, David, *English Neoclassical Art: Studies in Inspiration and Taste*, Faber & Faber, London, 1966.

Justi, Carl, *Winckelmann und seine Zeitgenossen*, 3 vols., 5th ed., Cologne, 1956.

Knight, Douglas, *Pope and the Heroic Tradition: A Critical Study of his Iliad* [1951], Archon Books, New York, 1969.

Kuhn, A. J., 'English Deism and the Development of Romantic Mythological Syncretism', *Publications of the Modern Language Association*, lxxi (1956), 1094–1115.

Landy, Jacob, 'Stuart and Revett: Pioneer Archaeologists', *Archaeology*, ix (1956), 252–9.

Lang, S., 'The Early Publications of the Temples at Paestum', *Journal of the Warburg and Courtauld Institutes*, xiii (1950), 48–64.

Larrabee, Stephen, *English Bards and Grecian Marbles: the Relationship between Sculpture and Poetry, especially in the Romantic Period*, Columbia University Press, New York, 1943.

Lawrence, Lesley, 'Stuart and Revett: their Literary and Architectural Careers', *Journal of the Warburg Institute*, ii (1938–9), 128–46.

Leppmann, Wolfgang, *Pompeii in Fact and Fiction*, Elek Books, London, 1966.

Levin, Harry, *The Broken Column: a Study in Romantic Hellenism*, Harvard University Press, Cambridge, Mass., 1931.

Lombard, A., *Fénelon et le retour a l'antique au xviiie siècle*, Mémoires de l'Université de Neuchatel, Neuchatel, 1954.

Lovejoy, Arthur O., 'The Parallel of Deism and Classicism', *Modern*

Philology, xxix (1932), 281–99.

Macaulay, Rose, *Pleasure of Ruins*, Weidenfeld & Nicolson, London, 1953.

Malakis, Émile, *French Travellers in Greece, 1770–1820; An Early Phase of French Philhellenism*, Philadelphia, Pa., 1925.

Man, Paul de, 'Keats and Hölderlin', *Comparative Literature*, 8 (1956–7), 28–45.

Mango, Cyril, 'Byzantium and Romantic Hellenism', *Journal of the Warburg and Courtauld Institutes*, xxviii (1965), 29–43.

Manuel, Frank E., *The Eighteenth Century Confronts the Gods*, Harvard University Press, Cambridge, Mass., 1959.

Mason, H. A., *To Homer Through Pope: an Introduction to Homer's* Iliad *and Pope's Translation*, Chatto & Windus, London, 1972.

Miller, Helen Hill, *Greece Through the Ages: as Seen by Travelers from Herodotus to Byron*, Funk & Wagnalls, New York, 1972.

Miller, William, *The English in Athens before 1821*, Anglo-Hellenic League, London, 1926.

Morritt, J. B. S., *The Letters of John B. S. Morritt of Rokeby descriptive of Journeys in Europe and Asia Minor in the Years 1794–1796*, ed. G. E. Marindin, John Murray, London, 1914.

Newsome, David, *Two Classes of Men: Platonism and English Romantic Thought*, John Murray, London, 1974.

Notopoulos, James A., *The Platonism of Shelley: a Study of Platonism and the Poetic Mind*, Duke University Press, Durham, N.C., 1949.

Novotny, Fritz, *Painting and Sculpture in Europe, 1780 to 1880*, Allen Lane, Harmondsworth, 1960.

Ogilvie, R. M., *Latin and Greek: a History of the Influence of the Classics on English Life from 1600 to 1918*, Routledge & Kegan Paul, London, 1964.

Osborn, James M., 'Travel Literature and the Rise of Neo-Hellenism in England', *Bulletin of the New York Public Library*, 67 (1963), 279–300.

Pater, Walter, 'Winckelmann' (1867) in *Studies in the History of the Renaissance*, Macmillan, London, 1873.

Pevsner, Nikolaus and Lang, S., 'Apollo or Baboon', *Architectural Review*, civ (1948), 271–9.

——, 'Richard Payne Knight', *Art Bulletin*, xxi (1949), 293–320.

Pierce, F. E., 'The Hellenic Current in English Nineteenth Century Poetry', *Journal of English and Germanic Philology*, 16 (1917), 103–35.

Pinkerton, John, *A General Collection of the Best and Most Interesting Voyages and Travels in All Parts of the World*, 17 vols., London, 1808–14 (1–6, Europe).

Praz, Mario, 'Herculaneum and European Taste', *Magazine of Art*, xxxii (1939), 684–93, 727.

Raine, Kathleen, *Blake and Tradition*, 2 vols., Bollingen Series XXXV, Princeton University Press, Princeton, N.J., 1969.

Raine, Kathleen, *Blake and Antiquity*, Routledge & Kegan Paul, London, 1977 (shorter version of *Blake and Tradition*).

——, 'Taylor, Blake, and the English Romantic Movement' in *Blake and the New Age*, Allen & Unwin, London, 1979.

Rawson, Elizabeth, *The Spartan Tradition in European Thought*, Clarendon Press, Oxford, 1969.

Rogers, Stephen, *Classical Greece and the Poetry of Chénier, Shelley, and Leopardi*, University of Notre Dame Press, Notre Dame, Ind., and London, 1974.

St Clair, William, *Lord Elgin and the Marbles*, Oxford University Press, London, 1967.

——, *That Greece Might Still be Free: the Philhellenes in the War of Independence*, Oxford University Press, London, 1972.

Schultz, Arthur, *Winckelmann und Seine Welt*, Berlin, 1962.

Seznec, Jean, *The Survival of the Pagan Gods: the Mythological Tradition and its Place in Renaissance Humanism and Art*, tr. Barbara F. Sessions [1953], Harper Torchbooks/The Bollingen Library, Harper & Row, New York, 1961.

Smith, A. H., 'Lord Elgin and his Collection', *Journal of Hellenic Studies*, xxxvi (1916), 163–372.

Smith, Bernard, *European Vision and the South Pacific 1768–1850: a Study in the History of Art and Ideas*, Oxford University Press, London, 1960.

Smith, Cecil Harcourt, *The Society of Dilettanti: its Regalia and Pictures*, Society of Dilettanti, London, 1932.

Spencer, Terence, *Fair Greece, Sad Relic: Literary Philhellenism from Shakespeare to Byron* [1954], Cedric Chivers, Bath, 1974.

——, 'Robert Wood and the Problem of Troy', *Journal of the Warburg and Courtauld Institutes*, xx (1957), 75–105.

Stanford, W.B., *The Ulysses Theme: a Study in the Adaptability of a Traditional Hero*, 2nd ed., Basil Blackwell, Oxford, 1963.

Stern, B. H., *The Rise of Romantic Hellenism in English Literature 1732–1786*, George Banka Publishing Co., Menasha, Wis., 1940.

Swedenberg, H. T., Jr., *The Theory of the Epic in England 1650–1800* [1944], Russell & Russell, New York, 1972.

Taylor, Thomas, *Thomas Taylor the Platonist: Selected Writings*, ed. Kathleen Raine and George Mills Harper, Bollingen Series, LXXXVIII, Princeton University Press, Princeton, N.J., 1969.

Tillyard, E. M. W., *The English Epic and its Background*, Chatto & Windus, London, 1954.

Tregaskis, Hugh, *Beyond the Grand Tour*, Ascent Books, London, 1979.

Trickett, Rachel, 'The Augustan Pantheon: Mythology and Personification in Eighteenth-Century Poetry', *Essays and Studies*

(1953), 71–86.

Vermeule, Cornelius, *European Art and the Classical Past*, Harvard University Press, Cambridge, Mass., 1964.

Walpole, Robert, *Memoirs relating to European and Asiatic Turkey*, edited from manuscript journals, Longman *et al.*, London, 1817 [includes *Account of a Journey through the District of Maina in the Morea* by Morritt].

Walpole, Robert, *Travels in Various Countries in the East; being a continuation of Memoirs relating to European and Asiatic Turkey*, Longman, London, 1820.

Watkin, David, *Thomas Hope, 1769–1831, and the Neo-Classical Idea*, John Murray, London, 1968.

Webb, Timothy, *Shelley: a Voice Not Understood*, Manchester University Press, Manchester, 1977, Chapter Seven.

——, 'Shelley and the Religion of Joy', *Studies in Romanticism*, 15 (1976), 357–82.

——, *The Violet in the Crucible: Shelley and Translation*, Clarendon Press, Oxford, 1976, Chapters II and III.

Weber, S. H., *Voyages and Travels in Greece, the Near East and Adjacent Regions previous to the year 1801*, Catalogue of the Gennadius Library, American School of Classical Studies at Athens, 1953.

Whitney, Lois, *Primitivism and the Idea of Progress in English Popular Literature of the Eighteenth Century*, Johns Hopkins Press, Baltimore, Md., 1934.

——, 'Eighteenth Century Primitivistic Theories of the Epic', *Modern Philology*, xxi (1924), 337–78.

Wiebenson, Dora, *Sources of Greek Revival Architecture*, Zwemmer, London, 1969.

——, 'Subjects from Homer's *Iliad* in Neoclassical Art', *Art Bulletin*, xlvi (1964), 23–37.

Winckelmann, Johann Joachim, *Winckelmann: Writings on Art*, selected and ed. David Irwin, Phaidon, London, 1972.

Wood, A. C., *A History of the Levant Company*, Oxford University Press, London, 1935.

Zwerdling, Alex, 'The Mythographers and the Romantic Revival of Greek Myth', *Publications of the Modern Language Association*, lxxix (1964), 447–56.

——, 'Wordsworth and Greek Myth', *University of Texas Quarterly*, 33 (1963–4), 341–54.